HEROES
Among US

Deep Within Each of Us Dwells the Heart of a Hero.

JIM RYUN & SONS

Treasure House

An Imprint of
Destiny Image® Publishers, Inc.
P.O. Box 310
Shippensburg, PA 17257-0310

"For where your treasure is, there will your heart be also."
Matthew 6:21

ISBN 0-7684-3005-4

For Worldwide Distribution
Printed in the U.S.A.

First Printing: 2002   Second Printing: 2002

This book and all other Destiny Image, Revival Press, MercyPlace,
Fresh Bread, Destiny Image Fiction, and Treasure House books are available
at Christian bookstores and distributors worldwide.

For a U.S. bookstore nearest you, call **1-800-722-6774**.
For more information on foreign distributors, call **717-532-3040**.
Or reach us on the Internet:
www.destinyimage.com

"*Lives of great men all remind us*
We can make our lives sublime,
And departing, leave behind us
Footprints on the sands of time."

Henry Wadsworth Longfellow

DEDICATION

To Anne, the wife and
mother of the Ryun clan.

ACKNOWLEDGMENTS

No book is ever truly written alone, and many people have helped bring this book into being. It is with gratefulness that we acknowledge: Mike and Judy Phillips, who not only were the catalyst behind our writing, but who also gave us hope that this book would be published, the staff of the Library of Congress for their help with the sources used for this book; Kevin Belmonte, Director of the Wilberforce Project at Gordon College, for his assistance in not only providing guidance, but also some valuable resources on Wilberforce; David Barton of Wallbuilders; Joel Leftwich and Nathanael Bennett of Congressman Ryun's staff for their help with this project; Tom Pratt, Chris Nagel, and friends at the White House for their help with the title; and the many friends who gave assistance in reading, providing feedback, and, in general, putting up with Ned and Drew talking about this book all the time.

Endorsements

"These stories of men and women who had the courage to stand up for their beliefs are worth remembering; the stories honor their deeds and remind us of how we are called to act."
—William J. Bennett
Editor of *The Book of Virtues*

"The heroes in this book show us what it is to be noble, to be brave, to do what is right despite the cost. They also show us what it is to be good. And if we emulate their goodness, we as a nation will not only continue to be good, we will continue to be great."
—Congressman J.C. Watts, Jr.

"A book about heroes is especially appropriate when it comes from my friend Jim Ryun. In his own way, Jim was a hero to me and many others when as an athlete he stood up publically for his convictions as a Christian, placing those convictions even above his own quest for Olympic gold. It is an honor and pleasure to recommend this book by the Ryuns, in which they recount stories of other Americans who likewise did not falter or waver at those crucial moments when their own convictions were tested, and became heroes among us."

—Michael Phillips
Best-selling author

"Americans love to have heroes—heroes to whom we can relate. Thankfully, the Ryuns have dug back into the treasures of our heritage and brought to life the stories of such heroes: Elijah Lovejoy, Angelina Grimké, Richard Allen, Christopher Greene, and others. These were once the heroes among us; and their lives can still inspire us today to become heroes for following generations."

—David Barton
Author of *Original Intent*
Founder, President of WallBuilders.

CONTENTS

Authors' Note

The men and women dealt with in this book are real people. The dialogue and the circumstances covered in this book are from firsthand accounts, journals, diaries, or letters, and as such adhere closely to what took place. These real people lived amazing lives, and it would take hundreds of pages to truly tell each one of these hero's stories. But we have attempted to show in limited space examples of courage that will hopefully inspire those who read this book.

It goes without saying that there are likely to be errors. For these the authors offer neither defense nor excuse, save that they have presented these heroes as faithfully as they could.

INTRODUCTION

"Enter the Heroes"

★ ★ ★

My search for heroes began years ago when I was a young boy growing up in Wichita, Kansas. I was enthralled with the black and white TV version of Superman. It fascinated me that Superman could leap tall buildings with a single bound, rescue the beautiful heroine, and beat the bad guys every time. I wanted to be Superman. I wanted to be a hero.

One day I decided I would make a drink that would give me superhuman powers. I went to the kitchen, grabbed a tall glass, and proceeded to pour into it everything I could find: milk, orange juice, pickle juice, whatever was in our refrigerator.

I then calmly opened my mother's spice cabinet and put a shot of each spice into the drink. By the time I was done, the glass was full and smelled awful, but I figured it was a small price to pay for superhuman powers. In my youthful naiveté and innocence, I was convinced that this drink would make me into the next Superman.

I walked out onto the back porch and took a swig of the brew, managed to swallow it, and then calmly stretched my hands past my head and bent over at the waist, fully expecting to fly. Seeing as I had never flown before, my chief concern was whether I could manage to bank around the trees in the backyard. But after a few moments passed and nothing happened, I realized what my mistake had been: I'd neglected to drink the "Superman brew" in its entirety. So, mustering up my courage, I drained the glass. Much to my disappointment, still nothing happened. I never became Superman.

Nearly 50 years later, as I walk the halls of Congress, with my glory days of Olympic and world record running behind me, my search for heroes continues. Now, more than ever, America needs heroes—not superheroes, but real men and women of character who will stand up and with conviction make right, and often hard, decisions.

Before September 11, 2001, it appeared to me that twenty-first century Americans had lost sight of who a hero was. Good eye/hand coordination or quick feet seemed to define one as a hero or a role model. Celebrities were paraded across the big screen and on news and sports broadcasts as though somehow their beauty and fame should give us cause to emulate them.

But heroism isn't defined by one's eye/hand coordination or by beauty or popularity, and on September 11 people woke up to this fact. Thousands died that day, and hundreds of New York City firefighters and police officers lost their lives, but they lost them because they were trying to save the lives of others. It is this ideal of self-sacrifice, the laying down of one's life for someone or something else, that defines heroism. John F. Kennedy wrote in *Profiles in Courage*, "A man does what he must—in spite of personal consequences, in spite of obstacles and dangers and pressures—and that is the basis of all human morality."[1] Even more importantly, heroes are evidence that there is a moral structure in society—if there was no good or evil, there would be no heroes.

The *Random House Dictionary* defines a hero as "a man of distinguished courage or ability, admired for his brave deeds and noble qualities." This definition says nothing of material success or athletic ability, but speaks of character qualities such as courage, bravery, and nobleness. Where do these "noble qualities" come from? Is one born a hero, or are heroes made? I cannot help but think that one becomes a hero through consistently making small decisions that build one upon the other, fortifying one's character through a lifetime of right choices. Aristotle once wrote, "Men acquire a particular quality by constantly acting a particular way...you become just by performing just actions, temperate by performing temperate actions, brave by performing brave actions." It is the little decisions built one upon the other that make the man. When the moment of crisis comes, there is already the fortitude of character that is strong enough to make the right decision even in the midst of the most trying circumstances.

And what gave the heroes in this book the basis and foundation upon which to make right choices? Faith. Faith in God and faith in Christ. It is this faith that motivated these heroes to greatness, for their faith gave them the ideal of self-sacrifice, of the strong sacrificing for the weak. Their faith gave them a moral foundation from which to view the world around them and it gave them the courage to act rightly. Dr. Henry Van Dyke wrote several days after the sinking of the *Titanic*: "Only through the belief that the strong are bound to protect and save the weak because God wills it so, can we hope to keep self-sacrifice, and love, and heroism, and all the things that make us glad to live and not afraid to die."[2]

This book is about men and women of the past, many of whom have been relegated to the dusty shelves of history. Some of the lives recorded on these pages may be familiar, but for the most part these men and women are heroes who have been forgotten by popular culture. Nevertheless, their stories are well worth the telling.

The lives of these men and women inspire us. As this book unfolds, and the men and women within rise to life from the black and white of these pages, we will see real people like us—people who saw the same sun rise and set, who experienced the kaleidoscope of human emotions, and who were faced with tremendous challenges.

Yet, what sets them apart is the decisions they made—decisions to stand firm in the face of tyranny, to give their lives for others, to right the wrongs of social injustices, to slay the dragons of their day. Their lives show us what it is to be good, to be brave, to be guided by conscience and character.

Introduction

They are the stars that guide us in the dark nights, the wind at our backs, whose courage shows us the way in which we should go.

Notes

1. Kennedy, *Profiles in Courage*, 24b.
2, Marshall, *The Sinking of the Titanic and Great Sea Disasters*, 3.

Chapter 1

Dr. Joseph Warren

"Act worthy of yourselves!"

Hc was not in the healing business today.

No, thought Dr. Joseph Warren as he stared at the musket gripped in his hands. *I am not here to heal men today.*

It was June 17, 1775—a hot, sticky day.

Peering over the redoubt at the summit of Breed's Hill just outside of Boston, Warren saw line after line of British soldiers forming at the base of the gently sloping hill. It was clear that they had one objective in mind—to push the American militia off the heights that dominated the city of Boston and its harbor.

Still feverish from illness and battling a severe headache, Warren slumped against the dirt wall the men around him had built during the night. Only hours before he had borrowed a musket from his friend James Brickett and walked from Cambridge to Breed's Hill. Arriving at the scene of the coming conflict, he saw the acting American commander, General Israel Putnam, surrounded by his officers.

"What orders do you have for us, General?" Putnam asked, referring to Warren's recent commission from the Massachusetts Provincial Congress.

"I am only here as a volunteer," Warren replied. "I know nothing of your dispositions; nor will I interfere with them. Tell me where I can be most useful."[1]

"At the redoubt," Putnam replied, pointing to the top of Breed's Hill where a wall of freshly dug dirt made a barrier for the militia to fight behind. "There you will be covered."

Warren smiled. He had come to fight, not be safe.

"Tell me where the onset will be most furious."

"The redoubt," Putnam replied again. With a handshake, Warren left Putnam behind, striding up the hill toward the American line of defense.

As he approached, one of the men behind it exclaimed, "It's Dr. Warren!"

Cheers rose from the gathered men.

Moments after arriving, Colonel William Prescott, the commander of the militia atop Breed's Hill, appeared at Warren's side.

"Does the General have any orders?"

Warren smiled again. "I am not here to take command. I have not yet received my commission. I have come as a volunteer, with my musket, to serve under you. I shall be happy to learn from a soldier of your experience."

Prescott, a grizzled New Englander of few words, nodded at the tall, blond doctor and moved on. Warren thought he had seen the hint of a smile play on Prescott's lips as he glanced at Warren's silk shirt and jacket. Having come directly from a meeting of the Provincial Congress in Cambridge, Warren had had no time to change.

Now, as he leaned against the cool soil of the dirt wall, Warren turned his head around to see Prescott atop it, his broad-brimmed hat pulled low over his eyes, looking down the hill. And then, with a thunderous crash, the British ships in the harbor began to bombard Breed's Hill.

"Here they come, boys!" Prescott shouted as he leapt down from the redoubt.

The skirmishes at Lexington and Concord on April 19 had been only the beginning. It was clear now that if the colonies wanted independence, they were going to have to fight for it against the greatest army in the world.

Warren pushed himself to his feet and glanced down the line of defenses. At best, the men with him were poorly armed, untrained, and inexperienced in the art of war. And they had little ammunition.

Below Warren and the defenders of Breed's Hill lay Charlestown. He watched as the left flank of the British attack hit the small town. The American defenders there put up a spirited fight, but a short while later, flames began licking hungrily at the dry timber of the closely built houses. Now both flanks of the British attack were directed at the defenders atop Breed's Hill. A few men began firing prematurely.

"Save your ammunition!" Prescott's voice boomed along the line. He was again atop the redoubt, this time conversing with a fellow officer whom Warren did not know. Calmly, as if taking a Sunday stroll, the two walked and talked, seemingly oblivious to the British cannonballs and the American cheers. Their courage steadied the strained nerves of the inexperienced American militia.

"Do not fire until you see the whites of their eyes!" Prescott yelled. "We will make every shot count."

Another voice cried out, "Shoot the officers first!"

Warren watched the distant lines of British regulars draw closer, their red coats blazing, their white trousers moving in mesmerizing unison. He heard the sounds of the fife and drum as the British musicians played a merry tune. He heard the shouted commands of the British officers and felt his knuckles whiten as he gripped his musket even tighter.

This is why he had come. This is what he had lived for, and if this struggle for independence could not be settled by peaceful means, then he was prepared for war. The words of the speech he had delivered so many years ago echoed in his mind.

> *May the Almighty Being graciously preside in all our councils! May he direct us to such measures as he himself shall approve and be pleased to bless! May we ever be a people favored of God! May our land be a land of liberty, the seat of virtue, the asylum of*

the oppressed, a name and a praise in the whole earth, until the last shock of time shall bury the empires of the world in one common undistinguished ruin.[2]

"Ready!" Prescott yelled.

Warren and the men around him rose as one, their muskets flying to their shoulders. Staring down the smooth musket barrel, Warren watched as the British troops drew nearer. Visions of his deceased wife and his young children flashed through his mind.

Fifty yards…40 yards…and still no command from Prescott.

Awake! Awake, my countrymen! And by regular and legal opposition, defeat the designs of those who would enslave us and our posterity.[3]

Warren's breath whistled through his clenched teeth.

The British were 30 yards away now. Warren could see their eyes, their grim faces, the sun gleaming on their bayonets.

He heard Prescott yell, "Fire, boys!"

With a roar of voices and the *pop, pop, pop* of musket fire, the British troops disappeared behind a cloud of black gunpowder smoke.

It was late September of 1765 and the light shining in the window indicated that the doctor was awake.

In the quiet recess of his study, Joseph Warren sat staring at the parchment on his desk, the ink from the quill in his hand dripping dark blotches on the white paper. The events that would forever change his life and set in motion a political career that would eventually lead him to Breed's Hill ten years in the future were just unfolding.

As a young doctor, he was successful. During the smallpox epidemic the year before, he and a handful of other doctors had used inoculations—progressive medicine for his day—to curb the dreaded disease. Now, as his reputation grew, so did his practice. Warren listed among his patients Thomas Hutchinson, the lieutenant governor of Massachusetts, John Hancock, and other leading citizens of Boston. His favorites were John and Abigail Adams. In future years, he would deliver their children.

But it was not his medical practice that kept him awake late this night while his young wife Elizabeth slept; it was a political matter, the Stamp Act passed only months before by the British Parliament. Sponsored by George Grenville, the Stamp Act was the first direct tax imposed by Britain on its American colonies. Levied on the colonies to help defray the cost of maintaining troops in America, the new act taxed legal and commercial documents as well as newspapers, brochures, and paper, all of which had to carry a special stamp.

The colonists reacted violently to the Act. Lawyers and printers refused to use the stamps or stamped paper. In New York, a mob of angry colonists destroyed the house of a British officer who had threatened to "cram the stamps down American throats at the point of his sword." Whispers of "No taxation without representation" began to circulate through the colonies. It was the Stamp Act that began to spark in the mind of Joseph Warren the concept of self-rule.

As he sat staring at the parchment, the words he wished to write for the *Boston Gazette* began to flow.

"Start, O start from your trance!" he whispered intensely to his unseen audience, his quill scratching feverishly across the parchment. Warren leaned back in his chair for a moment and stared out the window into the dark night. Then he began again, the words pouring from his heart onto the parchment.

> By the unconquerable spirit of the ancient Britons; by the genius of that constitution which abhors every species of vassalage; by the august title of Englishmen; by the grand prerogatives of the human nature; the lovely image of the Infinite Deity; and what is more than all, by the liberty wherewith Christ has made you free; I exhort you to instruct your representatives against promoting by any ways or means whatsoever, the operation of this grievous and burdensome law.[4]

When he finished, Warren quickly read the letter, dusting it with sand to dry the ink. Folding it, he carefully put it in his pocket and walked out the door to the printer's. One week later, his letter appeared in the *Boston Gazette*, and Warren's words quickly moved him into the realm of politics. In the midst of a city just beginning to be torn by political strife, battle lines were being drawn. The group soon to be dubbed the Sons of Liberty, headed by Samuel Adams, and fighting for American sovereignty, quickly recruited the bright young doctor to its side.

Though the Stamp Act was repealed within the year, the intensity of the political struggle between England and her American colonies escalated with the Townshend Revenue Acts of 1767. Designed to assert imperial authority in the colonies, the Acts imposed duties on paper, glass, and tea, created a Board of Customs, and authorized the use of blank search warrants called Writs of Assistance. As they did with the Stamp Act, the colonists reacted violently. There were petitions, riots, boycotts of taxed goods, and even the tar and feathering of custom officials. The rejection of this parliamentary taxation by the colonists was not tolerated by the British government.

On October 1, 1768, a fleet of British men-of-war appeared in Boston Harbor, guns loaded, prepared for action. Aboard the ships were two full regiments, the Fourteenth and the Twenty-Ninth, as well as a portion of the Fifty-Ninth. With drums rolling and fifes blaring, the British soldiers marched brazenly through the midst of Boston and bivouacked on the Boston Commons.

In March of 1769, Warren was a member of the committee that adopted a petition to George III, requesting the removal of these troops. The petition expressed sincere loyalty to the Crown, yet decried the unconstitutional use of troops against citizens of the Crown. It was met with silence. And all the while tensions mounted in the city of Boston until the night of March 5, 1770.

At eight p.m. on that day, the insults that had been traded all day long between British soldiers and some young men of Boston escalated into a fight. A barber's apprentice named Edward Garrick shouted an insult at the British sentry standing guard in front of the Customs House. For the young apprentice's pains, the British sentinel on guard of the barracks knocked him down with the butt of his musket. A young, unnamed boy quickly rang the warning bell at the Old Brick Meetinghouse and shots were fired as the civilians drove the soldiers back into their barracks. Things might have ended there were it not for a late arriving party of Bostonians. Having heard the ringing of the warning bell, they had rushed to the scene of the earlier fight.

"There he is!" cried Edward Garrick. "That's the soldier who knocked me down with the butt-end of his musket."

The crowd began reassembling. Someone in the crowd yelled, "Kill him! Knock him down!" Objects were hurled at the sentinel, who loaded his gun and cried out for help. Reinforcements came in the form of an officer, a sergeant, and seven soldiers. Soon the officer of the day, Captain John Preston, joined his men, who were roughly pushing the crowd away from the sentry box. Snowballs with rocks in them were then hurled at the soldiers, who began using their bayonets to push the crowd back.

Then, in the cacophony of sound, a musket discharged. And then another, until all the soldiers had fired. In the stunned silence, the Bostonians retreated a short distance as the soldiers began reloading. Five men were dead and six wounded, the snow stained with their blood.

Captain Preston rushed among his men, stopping their efforts to fire again. The mob in front of them was growing, preparing to rush them once more. But as it did, drums rolled and several companies of the Twenty-Ninth appeared, the front line of them kneeling, ready to fire. In moments, thousands of Bostonians gathered, having heard the news that the British soldiers had begun killing their fellow citizens. Thomas

Hutchinson, now governor of Massachusetts, rushed to the scene and pleaded with the people to refrain from any further violence. After a short consultation with the officers in command, the troops were ordered back to their barracks and the crowd began to disperse. But the damage had been done.

In an attempt to soothe the unrest, Hutchinson had Captain Preston and his soldiers arrested to stand trial. A committee of the leaders of Boston gathered to meet with Hutchinson, asking for the immediate removal of the troops. Seven men were chosen for this committee; John Hancock, Samuel Adams, and Joseph Warren were among them. They informed Hutchinson that his offer to remove the Twenty-Ninth from Boston proper to Castle William in Boston Harbor while leaving the Fourteenth was unacceptable. Nothing would satisfy the people, or the members of the committee, except the total removal of the troops. Hutchinson refused. Samuel Adams rose to respond. All eyes were riveted on him as he spoke.

"It is well known that, as acting governor of this province, you are, by its charter, the commander-in-chief of the military forces within it," Adams said. "If you have the power to remove one regiment, you have the power to remove both; and nothing short of their total removal will satisfy the people or preserve the peace of the province." Although his voice remained calm, Adams' words were ominous as he studied Hutchinson. "The voice of ten thousand freemen demands that both regiments be forthwith removed. Their voice must be respected—their demand obeyed. Fail, then, at your peril, to comply with this requisition. On you alone rests the responsibility of this decision. The committee have discharged their duty, and it is for you to discharge yours."[5]

Under the gaze of Adams, Hutchinson grew pale as Lieutenant Colonel William Dalrymple, commander of both regiments, exclaimed to Adams, "The information of the intended rebellion is sufficient reason against the removal of His Majesty's troops."

He then turned to Hutchinson, "I am ready to obey your orders."

Hutchinson paused, asking the committee to remove itself so he could counsel with his officials. When the committee was summoned again, they received the answer they had sought. Both regiments would be removed from Boston and quartered at Castle William.

For Warren, the events of March 5 left an indelible imprint on him. In later years he would speak of the massacre with sadness. "The sanguity theatre again opens itself to view. The baleful images of terror surround me; the discontented ghosts, with hollow groans, appear to solemnize the anniversary of the Fifth of March."[6]

John Adams, who would defend the British soldiers on trial for the killing of the five men, wrote, "On that night [March 5], the foundation of American independence was laid....Not the Battle of Lexington or Bunker's Hill, not the Surrender of Burgyone or Cornwallis, were more important events in American history than the Battle of King Street, on the 5th of March, 1770."[7]

Despite Hutchinson's act of appeasement, the British administration demanded that the colonies bend to its will. In

1773 the Parliament passed the Tea Act, authorizing the East India Company to export tea to America, which, while duty free in England, carried a three pence tax in America. Again, it was an act designed solely to show the supremacy of the British Parliament.

The colonists exploded with anger. A British officer stationed in New York wrote to a friend in London, "All America is in a flame on account of the tea exportation. The New Yorkers, as well as the Bostonians and Philadelphians, are, it seems, determined that no tea shall be landed."[8]

A short time later, a letter began to circulate around the colonies from a group called the Boston Committee of Correspondence. "We are far from desiring that the connection between Great Britain and America should be broken. *Esto perpetua* is our ardent wish, but upon the terms only of equal liberty."[9] Clearly, the pen that had worked so late into the night years before was active again—Joseph Warren was the head of the committee.

On October 23, 1773, Warren again took up his pen and wrote that he and others "would oppose with their lives and fortunes the vending of any tea."[10]

Yet, in spite of the rhetorical resistance to the tea, word spread like wildfire through Boston on November 28. The first of the tea ships, the *Dartmouth*, was in the harbor. Just over a week later, another tea ship, the *Gazette*, arrived in Boston Harbor, followed shortly by a third. On December 11, the owner of the *Dartmouth*, Francis Rotch, was summoned before a committee of Boston's leading citizens, chaired by Samuel Adams.

"Why," Adams asked, "have you not kept your pledge to send the ship and the tea back to London?"

"It is out of my power to do so," Rotch replied.

"The ship must go: the people of Boston and neighboring towns absolutely require and expect it."

Yet, when Rotch applied several times for a pass to have his ship leave the harbor, Governor Hutchinson refused his requests. On December 16, all three tea ships were still anchored in Boston Harbor.

Leaving the governor after his last attempt to secure a pass, Rotch returned to the Old South Meetinghouse at six in the evening of December 16, where seven thousand men of Boston had gathered to discuss the tea problem. While the others met inside, Warren and other Sons of Liberty were outside under the cover of night, smearing boot black on their faces and fixing headbands and feathers on their heads. Then they stood silently, like men waiting for a signal to spur them into action.

All eyes were on Rotch as he entered the Meetinghouse.

"He has refused me again," Rotch said.

The room exploded with loud cries.

In the corner of the room, Samuel Adams rose, motioning for silence.

"This meeting can do nothing more to save the country," he said.[11]

Outside, a loud whoop arose as Warren and his men, numbering between 40 and 45, dressed as Mohawk Indians, raced toward the harbor. There the three ships sat under the guard of the British admiral's 64-gun ship. Impervious to the danger, the "Mohawks" raced aboard the *Dartmouth* and brought the chests loaded with tea onto the deck.[12]

"Open it up and throw it in the harbor," Warren cried, his hatchet already beginning to bite into the pine wood of the crate beneath him. Feverishly, he and the others split open crate after crate, dumping 80 whole chests and 34 half chests of tea into the harbor. They quickly boarded the other two ships and dumped their tea into the harbor. In all, the marauders dumped 342 chests of tea into the Boston Harbor that night.

In a letter dated December 17, 1773, John Adams wrote, "All things were conducted with great order, decency, and with perfect submission to the government."[13]

On May 10, 1774, news of the British Parliament's and the Crown's response regarding the destruction of the tea arrived. The Boston Port Act forbade the landing or shipping of any merchandise from Boston. To enforce this act, another British fleet was being sent to blockade the port of Boston for several weeks.

The Sons of Liberty gathered again.

"This act fills me with indignation!" Warren cried as the others sat silently around the table. "This attack, although made immediately upon us, is doubtless designed for every other colony who will not surrender their sacred rights and liberties into the hands of an infamous ministry. Now is the time when all should be united in opposition to this violation of the liberties of all."[14]

Samuel Adams and the others glanced at each other.

"Put it on paper, Joseph, and send it to the king. Let us see what his response is," Adams said.

As if anticipating this response from Boston, Parliament and the Crown acted quickly. Only days after Warren and his companions had drafted the response, long before any news of it could have reached England, General Thomas Gage landed in Boston Harbor. In his hand he held the royal appointment of governor, thus replacing Thomas Hutchinson. He was under direct instruction to arrest, for trial and transportation, Samuel Adams, John Hancock, Joseph Warren, and other popular leaders. The political stakes that had already been high became even higher. The lives, fortunes, and reputations of some of Boston's leading citizens were imperiled. Gage was now governor and commander-in-chief of all British military forces in North America. For all intents and purposes, America was under martial law.

In late May of that year, Warren again picked up his pen. If the Crown and Parliament would not listen, then he and the Sons of Liberty would appeal to the masses. The time for words and small actions was over. It was fast becoming time for action on a much larger scale.

"Mind it, O ye colonies," Warren wrote, "be it remembered by future generations—that the event of this struggle insures happiness and freedom or miserable slavery to this continent. Act, then, like men. Unite as a firm band of brothers, and ward off the evil intended."[15] Days later his letter appeared in the *Boston Evening Post*.

In time, the uniting that Warren called for came in the form of the Massachusetts Provincial Congress, which assembled for the first time on October 11, 1774, in Concord, Massachu-setts. The tone of the Congress was evidenced in a letter from Joseph Warren to his friend Josiah Quincy, Jr., on November 21.

> If the late Acts of Parliament are not to be repealed, the wisest step for both countries is to fairly separate, and not spend their blood and treasure in destroying each other. It is barely possible that Britain may depopulate North America; but I trust in God she can never conquer the inhabitants.[16]

It was a call for independence. Only days earlier, Gener-al Gage declared the Provincial Congress an unlawful body that tended toward riot and rebellion. In response to his decla-ration, the Congress reconvened on November 23. On Decem-ber 10, the Congress explained why it had convened, citing as its major grievance against the Crown the increase of British military to enforce the Acts that destroyed the freedom of Americans. Tensions mounted as both sides watched each other.

Warren, as head of the Committee of Correspondence, watched as British troops became more active. In the midst of this mounting tension, he gave an oration to commemorate the fifth anniversary of the Boston Massacre.

The Old South Meetinghouse was teeming with people as Joseph Warren rose behind the speaker's podium. He looked out over the crowd. Directly below him, seated in the places of honor, were the British officers who had come in hopes of in-timidating him. Warren acknowledged the crowd and began.

"It is not without the most humiliating conviction of my want of ability that I now appear before you," he said, "but the sense I have of the obligation I am under to obey the calls of my country at all times."[17]

Whistling accompanied by laughter arose from where the British officers sat.

Warren ignored them and continued his speech, laying out the cause for grievance the colonists had with their mother country. "The right of the House of Commons of Great Britain to originate any tax or to grant money is altogether derived from their being elected by the people of Great Britain to act for them, and the people of Great Britain cannot confer on their representatives a right to give or grant anything which they themselves have not a right to give or grant personally."

In the back of the room, a cry rose. "Hear, hear."

Warren smiled and continued, shifting to the topic that had brought them all together on this anniversary of the Boston Massacre. "Martial law and the government of a well regulated city are entirely different, that it has always been considered improper to quarter troops in populous cities, as frequent disputes must necessarily arise between the citizen and the soldier, even if no previous animosities subsist."

Warren glanced down from his podium to see the British officers glancing at each other, clearly agitated. He continued.

"And it is further certain from a consideration of the nature of mankind, as well as from constant experience, that standing armies always endanger the liberty of the subject."

Warren's voice choked as he related again the events of the Boston Massacre five years before—the firing of the troops, the bayoneting of wounded men. The crowd in the Hall grew quiet as he spoke.

37

"We wildly stare about ourselves, and with amazement ask, who spread this ruin round us?" Warren exclaimed, fixing his gaze on the British officers, many of whom glared back in defiance. "What wretch has dared deface the image of God?!"

His words hung in the air as he watched one of the British officers reach into his pocket.

Warren tensed, expecting the worst. But instead of a pistol, the officer pulled out a handful of pistol bullets and began rolling them around in his hand. His eyes bore into Warren's. Warren, his eyes fixed on the officer, seemed to read his mind. It was becoming increasingly clear that the British officers wanted action.

After a moment, Warren reached inside his coat pocket and pulled out a white handkerchief. Quickly, he walked down from the podium to stand before the officer.

Covering the hand with the bullets in it with his handkerchief, Warren said, "Now is not the time for this."[18] Taken aback at Warren's boldness, the officer muttered, "Continue, continue."

Yet when he had finished his speech, Warren knew one thing—the enmity between Great Britain and its colonies was progressing beyond rhetoric. As head of the Committee of Safety, Warren called a meeting. When all were assembled, Warren spoke. "Gentlemen," he said slowly, but firmly, his eyes scanning the room. "We must begin thinking about raising an army."

His words brought momentary silence to the room.

"An army," someone sputtered. "For what purpose? Why?"

"Because the Crown and Parliament will not let us go peacefully. If we are to have freedom and independent rule, we will have to fight for it." A colonial army. The thought weighed heavily on the men in the room. The British Army was the best disciplined, best equipped, and most feared fighting force in the world. Yet, when the meeting was over, all had agreed. An army must be raised.

Appointing 30 men to spy on the British troops, Warren was determined that when the British moved, the colonials would not be taken by surprise. By late March, British papers began running stories that on April 10, 1775, an army of 13,000 British troops would descend on Boston, commanded by three major generals. Fearing for the safety of John Hancock and Samuel Adams, Warren persuaded them to retire from Boston to the home of Reverend Jonas Clarke in Lexington so that they might be out of harm's way. As for himself, Warren refused to leave Boston. On one evening in early April, a friend warned him of parties of British officers on the watch for him and pleaded with him not to visit his patients. Warren, placing his pistols in his pockets, replied, "I have a visit to make in Cornhill this evening, and I will go at once: come with me."

Only a week later, as he was passing a place called the Neck in Boston, a place of public execution, three British officers taunted him. "Go on, Warren: you will soon come to the gallows!"

Warren spun on his heel and approached the three. "Who among you just said that?" The three looked at the grim face of Warren and backed away, saying nothing.[19]

On the evening of April 18, the struggle between England and her American colonies began in earnest. That night a hard knocking on the door of Warren's home roused him from his bed. Cracking the door open, he saw one of his informers.

"What is it?" Warren said, pulling the man into the safety of his home. It was clear the man had been running. His sweaty hair was matted to his head and his words came out in gasps.

"The British are marching. They've left their barracks and are marching to the Commons."

"Where are they going?" Warren demanded as the man sought to catch his breath.

"Lexington and Concord. It is said they are going to destroy the gunpowder and arrest Hancock and Adams." The man's words only confirmed what Warren had been told earlier in the day—the British were on the move. Warren had sent one rider already, William Dawes, to warn Hancock and Adams, but he needed to be sure they received the warning.

"Get Revere and send him to me," Warren ordered. As the man retreated back into the night, Warren strode back up the stairs to his room, throwing off his bedclothes and quickly dressing. He was waiting in his sitting room when the knock came. Outside was Paul Revere.

"You know why I have sent for you. Go. If the British go by land, look for one lantern in the belfry of Old South Church. If they are going by sea, look for two. We must save the gunpowder and warn Adams and Hancock." Grasping Revere's hand, Warren sent him on his way. With a clatter of hooves on cobblestone, Paul Revere rode off into the night.

A short while later, 800 British grenadiers and light infantry under Lieutenant Colonel Francis Smith stealthily boarded long boats to cross the harbor and march to Lexington. But their movements were soon announced throughout the countryside as watch fires, church bells, and signal guns proclaimed the warning.

At 4:30 on the morning of April 19, 1775, Lieutenant Colonel Smith and his men met and fired upon the colonial minutemen on Lexington Green. At 9 a.m., 120 British regulars, part of Smith's column, were soundly beaten in a skirmish at Concord Bridge. Having not found gunpowder or any other military stores, the British began to march back to Boston. A running battle ensued as the colonial militiamen harassed the retreating British.

When word reached Warren of the skirmish at Lexington, he ran out the door, leapt onto his saddled horse, and rode straight toward the heart of the fight. The countryside was ablaze with action. Hundreds of militia swarmed around the road on which the British soldiers marched. Hiding behind rock walls and trees, the militiamen were slowing decimating the British formation.

The day ended when Lord Percy, with 1,800 British soldiers and two cannon, marched from Boston and surrounded the beleaguered troops under Colonel Smith. Under this protection, still harassed by the militia, Smith's weary and beaten troops crawled back into Boston, leaving the countryside around the city in the hands of the victorious militia. The first battle of the American Revolution was over, but the war had just begun.

In the days that followed between April 19 and the next conflict on June 17, Warren was a flurry of action. He recommended that an army of nearly 14 thousand men be raised. The Mass-achusetts Provincial Congress voted in favor of his proposal.

On May 2, he was elected President of the Massachusetts Provincial Congress. On that same day, Warren, still a member of the Committee of Safety, appointed Benedict Arnold to cap-ture Fort Ticonderoga on Lake Champlain and thereby secure the cannons needed to drive the British from Boston. On May 22, word arrived that Fort Ticonderoga and its supply of can-nons were in the hands of Benedict Arnold, Ethan Allan, and his Green Mountain Boys.

On June 14, the Massachusetts Provincial Congress voted to make Joseph Warren one of its two commissioned major-generals. On June 15, heeding the advice of General Is-rael Putnam, the Provincial Congress voted to send Colonel William Prescott and one thousand colonial militia to the heights above Boston and drive the British out of the city.

One voice of dissent was Warren himself.

"We do not have enough ammunition and we cannot find a way to move the cannons from Ticonderoga. How will we supply the men? How will we fight?"

"We will take the high ground and make the British come to us," answered Israel Putnam.

"You almost persuade me, General Putnam," Warren said, standing behind his chair, his hands gripping its back. "But I must still think the project a rash one. Nevertheless, if it be adopted, and the strife becomes hard, you must not be sur-prised to find me near you in the midst of it."[20]

When the Congress had voted, Warren was among the few who voted against challenging the British in Boston. But he would acquiesce to the voice of the majority.

"Where shall we send the men?"

"To Bunker Hill and the hills near it."

J oseph Warren could scarcely believe his eyes. The soldiers of the greatest army on earth were retreating, leaving the ground near the redoubt littered with dead and wounded.

"They will return!" Prescott yelled. "Reload and wait."

Warren watched as the British troops reached the base of the hill and reformed. Again the drums beat a marching tune, again the fifes whistled a merry tune, and again the British troops advanced up the hill.

"Steady! Steady!" Prescott yelled. Warren watched as Prescott, impervious to his own danger, ran along the American lines, shouting encouragement to his men.

As the British troops marched up the hill for the second time, Prescott roared his earlier order. "Wait until you see the whites of their eyes!"

Warren and the men around him waited. When the British were again within 30 yards, he and his fellow defenders fired. In the roar of gunfire and the haze of gun smoke, Warren feverishly reloaded, firing at the dim figures in front of him. Again he reloaded, again he fired.

In the midst of his battle fury, he heard another cheer. "They're retreating again!"

As the cloud of gun smoke cleared, he saw the British soldiers retreating again down the hill, leaving more dead and wounded behind.

But the American losses were mounting. All around Warren were dead and wounded men. Laying his musket down, he began caring for them.

"Dr. Warren!" It was Colonel Prescott. His voice was hoarse. "We are low on ammunition. Many of the men have only one round left, and we have no bayonets. I suggest you remove yourself from here."

Warren simply shook his head, thinking of the words he had told his friend Eldbridge Gerry only that morning. *Dulce et decorum est pro patria mori*—It is sweet and becoming to die for one's country.[21]

On the third British assault, the American fire was sporadic. The men who were out of ammunition picked up rocks and began throwing them at the advancing British.

With a roar, tired of being cut to pieces by men behind a dirt wall, tired of marching up the hill in the heat, angry at being embarrassed by a group of provincial farmers, the British stormed over the redoubt with fixed bayonets.

All around Warren men began fleeing, throwing down their muskets. A few, himself included, gripped their muskets like clubs to meet the onslaught of bayonets.

With a grunt, he swung and felt the butt of his musket connect with the head of the soldier in front of him, shattering the musket's butt. Dropping the useless gun, Warren unsheathed his sword, stabbing, slashing, parrying. But, slowly, the Americans were being pushed back.

"Rally to me!" Warren cried to the men around him, not realizing that he was one of the last Americans on the hill.

He never saw the British officer grab the musket from a soldier's hands. He never saw the officer fire. He only felt, briefly, the bullet hit him behind the right ear. Instinctively, the sword dropped as his hand shot up to cover the wound.

He was dead before he hit the ground.

Though the British would take Breed's Hill and force the Americans to retreat, the victory was a Pyrrhic one. Of the 2,200 British soldiers and officers that charged up Breed's Hill that day, 268 were killed and 828 were wounded. The American loss totaled 115 dead and 305 wounded. No longer did the British sneer at the colonial militia. Coupled with the stinging defeat they suffered on April 19, the battle that took place on Breed's Hill proved that the Americans, if united under good leadership, could fight and fight well.

As the news of Warren's death spread throughout the colonies, there was a public outpouring of grief. Abigail Adams wrote her husband, "Not all the havoc and devastation they [the British] have made has wounded me like the death of Warren. We want him in the senate; we want him in his profession; we want him in the field. We mourn for the citizen, the senator, the physician, and the warrior."[22]

"This is a day of heroes," wrote William Tudor. "The fall of one will inspire the surviving glorious band to emulate his virtues, and revenge his death on the foes of liberty and our country."[23]

In a letter written in the year leading up to that fateful day on June 17, 1775, Warren had written to the men of Massachusetts.

"Our country is in danger now, but not to be despaired of. On you depend the fortunes of America. You are to decide the important questions upon which rest the happiness and the liberty of millions yet to be born. Act worthy of yourselves."[24]

Notes

1. All conversations taken from *The Battlefield of Bunder Hill (With a Relation of the Action by William Prescott)* by Richard Frothingham, and *Stories about General Warren* by a Lady of Boston, 67-70.

2. Frothingham, *Life and Times of Joseph Warren*, 177.

3. Ibid, 30.

4. Ibid, 30.

5. Ibid, 145.

6. Ibid, 150.

7. *John Adams' Works*, vii. 384, ix 352 as cited by Frothingham, 150.

8. Frothingham, *Life and Times of Joseph Warren*, 234.

9. Ibid, 237.

10. Ibid, 239.

11. Lewis, *The Grand Incendiary*, 184, and Thomas, *Tea Party to Independence*, 20.

12. Frothingham, *Life and Times of Joseph Warren*, 286.

13. Ibid, 281.

14. Ibid, 305.

15. *Boston Evening Post*, June 6, 1774, as cited by Frothingham, *Life and Times of Joseph Warren*, page 314.

16. Frothingham, *Life and Times of Joseph Warren*, 396.

17. Warren, *An oration delivered March 6, 1775.*

18. Williams, *Joseph Warren*.

19. Loring, *The Hundred Boston Orators*, 48.

20. Falkner, *Forge of Liberty*, 250.

21. Sparks, *Library of American Biography*, 158.

22. Frothingham, *Life and Times of Joseph Warren*, 521.

23. Ibid.

24. Warren, *An oration delivered March 6, 1775.*

Chapter 2

WILLIAM WILBERFORCE

"Ages yet to come will glory in his memory . . ."

"When I consider the magnitude of the subject which I am to bring before the House—a subject, in which the interests, not of this country, nor of Europe alone, but of the whole world, and of posterity are involved; and when I think, at the same time, on the weakness of the advocate who has undertaken this great cause—when these reflections press upon my mind, it is impossible for me not to feel both terrified and concerned at my own inadequacy to such a task."

It was May 12, 1789, and the "silvery voice" of the young man speaking filled the House of Commons. There were fellow members of Parliament seated before him who would be bitterly opposed to the motion he was about to present, and there were many men in the balcony above the House floor who would stop at nothing to see him defeated. He no doubt would be attacked for his views, mocked and scorned. But he was fully aware of all this. He had dedicated himself to a great cause and would not stop until he accomplished what he'd set out to do.

"When I reflect, however, on the encouragement which I have had, and how conviction has increased within my mind—when I reflect, especially, that, however adverse any Gentlemen may be now, yet we shall all, most assuredly, be of one opinion in the end." He paused, looking at the faces of his colleagues. "When I turn myself to these thoughts, I take courage—I determine to forget all my other fears, and I march forward with a firmer step, in the full assurance that my cause will bear me out, and that I shall be able to justify, upon the clearest principles, every resolution in my hand—the avowed end of which, Sir, is, the total Abolition of the Slave Trade."

A murmur rippled across the House floor as viewers in the gallery leaned over and began whispering to each other. It was one thing to abolish slavery in England. That had been done 17 years earlier. It was quite another to abolish the slave trade and remove the vehicle by which many Englishmen had been made wealthy. Between 1783 and 1793, slave traders from Liverpool alone transported over 300,000 slaves to the West Indies, selling them for a profit of 15,186,850 pounds.[1] Men and women of all classes, from attorneys to grocers to tailors, invested in the trade, and it was quite normal to turn a one hundred percent profit in little time. It could not be denied that the slave trade was a mainstay of nineteenth-century British economy.

But these facts did not sway the young man in his purpose. For more than three hours he presented evidence against the slave trade, showing "the flagrant evils, the wars, the cruelties, the barbarisms which it engendered," and how it degraded not only those enslaved, but also those who advanced the trade. As he closed his speech, he looked at his colleagues.

> Policy…is not my principle, and I am not ashamed to say it. There is a principle above every thing that is political; and when I reflect on the command which says, 'Thou shalt do no murder,' believing the authority to be divine, how can I dare to set up my reasonings of my own against it? And when we think of eternity, and of the future consequences of all human conduct, what is there in this life that should make any man contradict the dictates of his conscience, the principle of justice, and the laws of religion, and of God? The nature and all the circumstances of this trade are now laid upon us; we can no longer plead ignorance—we cannot evade—it is now an object placed before us—we cannot pass it; we may spurn it, we may kick it out of the way, but we cannot turn aside so as to avoid seeing it; for it is brought now so directly before our eyes, that this House must decide, and must justify to all the world, and to their own consciences, the rectitude of the grounds and principles of their decision.[2]

The young man concluded his statements and resumed his seat. A fellow member of Parliament, Edmund Burke, praised the speech as equaling "anything he had heard in modern times, and was not, perhaps to be surpassed in the remains of Grecian eloquence." Yet, despite the moving speech, the

House dissolved itself into committee and voted to hear more evidence in the next Parliamentary session. Little did young William Wilberforce know that he had begun a fight that would entail nearly 20 years of labor to win.

In physical appearance, William Wilberforce did not look the type to take on such a fight. He was diminutive at 5 feet 4 inches, and his frail body was supported for most of his life by an iron brace. His eyesight was poor even from a young age, and he was to struggle with health problems all his life.

But when he opened his mouth and spoke, William Wilberforce was a different man. In 1784, Wilberforce rose and spoke before a gathered assembly in York County to persuade the freeholders of the county to support the government of his good friend, Prime Minister William Pitt. He also was harboring hopes of somehow winning for himself one of the two Yorkshire seats in the House of Commons.

It was a gusty, rainy March day, and after 12 other speakers, Wilberforce clambered atop the wooden table from which the speeches were being made. As his voice boomed out to the farthest reaches of the crowd, a wet and chilled James Boswell, the biographer of Samuel Johnson, looked in amused wonder at Wilberforce. He recounted to a friend, "I saw a little fellow on a table speaking, a perfect shrimp. But presently the shrimp swelled into a whale."[3] It was said Wilberforce spoke "like an angel" that morning. To everyone's surprise, Wilberforce not only secured the county's support for Pitt, but he also gained one of the Yorkshire seats without spending a penny of his own money or an election even being conducted—and this in the largest county in England where successful elections often cost 100,000 pounds to win.[4]

It appeared Wilberforce led a charmed life. He was from a wealthy family in Hull, had graduated Cambridge, and had won his first seat in Parliament at the age of 21 when he defeated the incumbent from Hull. He was very popular in both political and social circles; his sons wrote of Wilberforce: "His ready wit, his conversation continually sparkling with polished raillery and courteous repartee, his chastened liveliness, his generous and kindly feelings; all secured him that hazardous applause which society rewards its ornaments and victims."[5] His eloquence and smooth, and melodious voice on the House floor soon won him the title of "the Nightingale of the House of Commons," and Pitt, considered to be one of the finest orators of the day, wrote, "Of all the men I know, Wilberforce has the greatest natural eloquence."[6] By the age of 24, Wilberforce was at the height of success politically and socially and could rightfully be considered one of the premier politicians of his day alongside Edmund Burke, Pitt, and Charles Fox.

However, something happened in the winter of 1784 that was to change Wilberforce's life forever. He took his mother, sister, and cousin to the Franco-Italian Riviera to spend the winter, and he asked Isaac Milner, a friend from his Cambridge days, to come along. As Wilberforce and Milner rocked and swayed along in their coach, they began to discuss biblical Christianity.

Wilberforce was a Unitarian at the time and had little trust in the Scriptures or the divinity of Christ. Milner, though from all appearances not a serious Christian, had a firm grasp on the intellectual case for Christ. The two men spent the entire trip to Nice discussing Christianity.

While in Nice, Wilberforce began to read Phillip Doddridge's *The Rise and Progress of Religion in the Soul*, and on their way home to England, having left the women on the Continent, Milner and Wilberforce discussed the book and passages from Scripture. Their debates sparked something in Wilberforce, and the next summer, as he and Milner traveled to retrieve the women, their debate on Christianity continued. By that fall, as they returned once more to England, Wilberforce reached a decision. Somewhere along the way, "intellectual assent developed into deep inner conviction."[7]

He wrote in his journal:

> Often while in the full enjoyment of all that this world can bestow, my conscience told me that in the true sense of the word, I was not a Christian. I laughed, I sang, I was apparently…happy, but the thought would steal across me, "What madness is all this; to continue easy in a state in which a sudden call out of the world would consign me to everlasting misery, and that, when eternal happiness is within my grasp!"[8]

He wrote soon afterwards, "It was not so much the fear of punishment by which I was affected, as a sense of my great sinfulness in having so long neglected the unspeakable mercies of my God and Saviour."[9]

This transformation of Wilberforce caused him to question whether he should continue in politics. He wrote Pitt in November of 1785 and told him as much. Pitt replied:

> …forgive me if I cannot help expressing my fear that you are nevertheless deluding yourself into principles which

have but too much tendency to counteract your own object, and to render your virtues and your talents useless
both to yourself and mankind...If a Christian may act in
the several relations of life, must he seclude himself from
them all to become so? Surely the principles as well as
the practice of Christianity are simple, and lead not to
meditation only but to action.[10]

Unsure of what direction to take, Wilberforce turned to
the former slave trader, John Newton. Meeting at night for fear
of being recognized and associated with a radical Christian,
Wilberforce laid out his dilemma to Newton.

"I wish to have some serious conversation with you about
religion," Wilberforce began as they sat in Newton's sitting
room.

The older man smiled. "I had always entertained hopes
that God would bring you to him," Newton said.

"What am I to do?" asked Wilberforce. "Am I to forsake
politics and pursue religious things?"

Newton shook his head. "No. I would suggest that you
avoid making too many religious acquaintances, and do not
separate yourself too much from old acquaintances. You must
stay good friends with Pitt, and above all, stay in Parliament.
There is the need for a moral voice in government."

As Wilberforce left that night, Newton paused at the door
and looked at him. "The Lord has raised you up for the good
of his church and for the good of this nation," he said. Taking
the outstretched hand, Wilberforce thanked Newton before
walking out into the dark night. He later recorded that when he
left Newton, "I found my mind in a calm and tranquil state."[11]

Several months later, on Easter, 1786, Wilberforce wrote his sister, Sarah: "...by degrees the promises and offers of the gospel produced in me something of a settled peace of conscience. I devoted myself for whatever might be the term of my future life, to the service of my God and Saviour, and with many infirmities and deficiencies, through his help I continue to this day."[12] It soon became clear to Wilberforce that Christianity was more than going to church on Sundays and living a decent life; it was a worldview that must be allowed to pervade and penetrate every aspect of his existence.

Wilberforce was a changed man when Parliament convened again in the spring of 1786. He had been afraid that his religious beliefs, and that his being associated with Newton and the most militant Christianity of his day, might ruin his career.[13] But there were no ill effects from his newfound faith. He became a member of the Evangelical Party, a group of Members of Parliament who belonged to different political parties but who were all Christians. They were called "The Saints" by their enemies for their moral stances on issues, and Wilberforce quickly became their leader.

In 1787, Wilberforce received a letter from Sir Charles Middleton, the Comptroller of the Navy and a member of the House of Commons. Middleton had been hounded by his wife to bring up the slave subject on the House floor. Doubting his abilities, Middleton had begun searching amongst his colleagues for a man who might possibly be up to the task. He settled on Wilberforce and wrote him, asking him to bring up the matter of slavery in the House of Commons. Wilberforce immediately responded, "I feel unequal to the task, but I could not possibly decline, because I feel the great importance of the subject."[14] The Committee for the Abolition of the Slave Trade also contacted Wilberforce and asked him to speak on the subject in the House. The final nudge for Wilberforce came one day as he and Pitt, along with Pitt's cousin, Lord Grenville, sat beneath an oak tree on Pitt's estate.

"I've done nothing with my first years in Parliament," Wilberforce said as the three sat there. "At least nothing of any good purpose."

"Wilber, why don't you bring up a motion on the subject of the slave trade?" Pitt asked from where he lounged against the oak tree.

"I have been asked by several sources to bring up the slave issue on the House floor," Wilberforce replied.

"It would be a subject well suited to your character and talents," Pitt said. "I would encourage you to do it."[15]

That fall, on October 28, 1787, Wilberforce wrote in his journal, "God Almighty has set before me two great objects, the suppression of the slave trade and the reformation of manners."[16] And so began the struggle that would last a lifetime.

Shortly before Christmas of 1787, he gave notice that he would bring the subject of the slave trade onto the House floor early in the next session. But, in February of 1788, Wilberforce came down with a serious case of ulcerated colitis. It appeared he was dying, and one doctor commented, "That little fellow with calico guts can not possibly last a twelve month."[17] Yet, Wilberforce regained his health and spent the next year compiling information concerning the slave trade. In the spring of 1789, he gave his first speech on the House floor concerning the abolishment of the slave trade. It was moved that the House form a committee and hold hearings on the matter. The House then promptly tabled the matter until the next session. Wilberforce was undeterred, and it quickly became evident that his speech was the opening volley of what would be a long and determined struggle.

As soon as Wilberforce began his crusade against slavery, the opposition began its attacks against him. The West Indies interests claimed that the abolishment of the slave trade would ruin the West Indies commerce, which in turn would strike a severe blow to the British economy. Admiral Lord Nelson, one of England's greatest heroes, wrote from his flagship, *Victory*: "I was bred in the good old school and taught to appreciate the value of our West Indian possessions, and neither in the field nor in the Senate shall their just rights be infringed, while I have an arm to fight in their defence [sic] or a tongue to launch my voice against the damnable doctrine of Wilberforce and his hypocritical allies."[18]

At one juncture in 1792, several captains of West Indian ships threatened Wilberforce with physical violence. Worried for his safety, friends urged him to procure bodyguards. When he traveled into Yorkshire a short time later, one of his friends, Lord Rokeby, accompanied him as an armed escort. Wilberforce wrote another friend, "…I will do all for my own security…I can't say I apprehend much, and I really believe, that if he [one of the ship captains] were to commit any act of violence it would be beneficial rather than injurious to the cause."[19] Treating the threat of harm with some levity, Thomas Gisborne, a friend of Wilberforce's from his Cambridge days,

wrote Wilberforce, "I shall expect to read of your being car-
banadoed by West Indian planters, barbequed by African mer-
chants, and eaten by Guinea captains, but do not be daunted,
for—I will write your epitaph!"[20]

Undeterred by the opposition facing him, Wilberforce
became more determined than ever. At one juncture in 1790,
he visited Gisborne's country house and the two of them spent
nearly ten hours a day studying the voluminous evidence gathered by the men whom Pitt had nicknamed "Wilber's 'white
negroes.' "

There were many like these "white negroes" who supported Wilberforce in his endeavors. In the early 1790s, Wilberforce and his friend Henry Thornton decided to move closer
together into Clapham, a village just south of London, to fa-
cilitate the twin aims of deeper personal commitment to Christ
and a more concerted influence on political and social affairs.
Soon a nucleus of talented individuals gathered around
Wilberforce. The men and women of the Clapham circle were
" 'a group whose brains could not be denied, even by those
who sneered at their religion,' and they possessed between
them an astonishing range of capacities: encyclopedic knowledge, a capacity for research, sparkling wit and literary style,
business sagacity, intimate knowledge of India and the West
Indies, legal ability, oratory and parliamentary skill."[21] One
historian noted that "No Prime Minister had such a cabinet as
Wilberforce could summon to his assistance." It was the support of this group that enabled Wilberforce to continue his determined struggle for abolition.

On April 18, 1791, Wilberforce once more brought the motion to abolish the slave trade to the House floor. As he began to speak, Colonel Banastre Tarleton, the infamous leader of Tarleton's Legion during the American Revolution, attempted to distract Wilberforce by pulling out a pen and paper and beginning to work in front of Wilberforce as he spoke. Wilberforce would have none of it and spoke for four hours.

"It becomes Great Britain, in every view, to take a forward part," Wilberforce said, looking at the quiet faces of his colleagues. "One half of this guilty commerce has been carried on by her subjects. As we have been great in our crime, let us be early in our repentance. If the bounty of Providence has showered its blessings on us in unparalleled abundance, let us show ourselves grateful for the blessings we enjoy, by rendering them subservient to those purposes to which they were intended." He paused, then raised his voice. "There will be a day of retribution, wherein we will have to give an account of all those talents and faculties and opportunities with which we have been entrusted. Let it not appear then that our superior power had been employed to oppress our fellow creatures, and our superior light to darken the creation of God!"

"Hear him! Hear him!" a voice cried out from the back of the floor. Wilberforce smiled, acknowledging the encouragement.

"I am comparatively indifferent as to the present decision of the House," he continued. "Whatever you choose to do, I am confident that someday the people of Great Britain will abolish the slave trade. As for me, I am engaged in a work which I will never abandon! The justness of my cause will carry me forward, even if I am alone!"

He had been speaking for nearly four hours now, but his voice was growing stronger. He looked to the fellow Saints sitting before him. "Let us not despair. This is a blessed cause, and success, ere long, will crown our exertions. We have already gained a victory for these poor creatures, the recognition of their human nature. Let us persevere, and our triumph will be complete." He looked toward Tarleton. "Never, never will we desist until we have wiped away this scandal from the Christian name, released ourselves from the load of guilt, and extinguished every trace of this bloody traffic."

Wilberforce looked to the sitting Chair. "I move that the chairman be instructed to move for leave to bring in a bill to prevent the further importation of slaves into the British colonies in the West Indies."[22]

As Wilberforce took his seat, Tarleton immediately rose. "Mr. Chairman, it would appear that the inspiration which began on that side of the House," he said sarcastically, pointing to Wilberforce, "the revelation has extended also to this side, and reached the height of fanaticism and frenzy!"[23] He shook his head. "Are we really to suppose that we can abolish this trade, a foundation of our economy and prosperity? Abolition would instantly annihilate a trade which annually employs 5,500 sailors, upwards of 160 ships, whose exports amount to 800,000 pounds sterling!"[24] He glared at Wilberforce. "Abolition will undoubtedly bring the West India trade to ruin, whose exports and imports amount to upwards of six million pounds sterling, and gives further employment to upwards of 160,000 tons of additional shipping and sailors in proportion!" Two days after the debate, a vote was taken.

Though Pitt, Burke, and Fox, some of the most revered states-
men of their day, all voted for Wilberforce's measure, it was
defeated 163 to 88.

Not to be dissuaded, Wilberforce brought the same motion to abolish the slave trade to the House one year later. Support was growing for abolition, but in the final bill, it was
moved that "gradual" be placed before "abolition." The bill
passed overwhelmingly, but it was not the victory Wilberforce
had fought for. Gradual abolition might actually mean no final
abolition. The measure, however, came to nothing in the
House of Lords.

During his continued struggle against the slave trade,
Wilberforce did not neglect the second of his two life goals:
the reformation of manners, or morals, in England. For him, it
was very clear that the "abolition of the slave trade could not
take place without a concurrent moral reform to strengthen the
consensus that the British trade was a tragic national sin."[25]
Wilberforce wrote his friend, Lord Muncaster, "It is not the
confusion of the parties...which makes me despair of the re-
public...but it is the universal corruption and [immorality] of
the times, which taking its rise amongst the rich and luxurious
has now extended its baneful influence and spread its destructive poison through the whole body of people."[26]

Viewing the upper classes as the key to reforming morals
in England, Wilberforce set out to make "goodness fashionable
among the leadership class."[27] For him this was simply the best
place to start: "Men of authority and influence may promote
the cause of good morals. Let them in their several stations encourage virtue and [discourage] vice in others...Let them

favour and take part in any plans which may be formed for the advancement of morality. Above all things, let them endeavor to instruct and improve the rising generation."[28] He formed a Society for the Reformation of Morals to further his crusade, and it was comprised of Members of Parliament and other leading citizens.

As part of his morality campaign, Wilberforce wrote *A Practical View of Christianity* and had it published in 1797. He hoped that it might prove a vehicle by which to share the gospel with many of his colleagues and those in the upper class. The publisher, Thomas Cadell, was a bit reluctant to publish the book, and only printed five hundred initially. Within weeks the book sold 7,500 copies and had an amazing effect on England. "It was read...by all the leading persons in the nation," wrote one person, while another commented, "Everyone talked about it...it was acknowledged that such an important book had not appeared for a century." It was a best-seller for 50 years, and by 1826, 15 editions had been printed in England and 25 in America. It was translated into French, German, Italian, Spanish, and Dutch.[29]

However, Wilberforce's reformation of manners was not well received by all. He was mocked by other Members of Parliament, called a hypocrite, and scorned in literature by Lord Byron and Boswell. Wilberforce took the attacks in stride. On one occasion, after a literary attack against him, Wilberforce remarked to Zachary Macaulay, a member of the Clapham sect, "Remember, that they will by-and-by appear only like the barking of cottage curs on our passing through a village, when on our progress in the journey of life."[30] The attacks against him seemed almost to spur him on, and Wilberforce either founded or was a member of numerous philanthropic organizations. He and his friends founded the British and Foreign Bible Society, believing that the spread of Scriptures would "impart the blessing of the Judeo-Christian heritage throughout the world.[31] In 1793, Wilberforce began another 20-year fight to convince the British government to allow the introduction of British missionaries into India, finally succeeding in 1813.

In the midst of his various efforts, the abolition of the slave trade continued to be in the forefront of his work. After his defeat in 1791, he continued to bring the motion for immediate abolition of the trade before the House. Further defeats followed in 1793, 1797, 1798, 1799, 1804, and 1805. Then in 1806 William Pitt died, and Lord Grenville, the third young man present when Pitt suggested Wilberforce take up the slavery issue, came to power. Grenville favored abolition, and it became apparent that Wilberforce's motion against the slave trade would pass.

On February 23, 1807, the motion to abolish the slave trade once again came to the floor. Support for it was overwhelming, and it quickly became evident that the bill for immediate abolition was going to pass. The final speaker that day was Sir Romilly, the Solicitor General of England. At the end of his speech, he gestured to where Wilberforce sat.

> When I look to the man at the head of the French monarchy [Napoleon], surrounded as he is with all the pomp of power...seeming when he sits upon his throne to have reached the summit of human ambition and the pinnacle of earthly power...and when I follow that man...to his

bed, and consider the pangs which his solitude must be tortured and his repose banished, by the recollection of the blood he has spilled and the oppressions he has committed—and when I compare with these pangs of remorse the feelings which must accompany my honourable friend from this House to his home, after the vote of this night shall have confirmed the object of his humane and unceasing labours...when he lays himself down on his bed, reflecting on the innumerable voices that will be raised in every quarter of the world to bless his name, how much more pure and perfect felicity he must enjoy, in the consciousness of having preserved so many millions of his fellow-creatures...Who will not be proud to concur with my honoured Friend, in promoting the greatest act of national benefit, and securing to the Africans the greatest blessing which God has ever put in the power of man to confer on his fellow-creatures?"[32]

When Romilly finished, the House, forgetting the "time honored custom" of no cheering or applause in the House chamber, broke into loud cheering and applause. As his fellow members gave him three hurrahs, Wilberforce sat and wept. The struggle had taken nearly 20 years, but it had been accomplished. The bill abolishing the slave trade was passed 283 to 16, and within days received the Royal Assent and became law. That night, as he and his friend Henry Thornton basked in the glow of victory, Wilberforce turned to Thornton and asked, "Well, Henry, what shall we abolish next?"

Wilberforce's work was not done with the abolishing of the slave trade. He and others worked tirelessly to ensure that the law was enforced and that any illegal trading was shut down. In 1812, due to poor health, Wilberforce stepped down from his Yorkshire seat and took another with a much smaller constituency. The last years in Parliament were spent pursuing emancipation for the slaves, and in 1823 the freedom of the slaves in Britain's West Indies became his next battle. He wrote an *Appeal in Behalf of the Negro Slaves in the West Indies*, which had a profound impact on Britain and Europe.[33] His fight for emancipation was limited by poor health, and he realized his days in Parliament were nearing an end. He wrote his young friend, John Harford:

> When I consider how my public life is nearly expired, and when I review the many years I have been in it, I am filled with the deepest compunction from the consciousness of my having made so poor a use of my talents committed to my stewardship...We alone know ourselves the opportunities we have enjoyed and the comparative use we have made of them...Well, it is an unspeakable consolation that we serve a gracious Master, who giveth liberally and upbraideth not.[34]

In February of 1825, having served in the House for nearly 45 years, Wilberforce retired from public life. The later years of his life were spent in poor health, and Wilberforce fell on hard times financially due to his eldest son's poor investments. But despite his hardships, he would still speak out on the slave issue whenever given the chance.

In the spring of 1833, he was asked to propose another petition for the emancipation of slaves. As Wilberforce rose to speak before the assembly in the town of Maidstone, it was like an old champion rising to fight one more time. His body was stooped over by the years, his back was crooked, and his head drooped on his chest. His voice was weak, but his spirit was still strong.

"I never thought to appear in public again," he began with a smile. "But it shall never be said that William Wilberforce is silent while the slaves require his help. I say, and say honestly and fearlessly, that the same Being who commands us to love mercy, says also, 'Do justice.' "

As he reached his conclusion, he looked out over the assembly. "I trust I now approach the end of my career," he started. Then suddenly a beam of sunlight burst through the window and illuminated his face. "The object of emancipation is bright before us!" he cried, pointing to the sunshine. "Look, the light of heaven beams on it, and is a promise of success!"[35]

One month later, Wilberforce grew ill again, and by July, though able to receive visitors, he was in a weakened state. One of his last visitors was William Lloyd Garrison, who would quickly become one of America's leading abolitionists. Another was the young William Gladstone, who would later become one of England's greatest Prime Ministers. Gladstone later recounted in his journal, "He is cheerful and serene, a beautiful picture of old age in sight of immortality. Heard him pray with his family. Blessing and honour are upon his head."[36]

On July 26, 1833, the House of Commons passed a law that decreed that all slaves in the Empire were to be freed in one year's time, though they then had to serve seven year's apprenticeship with their masters. Their masters were to be given 20 million pounds sterling as compensation. When he heard the news, Wilberforce declared, "Thank God that I should have lived to witness a day when England is willing to give twenty millions sterling for the Abolition of Slavery."[37]

The very next day, Wilberforce grew suddenly weaker. Early on the morning of July 29, he whispered to his son, Henry, "I am in a very distressed state."

"Yes, but you have your feet on the Rock," Henry whispered back.

"I do not venture to speak so positively," Wilberforce murmured back. "But I hope I have." A few moments later he breathed his last.

His friend, Thomas Buxton, later recounted, "It is a singular fact, that on the very night on which we were successfully engaged in the House of Commons in passing the clause of the Act of Emancipation—one of the most important clauses ever enacted...the spirit of our friend left the world. The day which was the termination of his labours was the termination of his life."

Wilberforce was laid to rest in the north transept of Westminster Abbey, close to the tomb of his great friend, William Pitt. All of England mourned his passing, and the highest-ranking bishops of the Church of England, royal princes, numerous members of Parliament, and the Duke of Wellington came to his funeral. Wilberforce was called "great among the good and good among the great," and it was said that "ages yet to come will glory in his memory." John Pollock wrote of Wilberforce:

> His life gives us an example of how to create the momentum that leads to a positive change. His life was proof that a Christian statesman...can change the times in which he lives; though he cannot do so alone. It is a matter of history that for two generations at least after Wilberforce the British character was molded by attitudes that were essentially his. Under his leadership, a

William Wilberforce

Christian social conscience attacked prevalent social ills while at the same time seeking to better the lives of those affected by them.[38]

Notes

1. Lean, *God's Politician*, 2.
2. Wilberforce, *The Speech of William Wilberforce, Esq.*, n.p.
3. Lean, *God's Politician*, 28.
4. Ibid, 26.
5. Robert and Samuel Wilberforce, *Life of William Wilberforce*, Vol. 1, 29.
6. Harford, *Recollections of William Wilberforce*, 140.
7. Lean, *God's Politician*, 35.
8. Robert and Samuel Wilberforce, *Life of William Wilberforce*, Vol. 1, 88.
9. Ibid, 89.
10. A.M. Wilberforce, ed., *Private Papers*, 13.
11. Robert and Samuel Wilberforce, *Life of William Wilberforce*, Vol. 1, 97.
12. Ibid, 112.
13. Lean, *God's Politician*, 39.
14. Robert and Samuel Wilberforce, *Life of William Wilberforce*, Vol. 1, 147.
15. Ibid, 84.
16. Ibid, 148-49.
17. Pollock, *Wilberforce*, 78.
18. Lean, *Brave Men Choose*, 10.
19. Ibid, 359.
20. Robert and Samuel Wilberforce, *Life of William Wilberforce, Vol. 1*, 218.
21. Lean, *God's Politician*, 104.
22. *The Parliamentary History of England*, Vol. XXIX.
23. Allen, *Life of William Allen*, Vol. 1, 13-14.
24. Lean, *God's Politician*, 3.
25. Belmonte, *Hero for Humanity*, 86.
26. Robert and Samuel Wilberforce, *Life of William Wilberforce*, Vol. 1, 150-51.
27. Belmonte, *Hero for Humanity*, 89.
28. William Wilberforce, *A Practical View of Christianity*, 215.

29. Lean, *God's Politician*, 134.

30. Ibid, 97.

31. Belmonte, *Hero for Humanity*, 97.

32. Romilly, *Sir Samuel Romilly*, 143.

33. Belmonte, *Hero for Humanity*, 153.

34. Robert and Samuel Wilberforce, *Life of William Wilberforce*, Vol. 5, 231.

35. Everett, *Freedom Fighter*, 103.

36. Lean, *God's Politician*, 178.

37. Belmonte, *Hero for Humanity*, 197.

38. Pollock, "The Little Abolitionist, William Wilberforce," 23.

Chapter 3

CHRISTOPHER GREENE

"Deeds of Desperate Valor"

It seemed an insignificant fort on the banks of the Delaware River—a rude structure, housing 425 American troops. But the 1,200 Hessians, the feared mercenaries of the British Army surrounding the fort, had been ordered to take it at all costs.

Under a flag of truce, a Hessian officer met with Leiutenant Colonel Jeremiah Olney of the Second Rhode Island Regiment.

The two officers eyed each other coldly.

"The King of England orders his rebellious subjects to lay down their arms," the Hessian officer said from his lofty position astride his horse.

"And my commander, Colonel Christopher Greene, says he will defend the fort until the end," Olney replied coolly, his arms crossed as he looked up at the Hessian.

Taken aback, the other fell silent for a moment, his jaw clenched. "I insist that I speak to your commander."

Olney just stared at him.

"If you do not surrender," the officer snapped, "no mercy will be shown when we overrun the fort."

"Colonel Greene neither asks for nor expects any quarter from your commander. We shall defend the fort to the last extremity."

"Very well."

With that, the officer, his white flag of truce fluttering over his head, returned to his lines, reporting his conversation to his commander, Count Von Donop.[1]

Inside Fort Mercer, the tall, powerfully built Christopher Greene met Olney.

"He said they would give no mercy," Olney said. "And I said you neither sought nor asked for any."

Greene nodded. In a fort built for 1,500 men, he had only 425. They had marched hard to get here—35 miles in one day. Only days before, under orders from General Washington, he had sent 150 of his men under Major Simeon Thayer to help with the defense of Fort Mifflin. A superior force of 1,200 men faced him. As he barked orders, the enemy cannons opened fire.

It could be said that 1777 had been a year of ups and downs for the Americans in their War for Independence. First in January, after his bold victory at Trenton, General Washington led his army to Princeton, soundly defeating the British yet again.

Then in June, a large British army under General Burgoyne invaded from Canada as part of a plan to cut off New England from the rest of the colonies. In his first action, Burgoyne captured Fort Ticonderoga, a serious loss for the American forces as Ticonderoga held military supplies desperately needed by Washington and his army. In September, General Howe and his British army defeated Washington at Brandywine Creek and marched into Philadelphia.

The few days in October epitomized the American struggle. On October 7, 1777, Generals Horatio Gates and Benedict Arnold dealt the British a crushing blow at the Battle of Saratoga, forcing General Burgoyne and his 5,700 troops into complete surrender.

But earlier on October 4, the American cause had suffered yet another setback. It began as a well planned, daring attack on General Howe's nine thousand troops at Germantown, a small town outside of Philadelphia. Using four columns, General Washington surprised the British forces in the early morning hours. However, the battle plan relied on precise timing among the four columns, and things went badly when one of the four columns lost its way in the gunfire smoke and fog and Americans began firing on Americans. The tide turned quickly, and the British drove the Americans from Germantown.

As he retreated, Washington reinforced the forts the Americans held along the Delaware River. Howe and the British controlled Philadelphia and the surrounding countryside, but unless they could ship supplies down the Delaware to Philadelphia, theirs was a lost cause.

Howe, realizing the importance of the forts, began to lay plans to seize them. On the New Jersey side sat Fort Mercer—it would have to be taken by land. North of Fort Mercer sat Fort Mifflin on Mud Island and would have to be taken by British ships.

Now, in the afternoon of October 22, 1777, 1,200 Hessian troops under Count Von Donop surrounded the Americans at Fort Mercer. Within minutes of the opening carronade, two columns of Hessians advanced from the north and south of the fort. Breaking through the outer breastworks, they encountered little opposition.

Cheering their victory, the Hessians advanced toward the inner breastworks, their drummer snapping out a lively tune.

Through a crack in the rough palisade of the inner breastworks of the fort, Christopher Greene watched their advance. He thought of the letter he had received from Alexander Hamilton only days before.

"The enemy's attempt will probably be sudden and violent," Hamilton had written. "It is of infinite importance to disappoint their intentions."[2]

Greene had every intention of doing so. His reply to Hamilton and Washington was simple: "The post I have in charge I am determined to defend with the small number I command to the last extremity."[3]

"Steady," he whispered to his men. He had been with the Kentish Guards at Bunker Hill. He knew the withering effect of fire at close range, and he had seen the British mowed down at close range by the American volleys.

"Fire low, men," he said in a hushed tone, "they have a broad belt just above the waist—aim at that."

He heard his command quietly repeated down the line.

With the Hessians nearly upon them, the Rhode Islanders still crouched silently, fingers nervously rubbing the triggers of their muskets. When the Hessians were within 30 yards, and one of them beginning to plant their flag on the fort's ramparts, Greene rose to his feet, his sword held high above his head.

"Now!" Greene cried, waving his sword above his head. "Now!"

As one, the Rhode Islanders rose, their line erupting in a blaze of gun and cannon fire. Musket balls and grapeshot from the cannons ripped through the surprised Hessian lines. To their credit, the Hessians did not break and run—they advanced.

Through the smoke, Greene saw them coming. "Fix bayonets!" He yelled above the gunfire. The few men that heard him did so and soon the fight became hand-to-hand combat.

For 45 minutes, the Americans and Hessians fought, the Hessians seeking to clamber up the wall of the palisade, and the Americans seeking to throw them off.

In the end, the Hessians retreated, totally demoralized by the fierce encounter. As they retreated, they left behind almost 400 casualties to the Americans' 37. Among the Hessian dead was Count Von Donop, mortally wounded in the charge.

For the time being, the Americans held Fort Mercer. As Christopher Greene stared over the devastation of the battlefield, he knew no more assaults would be made on the fort for some time.

Two days later a letter came from General Washington himself.

"I heartily congratulate you upon this happy event, and beg you will accept my most particular thanks, and present the same to your whole garrison, both officers and men...I am, Sir, Your most obedient Servant, George Washington."[4]

Greene allowed himself a slight smile as he read the letter. He knew Washington probably had not heard of the destruction of the British ship of war, the *Augusta*.

After running aground in seeking to aid Von Donop and his attack, the British ship was stranded. Hit by a heated cannonball from one of the American cannons, the ship caught fire. When the fire reached the gunpowder magazine of the 64-gun ship, the explosion could be heard for 30 miles.

Greene almost laughed out loud at the fact that days later his ears were still ringing from the thunderous explosion. Upon the heels of Washington's letter came one from his cousin and friend, General Nathanael Greene.

"With the greatest pleasure I congratulate you on your late brave and successful defense, the attempt was bold and the defence [sic] noble. Honnor [sic] and laurels will be the reward of the garrison."[5]

In later years, Secretary of War Henry Knox, himself a general during the War for Independence, said, " [the defense at Fort Mercer was] one of the most brilliant feats of the war."[6]

The defense of Fort Mifflin, just over a mile up the river, would be a different story.

The small garrison of American soldiers at Fort Mifflin was prepared for the British attacks. For nearly three weeks they held the fort until November 15. Then the British seized a small island near the fort and set up a battery of cannons. As they began to barrage the American fort, seven British ships sailed down the Delaware, joined by a barge loaded with cannons. The warships sailed so close to the fort that grenades were lobbed into it from the tops of the warships' masts.

The Americans fought until the walls of the fort were leveled to the ground and their cannons silenced. Of the 300 men defending Fort Mifflin, 250 were killed or wounded.

At midnight on November 15, Major Thayer, the last American officer standing, spiked the cannons, set fire to the remains of the barracks, and took the survivors to safety across the river to Fort Mercer. He was the last man to leave the island. The battle the British expected to last one day had lasted over three weeks.

When he reached Fort Mercer, Thayer found Colonel Greene. As they clasped hands, Greene said, "I am glad to see you alive and well. You are just in time. Cornwallis is coming with 2,000 fresh British troops. New orders have come. We are to march to meet General Washington."

"Where?" Thayer asked.

"At Valley Forge."

"And the British forces that surround us?"

"We will simply have to avoid them," Greene replied.

Greene and his men miraculously avoided the British troops and arrived safely at Valley Forge in December of 1777.

Now, as he walked the sentry lines at Valley Forge, Christopher Greene was lost in thought. Only a few years before he had been a state legislator in the Rhode Island General Assembly, still actively involved in his family's ironwork and sawmill business. Now he was a far cry from the legislature or his family's business. He was a colonel in the Continental Army.

It was rumored that the First and Second Rhode Island Regiments were going to be combined due to low enlistment numbers. Too many men had died or simply gone home to their families and farms.

Beating his hands together to fight the intense cold of the Pennsylvania winter, Greene stopped at the fire the sentries had built, nodding at the Rhode Island men standing there. Nineteen-year-old Jeremiah Greenman was one of the sentries.

"Cold night, isn't it, sir?"

Greene nodded. "Not quite as cold as Quebec," he replied. Greenman nodded in reply. He had been there. He knew.

It had been cold up in Canada. *Cold and ill-fated from the beginning*, Greene thought as he gazed into the dancing flame of the fire.

On September 13, 1775, Greene and 1,000 other men under the command of Benedict Arnold began their march through the Maine wilderness to invade Canada and take the war to the British. After 38 days on the Kennebunk River, after losing 350 men to desertion, short on supplies, Arnold pressed ahead.

On November 8, Arnold reached Quebec City and laid siege to it, waiting for another American force under General Richard Montgomery. After taking St. Johns and Montreal, Montgomery appeared with only 350 men on December 3, leaving the rest of his force to occupy the recently taken towns.

The British General Carleton rebuffed their demand for the surrender of Quebec. Early on the morning of December 31, under the cover of a heavy snowstorm, the Americans attacked—Montgomery and his 350 men from the west, Arnold and his men from the east.

Greene had been with Arnold. A lieutenant colonel at the time, he stood shivering with his men in the cold, watching the rockets Montgomery launched cut through the murky darkness of the blizzard. It was the signal for the attack. It was now 4 a.m.

Though he didn't know it at the time, Greene would find out later that the British had been waiting all night for the American assault, warned by an American deserter.

Montgomery never entered Quebec. He died in the initial charge along with his two lieutenants.

Suffering heavy casualties, the Americans in the west retreated, leaving Arnold to attack alone from the east. Arnold fell in the initial charge, hit in the leg by a musket ball. Christopher Greene, the ranking officer, took command.

Without hesitation, he and Daniel Morgan, the Virginia rifleman, led the men over the British barricade and began fighting their way through the streets of Quebec, waiting to see Montgomery and his men. They never came.

As Morgan and Greene pressed ahead, the British forces enveloped them and the battle became a running skirmish through the streets and houses of Quebec. Slowly, but surely, the Americans were isolated into small pockets and forced to surrender.

Greene snapped out of his reverie to glance at Jeremiah Greenman. Greenman had been with him in the last hours, had heard Greene and the other officers conferring that cold morning of December 31, 1775.

"Sir," Major Bigelow shouted above the gunfire, "We are trapped. We will all be killed unless we surrender now."

Peering out the window of the house they were trapped in, Greene saw the British soldiers, moving from house to house, drawing closer. A bullet whined near his head and smacked into the wall behind him as he ducked. He crouched on the floor, looking at Major Bigelow. He glanced over at Major Meigs, who simply nodded.

To continue to fight would mean the needless deaths of his men. *Where is Montgomery?* he thought. *And where is Daniel Morgan?* he wondered, glancing out the window one more time. Greene had not seen the tall Virginian rifleman for hours.

"Very well." he said, resigning himself to the fact that they were outnumbered and now beaten.[7]

In the end, almost the entire American force surrendered. Even now Greene smiled at the stories he had heard of Morgan's surrender. Daring the British to shoot him, Morgan refused to surrender, cursing them with all the vigor of a Virginian woodsman. His men pleaded with him to drop his sword, but it was not until a French priest arrived that Morgan surrendered, handing his sword to the priest because he refused to surrender it to the British.

For more than a year, Greene and the others who surrendered with him languished in the citadel of Quebec until a prisoner exchange returned them home. But his days in prison forged within Greene a new resolve—he would win this war for independence or he would die fighting. There was no surrender.

And now he was here at Valley Forge, shivering in front of a fire in a bitter wind, still fighting for the cause of independence that was faltering. While the British officers were enjoying the warmth of Philadelphian homes and society, Greene and the other American officers, along with their men, were living in rude wooden huts that the bitter wind whistled through at night. Nightly, dozens of men deserted the American cause.

Only days before Greene and fellow Rhode Islander General James Varnum had proposed something new, often debated in the American ranks. It was well known that the British were utilizing slaves in their southern campaign. Pledging the slaves freedom if they fought under British colors, Dunmore's Ethiopian Regiment was formed in 1775. American slaves left their masters in droves.

Why, Christopher Greene and James Varnum argued to General Washington and his staff, *can we not do the same?* Given the shrinking numbers in the Rhode Island regiments, something had to be done. White men were not enlisting. If slaves were promised their freedom to enlist, then something might be done to resolve the problem. What the Continental Army needed now were able-bodied men who could fight.

It was evident that Washington was unsure at first. In November of 1775, he had issued an order barring black enlistment in the Continental Army. Within a year, seeing the success of the Dunmore's Regiment, he began to change his mind. With Alexander Hamilton, Nathanael Greene, James Varnum, and now Christopher Greene pressing for black enlistment, Washington acquiesced.

In a letter dated January 2, 1778, Varnum wrote Washington.

> The two battalions from the State of Rhode Island being small, Field Officers have represented the propriety of making one temporary battalion from the two that an entire corp of officers may repair to Rhode Island...It is imagined that a battalion of Negroes can easily be raised there. Should that measure be adopted...the Service will be advanced. The field officers who go upon this command are Col. Greene, Lt. Col. Olney and Major Ward.[8]

Washington took immediate action. In a letter dated the same day, he wrote Rhode Island governor Nicholas Cooke:

> Inclosed [sic] you will receive a copy of a letter from Gen. Varnum to me, upon the means which might be adopted for completing the Rhode Island troops to their full proportion in the Continental Army. I have nothing to say in addition....But desire that you give the officers employed in this business all the assistance in your power.[9]

It was August 29, 1778, now. Nicholas Cooke's reply to Washington's letter had been hesitant, but in the end he assisted the attempt to recruit slaves. The proposed measure was debated acrimoniously in the Rhode Island General Assembly, a body of men connected extensively to Rhode Island's widespread slave trade, some of whom were also slave holders.

But Cooke and the majority of the members overrode the protest of the slaveholders and the measure passed, the Assembly permitting "every able bodied Negro, Mulatto or Indian slave" to enlist in either of the two state regiments. For the black slaves, the Assembly declared that every slave enlisting, "upon passing his muster, he is absolutely made free, and entitled to all the wages, bounties, and encouragements given by Congress to any soldier enlisting."[10]

The recruiting had been slower than expected, but a regiment of 225 blacks was formed, some freedmen, some former slaves. There had been little time to train the men, but Greene, Olney, and Ward drilled them mercilessly, using the manual Baron von Steuben wrote while at Valley Forge.

Now from where he stood at the base of Butt's Hill outside of Newport, Rhode Island, Christopher Greene squinted through the summer haze into the distance.

In their withdrawal from their lines outside of Newport, the American forces had made an orderly retreat. But word had just come from the scouts. The British and Hessian troops were advancing, intent on catching the retreating Americans off guard.

Only weeks before, the French fleet under D'Estaing had destroyed the British fleet off Newport, Rhode Island, in a joint effort with General Sullivan's American troops to recapture the city. With the British ships gone and supplies cut off, victory seemed imminent for the new allies. That was, until a summer storm damaged the French fleet to such an extent that D'Estaing had to return to Boston for repairs, leaving Sullivan and his troops to face the superior British and Hessian force alone. He opted to retreat.

As the British and Hessian forces drew closer, the American retreat stopped and turned to face them at the hills outside of Newport.

Commanding the center of the American force was Sullivan himself. To his left was General Lafayette and to his right was General Nathanael Greene. It was under his cousin's command that Christopher Greene now stood with the Rhode Island militia and his First Rhode Island Regiment.

The struggle to raise this regiment had not been an easy one. First had come the acrimonious debate in the Assembly, then the public outcry against arming slaves. To make matters worse, white men had gathered around Greene and his officers at the recruiting table, seeking to discourage any slaves that sought to enlist. The loudest had been Hazard Potter.

You will be used as barricade for the white soldiers to hide behind!" he yelled as the slaves sought to enlist. "You will always be put in the places too dangerous for the white soldiers!"[11] In spite of Potter and others, Greene raised a regiment.

As Greene glanced down the line to see the First Rhode Island, he felt a surge of pride. These were his men. But not trained to the level he had wished for, and facing their baptism of fire, he was uncertain how they would fight.

He glanced farther down the line and caught the eye of Jack Sisson. A white, toothy grin split the man's face as he nodded at Greene. Greene smiled in return.

For a man as experienced as Sisson in the ways of war, he was still only a private. Yet, he had more experience than most officers Greene knew. Jack had been part of the daring raid that snatched the British Major General Richard Prescott right out of his bed in July of 1777. It was Jack who navigated one of the American whaleboats through the thunderstorm and past the British ships of war. It was Jack who had followed his commanding officer into Prescott's headquarters at the Overing house, four miles outside of Newport, Rhode Island. Making short work of the sentinel, the short but powerful Jack head-butted the door to the house open. Prescott's door received the same fate of the house's front door as Jack and his commanding officer, Lieutenant Colonel William Barton, grabbed Prescott, making him a prisoner of war. It had been a major coup for the Americans, who exchanged Prescott for one of their own captured generals, Charles Lee.[12]

Greene snapped out of his reverie as the British cannons at the top of Quaker Hill roared, followed by the Hessian ones atop Turkey Hill. The American cannons responded, and the battle began.

He saw his cousin, Nathanael, riding on his horse, surrounded by his staff. They were not only cousins, they were friends. Nathanael saw Christopher from a distance.

"A fine day for battle, is it not, Kitt?" Nathanael asked. It was the nickname he used for both his brother Christopher and his cousin.

"A strange place to find two Friends!" Christopher called in return. The fact that the two of them, along with their cousin Griffin, had been suspended from the pacifist Society of

Friends served only to strengthen the bond between them. The three, along with Nathanael's brother, had joined the Kentish Guards of Rhode Island to march in aid of the defense of Boston in 1775.

Knowing his men, both militia and the First Rhode Island, were raw recruits, Greene placed them behind a thicket in the valley at the base of Butt's Hill. As the enemy charged, Greene saw the Hessian uniforms of blue and yellow. They were headed straight for his position.

Along the American lines, gunfire erupted. Through the clouds of gun smoke, the Hessians burst upon Greene and his men. To the Hessians' surprise, they were driven back in a furious onslaught of fire. They regrouped and charged again. As one observer of the battle wrote, the Hessians "experienced a more obstinate resistance than they had expected."[13]

"Steady!" Greene shouted as the Hessians charged once more. Again, the American line erupted with musket fire. Again the Hessian line wavered as it charged and then collapsed. The men around Greene cheered as the Hessian soldiers retreated, leaving piles of dead and dying men behind them.

But, Greene knew they would be back. Ever since the beating Washington had given them at Trenton, and the defeat he had handed them at Fort Mercer, the Hessians seemed to have become even fiercer, more brutal, as if they had something to prove in battle.

And so they charged the American lines again.

By now, many of Greene's Rhode Islanders had thrown off their packs and stripped off their uniforms. Fighting in short-sleeve undergarments, blacks alongside whites, their muscular and sinewy arms glistening with sweat in the intense heat of the day, caused the remark later from the commanding officer of the Hessians: "We found obstinate resistance, the bodies of troops behind the work and at its sides, chiefly wild looking men in their shirt sleeves, and among them many negroes."

As was typical of their training, neither the British nor the Hessians removed their packs or uniforms. Greene could see they were suffering in the heat, yet they still charged.

He heard the commands barked out in German, heard the Hessians shouting encouragement to each other. Closer and closer they came. Greene knew it was on the third charge that the British won the day on Bunker Hill. This day would be different, though.

When the Hessians were so close Greene felt he could touch them, he snapped the command, "Fire!"

The front line of the Hessians literally disappeared, mowed down by the muskets of Greene's men. And just like that, their will to fight was gone. Throwing aside packs and guns, they turned and ran.

One of Greene's First Rhode Islanders, speaking years later at an abolition meeting, recounted the battle.

> ...the regiment to which I belonged [the First Rhode Island] was once ordered to what was called a flanking position—that is, upon a place where the enemy must pass in order to come around our rear...it was a post of imminent danger. They attacked us with great fury, but were repulsed. They reinforced and attacked us again, with more vigor and determination, and again were repulsed. Again they reinforced, and attacked us a third

time, with the most desperate courage and resolution, but a third time were repulsed. The contest was fearful. Our position was hotly disputed and as hotly maintained.[15]

Little did Greene and his men know that the first attack made that day by the British and their allies on the left front of the American forces was stymied. Regrouping, the British and their allies gathered all their forces and launched an attack on the right wing of the American lines, directly at Greene and his position, knowing they were raw troops. Had his men not held the line, the day would have been lost for the Americans.

To the wonderment of all, the First Rhode Island suffered only seven casualties—one dead and six wounded.

In later years, a Rhode Island historian wrote that "it was in repelling these furious onsets that the newly raised black regiment, under Col. Green, distinguished itself by deeds of desperate valor."[16]

On the night of August 30-31, the Americans quietly withdrew, moving by boat back to the mainland. Their timely withdrawal was none too soon. On September 1, Sir Henry Clinton reinforced the British and Hessian forces on Newport with ten regiments of infantry and two brigades of artillery. Although the attempt to re-take Newport had failed, General Lafayette wrote of the battle, "[It was] the best fought action of the war."[17] The Americans had defeated their pursuers with a loss of 211 men. The British and Hessians had lost 260.

In May 1781, due to the shrinking numbers of enlisted men, the Continental Congress combined the First and Second

Rhode Island Regiments into one unit. Christopher Greene was appointed commander of the new unit, with Jeremiah Olney and Ebenezer Flagg as his lieutenants. The heroes of Fort Mifflin and Newport, Simeon Thayer and Samuel Ward, were forced into retirement.

As his horse clopped along the road, Greene inhaled deeply of the fresh spring air of New York. He turned in his saddle to glance at the handful of men behind him. Remnants of the First Rhode Island, these men insisted on staying with him, calling themselves his bodyguards. It seemed that wherever he was, these loyal men were with him.

In the years since the Battle of Newport, the slaves Greene had recruited had become one of the best-trained units in the American army. Extremely loyal, unlike the white soldiers surrounding them, there were no desertions. But they had been left out of the action for some time, stationed to guard Rhode Island even after the British had turned their attentions elsewhere. The action had been so limited that Greene had written George Washington: "I should be very much pleased if your excellency could...order me southward with General Greene. I have no other motive than of having a better opportunity of serving my country than I can probably have here."[18] His request was denied, and yet, shortly thereafter, he and his men were stationed in New York.

Now it was the evening of May 13, 1781. Stationed on the Croton River 20 miles north of Manhattan Island, Greene's Rhode Islanders enjoyed a time of relative quiet.

The tide had turned—the American cause was nearing victory. Greene smiled as he thought of his cousin, Nathanael.

In the early months of 1781, his cousin and the British General Cornwallis fought bitterly, engaging at Guilford Courthouse, where Nathanael, though beaten, had inflicted heavy casualties on the British. And he was still alive, nipping at Cornwallis' heels.

As he rode, Greene was lost in thought. Though he and his troops were inactive and enemy seemingly elsewhere, he was anxious. He knew that Oliver DeLancey and his Loyalist cavalry were in the region. A firm supporter of King George III, the New Yorker had personally raised and funded three battalions of Loyalist troops to form his Brigade. Known for its bravery and fierceness, the Brigade was used extensively by the British, who sent it to fight in several major campaigns during the war.

Now, with his men forward on the American lines and DeLancy's Brigade only 20 miles away, Greene knew he had every right to be cautious. Earlier in the year, American General Samuel Parsons had raided and destroyed DeLancy's base camp, capturing 52 of the Loyalists. Greene knew they would be seeking revenge.

He had written to Samuel Ward, his former lieutenant, only days before. "I expect when I go to the lines to be more industrious and alert, otherwise I may be surprised; that, you know, I always held up as unpardonable to an officer."[19]

It was this premonition that had Greene and his bodyguards riding to the forward position of the Rhode Island battalion to meet with Major Flagg. When he arrived, his fears seemed unfounded. There was no reported activity, no sign of DeLancy's Brigade.

As Greene slept that night, DeLancy's Brigade was on the move. One hundred fifty mounted Loyalists, riding hard, crossed the Croton River, heading straight for the Davenport House where Major Flagg's headquarters were. They encountered no opposition until they reached the house.

Greene awoke suddenly to the sound of horses whinnying, men shouting and torches glaring. Rushing to his window, he saw the courtyard below filled with men in red coats, cutting down the American sentries. Some of the Americans had already surrendered. He saw Major Flagg leaning out his window, pistols in both hands. He fired twice and two of the enemy fell. As he tried to reload, he himself was shot dead.

Wheeling around, still in his bedclothes, Greene grabbed his sword. He heard boot steps on the stairs outside his door and gripped his sword even tighter. If the fighting between the British and Americans was fierce, the fighting between the Loyalist and American troops accorded a new level of brutality. No quarter was given and none was expected.

Bursting out his door, Greene saw his bodyguards at the head of the stairs, slashing, yelling, fighting. They were soon overwhelmed, and Greene entered the fray, one against many.

Several of the enemy fell beneath his sword until, wounded twice in his sword arm, with a bayonet thrust in his side and several sword slashes to the head, Greene succumbed through loss of blood—he did not surrender. Little else is known of the events at the Davenport House that night, save this—Greene, his bodyguard, and Flagg all went down fighting. It was written of the night that "the sabers of the enemy only reached [Greene] through the bodies of his faithful guard of blacks, who hovered over him to protect him, and every one of them was killed."[20] Later that morning, Greene's body was found, half naked, by the road where DeLancey's men had discarded it. He and Major Flagg were given heroes' funerals.

In the days following the surprise attack, General William Heath wrote to General Washington, "Intelligence received on the 14th, Colonel Greene of the Rhode Island Regiment...was surprised by a body of the enemy's horse...the Colonel, Major Flagg, two subalterns and twenty-seven men were killed...Colonel Greene was a brave and intrepid officer, and his loss is much regretted."[21]

As for Greene's First Rhode Island, command was given to Jeremiah Olney, who had been with Greene from the beginning. Dubbed Olney's Battalion, the regiment served through the remainder of the war. At Yorktown, due to their reputation for bravery and fierceness, General Lafayette handpicked 40 men from Olney's battalion for the final assault on Redoubt 10.

On November 1, 1783, Olney's Battalion was disbanded. For five years, the black men who formed the core of the battalion had fought and died for the American cause.

Not one of them ever deserted.

Notes

1. Lossing, *Pictorial Field Book of the Revolution, Volume II.*

2. Letter from ALexander Hamilton to Christopher Greene, October 15, 1777, *George Washington Papers at the Library of Congress, 1741–1799.*

3. Letter from Christopher Greene to George Washington, October 14, 1777, *George Washington Papers at the Library of Congress, 1741–1799.*

4. Letter from George Washington to Christopher Greene, October 24, 1777, *George Washington Papers at the Library of Congress, 1741–1799.*

5. Showman, ed., Letter from Nathanael Greene to Christopher Green, October 1777, *The Papers of General Nathanael Greene, Vol. II*, 181.

6. Raymond, "Colonel Christopher Greene," 141.

7. Description of expedition to Canada and the battle of Quebec taken from Bray and Bushnell, eds., *Diary of a Common Soldier,* 13-24.

8. Letter from General James Varnum to George Washington, January 2, 1778, *George Washington Papers at the Library of Congress, 1741–1799.*

9. Letter from George Washington to Nicholas Cooke, January 2, 1778, *George Washington Papers at the Library of Congress, 1741–1799.*

10. Rider, "The Black Regiment of the Revolution," 10-11, and Adams, "Deeds of Desperate Valor."

11. Greene, "Some Observations of the Black Regiment", 161.

12. Falkner, "Captor of the Barefoot General," 29-31, 98-100.

13. Kaplan, *The Black Presence*, 64.

14. Ibid, 65.

15. Nell, *The Colored Patriots*, 40.

16. Kaplan, *The Black Presence*, 65.

17. Ibid, 64.

18. Letter from Christopher Greene to George Washington, Ocotober 27, 1780, *George Washington Papers at the Library of Congess, 1741–1799*.

19. Raymond, "Colonel Christopher Greene," 143.

20. Kaplan, *The Black Presence*, 65.

21. Raymond, "Colonel Christopher Greene," 143.

Chapter 4

RICHARD ALLEN

"The Purest Friend of Civil and Religious Liberty"

★   ★   ★

It was a cool Sunday morning in November of 1787 as Richard Allen and his three friends strode down Philadelphia's streets toward the Old St. George's Methodist Society. Their leader was the 27-year-old Richard Allen, who had been asked the year before by an elder at St. George's to come back to his birthplace and minister to the black community. Allen now spent his days preaching four or five times a day as well as helping lay the floor and build the gallery of St. George's.

Now, as the four men entered the church, the sexton of St. George's met them at the door. Giving the men a cold smile, the sexton pointed to the stairs leading up into the gallery. "The gallery is open for you," he said. "You will see what seats you can use."

The black men exchanged a look among themselves. It hadn't been too long ago that they had been free to sit and worship wherever they pleased. But as more and more blacks began attending the church, due in great part to Allen's preaching, the white members had begun moving the blacks into the seats lining the wall. Now they were being segregated to the gallery above the sanctuary. Without saying a word, the four men climbed the stairs to the gallery and moved toward the unoccupied seats near the front railing.

Below, the service had already begun, and as the congregation sang the opening hymn, the black men took their seats. As the last strains of the music died away, the elder motioned for the congregation to kneel.

"Let us pray," he said.

The prayers had just begun when Allen heard considerable scuffling and low talking just to the side of him. Lifting his head, he looked over to see one of the church's trustees pulling at one of his companions, the Reverend Absalom Jones, trying to wrestle Jones to his feet.

"You must get up!" the trustee whispered harshly, tugging at Jones. "You cannot kneel here!"

"Can we not wait until prayer is over?" Jones asked, trying to free himself from the trustee's grasp.

"You must get up now, or I will call for aid and force you to get up!" the trustee replied, struggling to pull Jones from his knees. Allen watched in surprise, and then dismay, as the scuffle continued.

The hostility toward the blacks at St. George's had been growing, but he hadn't anticipated this. The trustee called over another of his colleagues, who began pulling at William White, another of Allen's companions. By now the noise in the gallery was noticeable on the church floor, and there were some members craning their necks to watch the scene unfolding above them.

The prayer ended, and Allen stood to his feet. He looked at the church trustees and, without a word, moved down the stairs and walked out onto the streets. Jones and White shrugged off the hands of the trustees, and along with their other companion, Dorus Ginnings, followed Allen out of the church. There was a stirring among the white members of the congregation, but not one of them said a word as they watched the blacks exit the church.[1]

The sun was setting low in the west as the two slaves toiled away in their master's field, stopping to watch as a horse and rider approached. It was their master.

"Richard, aren't you going to meeting tonight?" Master Stokely asked as he pulled up next to his slaves.

"No, sir," Richard replied, wiping the sweat from his brow as he and his brother shook their heads. "I figure we're behind on getting the crops in."

Every week Master Stokely allowed them to attend the Methodist meetings. But they wouldn't be going tonight. The master's neighbors had said this indulging of the slaves was going to ruin Stokely, so the Allens decided that they would prove the neighbors wrong. They would attend more faithfully to the master's business, so that it couldn't be said that religion made them bad slaves.

"Doesn't matter to me," Stokely replied. "I'd rather you go to your meetings. If I can't be good, I like to see you striving yourselves to be good."

Allen looked at his brother, then back at Stokely. "Thank you, sir. But we would rather stay and make sure all the crops get in."

Later, Stokely commented to Allen, "I think this religion has made you a better person—it has made you more honest and diligent in your work."

"Sir, would you mind if I asked one of the Methodist preachers to come preach up at the main house?" Allen asked.

Stokely nodded his head. "I would like that."[2]

For the next several months, a Methodist minister by the name of Freeborn Garrettson frequently preached in Stokely's home. One day, Garrettson spoke on the words, "Thou art weighed in the balance and found wanting." Stokely believed that he had been found wanting, was converted, and promptly realized that he could no longer in all good conscience own slaves. He told Allen as much, and proposed to the Allen brothers that they buy their freedom.

A short time later, the Allen brothers did so. And while they earned the money to buy their freedom, Stokely held prayer services in his parlor every morning, and had the Allen brothers attend them. Then, in 1780, after paying 2,000 Continental dollars apiece, the two of them left Stokely's place and were freedmen. As they left Stokely's home, he called after them, "Boys, if you're ever sick, or you're ever in need of a place to rest your head, my house is always open to you." But Richard Allen never looked back. He would write in his memoirs, "…slavery is a bitter pill, notwithstanding we had a good master."[3]

Life wasn't easy for the newly freed Allen. He began cutting cord wood to earn a living, then moved to working in a brickyard, and eventually hauled salt for the Continental Army during the American War for Independence. He became an itinerant Methodist preacher and would often preach in the evenings, many times in a clearing in the woods. But it was after the war ended that he began preaching in earnest, and for three years roamed New Jersey, Delaware, and Pennsylvania, preaching in many of the small villages, staying with whoever would open his door to him. Many of the people who came to hear Allen's sermons were white, but color didn't seem to matter to them. One of the men listening to one of Allen's sermon was overheard telling another: "This man [Allen] must be a man of God; I have never heard such preaching before."

In time Francis Asbury, the noted Methodist circuit rider, heard of Allen's preaching, and asked that Allen come and meet with him. Asbury asked Allen to accompany him into the southern states to help Asbury with his ministry there. But he stipulated that Allen not intermix with the slaves, and due to Allen's color, Allen would spend most nights in Asbury's carriage. Though the two parted as friends, Allen refused Asbury's offer, and in February of 1786 went to Philadelphia and St. George's.[4]

He was assigned the 5 a.m. time to preach in the pulpit at St. George's, the only time allowed for the blacks to have their own preacher and service. He had been planning on staying in Philadelphia for only a few weeks, but when he saw the need among his people, the weeks stretched to months, then to years. Allen made the most of his first years in Philadelphia, and wrote in his memoirs: "I frequently preached twice a day, at 5 o'clock in the morning and in the evening, and it was not uncommon for me to preach from four to five times a day. I established prayer meetings; I raised a society for forty-two members. I saw the necessity of erecting a place of worship for the colored people."[5]

On the last point, Allen met opposition, both from the white and black communities. Realizing that he could not start an independent black church, Allen and Absalom Jones formed the Free African Society in May of 1787. Though not technically religious in nature, the Society was a benevolent one, looking out for the interest of the blacks in Philadelphia. Members were required to pay regular dues, and in turn widows, orphans, and those in need were supported with weekly payments from the coffers of the Society. However, after that November morning in 1787, Allen and Jones realized there was a pressing need for an independent black church. They were no longer welcome at St. George's, despite the fact that their money and labor had helped finish the building.

Then two men came to the blacks' aid: Robert Ralston, a prominent citizen in Philadelphia, and Dr. Benjamin Rush, a signer of the Declaration of Independence and a member of the Constitutional Convention. Allen and Jones called upon the two men, who were known to be friendly toward the plight of the slaves and freedmen, and found in Ralston and Rush advocates for their cause. With their help, Allen and his companions began raising money for a new church. However, the members of St. George's did not look kindly upon Allen and Jones's work. One day an elder of St. George's, John McClaskey, called on the two freedmen.

"If you don't stop raising money for a new church, you and your friends will be turned out of the Methodist meeting," McClaskey threatened, glaring at Allen and Jones.

"Have we violated any rules of discipline by raising money?" Allen asked, looking at Jones, perplexed by McClaskey's words.

"I have been charged by the Methodist Conference to order you to stop. If you don't, you will be publicly read out of the meeting," McClaskey replied.

"We are willing to abide by the discipline of the Methodist church," Allen said. "If you will show us where we have violated any law of discipline of the church, we will submit. But if there is no rule violated, we will continue on."

McClaskey was growing irritated. "We will read you and all of your friends out!"

"If you turn us out contrary to the rule of discipline, we will seek redress," Allen shot back. "We were dragged off our knees at St. George's, treated worse than heathens! We will continue on, with the Lord as our helper!"

"You are not Methodists!" McClaskey retorted before leaving.

Several days later, McClaskey returned. "You are determined to build a new church?" he asked.

"Of course," Allen replied. "We have no place of worship right now. We will not go to St. George's again after that scandalous treatment we endured in front of the entire congregation. If you deny us our name, you cannot seal up the scriptures, nor can you deny us a name in heaven. Heaven is free for all who worship in spirit and truth."

"We will disown you from the Methodist connection," McClaskey stated.

"If we put our trust in the Lord; he will stand by us," Allen returned, ending the conversation.[6]

Allen and Jones began raising money in earnest, and on their first day raised $360. A church was built, and "the first African Church or meetinghouse was erected in the United States of America." When it came time to decide what the denomination of the new church would be, a vote was held. Though the majority voted that the church become Anglican, two men, Richard Allen and Absalom Jones, voted that the church be of the Methodist denomination. Allen wrote:

> Notwithstanding we had been so violently persecuted by the elder [McClaskey], we were in favor of being attached to the Methodist connection; for I was confident that there was no religious sect or denomination [that] would suit the capacity of the colored people as well as the Methodist; for the plain and simple gospel suits best for any people; for the unlearned can understand, and the learned are sure to understand; and the reason that the Methodist is so successful in the awakening and conversion of the colored people, the plain doctrine and having a good discipline....The Methodists were the first people that brought glad tidings to the colored people. I feel thankful that ever I heard a Methodist preach. We are beholden to

the Methodists, under God, for the light of the Gospel we enjoy.[7]

His words spoke volumes of his character. Instead of harboring bitterness against the Methodist church for the wrongs done to him and his companions by St. George's, Allen instead chose to focus on what was right with the Methodist denomination and not on the human frailties of some who were members of that church.

When he was asked to be the minister of the new African Church, Allen refused: "I was a Methodist. I was indebted to the Methodists, under God, for what little religion I had...was born and awakened under them." Instead, in 1793, Allen and ten others began their own Methodist church. Allen bought an old blacksmith shop, hooked it up to his team of horses, and hauled the building to a lot he had purchased at the corner of Sixth and Lombard. Hiring several carpenters to repair the old frame, Allen made the building fit for worship. Soon the building was outgrown, and borrowing $2,000, Allen built a brick church on the site. In July of 1794, he asked Bishop Asbury to dedicate the church. Asbury agreed and preached the dedication sermon. The church was named Bethel Church, and Allen became its head deacon.[8]

At this juncture, McClaskey approached Allen once more and proposed that he give the church over to the Methodist Conference. Allen refused. After some debate, McClaskey informed Allen that Bethel Church at least had to be incorporated. When he offered to draw up the incorporation papers to save the blacks money, Allen agreed. McClaskey promptly drew up the incorporation papers and incorporated Bethel

Church under the Methodist Conference, consigning all the church's property to the white members of the Methodist Connection. For ten years, Allen was unaware of the trickery used against him until a new elder, James Smith, was appointed to take charge of the Methodist church in Philadelphia.

Smith called upon Allen, and it quickly became evident that Smith was going to make things difficult. "You will turn over the keys and books of the church to me, and I forbid you to hold any meetings except by my orders," Smith began.

Startled by Smith's words, Allen refused to acquiesce to Smith's demands. "This church is ours. We bought it and paid for the refurbishing of it," Allen said.

"You are incorporated under the Methodist Connection. You will submit to my requests," Smith replied, "or I will have you read out of the Connection."

Allen, confused by the turn of events, sought legal counsel. To his dismay, the lawyer informed him that the incorporation papers written up ten years before had given all of Bethel's property to the white Methodists.

"Is there any way we can alter this?" Allen asked.

"If two-thirds of your society agree to sign a petition for a supplement to the incorporation papers, you can," the lawyer replied. "Then the supplement must be granted by the state legislature."[9]

Allen immediately called the society of Bethel Church together and laid the facts before them. They unanimously voted to change the incorporation papers, and before Smith was aware of the situation, the Legislature of Pennsylvania had granted the supplement. Allen had the African Supplement attached to the incorporation papers, effectively taking Bethel away from the Methodist Conference and placing it once again under the blacks' control. This move, in Allen's own words, "raised a considerable rumpus."

Smith and the St. George's trustees called the African Methodist society together and informed them that they must pay St. George's $600 a year for them to be supplied with a white preacher—Allen, who was only a deacon, could not administer the sacraments, only an ordained minister could. After some debate, the blacks informed St. George's that they would pay $200 a year for a white preacher to minister five times a year to them. But the white Methodists were displeased with this offer, and John Emory of the Methodist Academy published a circular letter, disowning Bethel Church from the Methodist Connection. The white Methodists even tried to form a new church down the street from Bethel in hopes of drawing away Bethel's congregation. That effort failed.

Ultimately, a new elder, Robert Birch, moved to Philadelphia, and the struggle between the Methodist Connection and Bethel Church came to a head. Though the blacks at Bethel enjoyed the freedom to run their own affairs, the Methodist Conference technically still owned the church. The church was put up for auction, apparently by the Conference, and Allen was forced to buy Bethel off the auction block for $10,125—a tremendous sum for that day.

In a final play for control over Bethel, Birch informed Allen that he would be giving a sermon from Bethel's pulpit regardless of Allen's wishes. But when Birch arrived at the church at a little before 3 p.m. on December 31, 1815, he found a meeting already taking place.

Allen related the incident to Daniel Coker, the minister of the black church in Baltimore: "When the day arrived that he [Birch] intended to preach, we began meeting a little after 2 o'clock. The house was crowded, and the aisles all filled with people and benches so that he could not get halfway up the aisle; for observe, he came about a quarter before 3 o'clock."

Birch, furious at the situation, interrupted the meeting, calling out to the black minister in the pulpit, "Jacob Tapsicoe, did you not know that it was my appointment?"

From where he stood behind the pulpit, Tapiscoe looked down at Birch. "Silence, sir! I am preaching in the name of my God, by the authority of the laws of my country!"

Shocked at the response, Birch sputtered a few words in reply, then promptly turned on his heel and left the building. The next day, Birch applied to the Supreme Court of Pennsylvania for a writ of mandamus, which would give him the right to preach at Bethel. Allen wasn't about to back down, and he met fire with fire. He sent lawyers to defend Bethel before the Court, and Mr. Binney, one of Allen's lawyers, argued that, "...the Rev. Mr. Burch [sic], nor any other elder in the connection, had any right to the pulpit of Bethel, contrary to the wish of the society; for any grant that had been made to the elder by the trustees might be taken from him at their pleasure...."[10]

The Supreme Court agreed with Binney and denied the writ, saying that nothing would be gained by forcing Allen and his church to listen to a preacher whom they opposed. The ruling in Bethel's favor ended the debate over who would run Bethel Church; St. George's was no longer its mother church and it was now free to run its own affairs.

However, frustrated by years of poor treatment by the Methodists, Allen and 15 other ministers from Philadelphia and Baltimore met together in April of 1816. After several days of debating their grievances, the delegates to the convention resolved: "That the people of Philadelphia, Baltimore... should become one body, under the name of the African Methodist Episcopal Church." It was the first independent black denomination in America, and "the Rev. Richard Allen, being seventeen years an ordained minister by the Rev. Bishop Francis Asury of the Methodist church,"[11] was elected as its first bishop.

There were other battles for Allen to face. By now he was the recognized leader of the free blacks in the North, and he used his influence to better the lot of his people. He became involved in moral reform, creating a society for the Suppression of Vice and Immorality among the black community. He helped create a temperance society and worked on behalf of women's rights. Knowing that education was vital for the future of his people, Allen started a school for black children. By 1811, there were 11 such schools throughout Philadelphia.

But his biggest struggle in his later years was against colonization, the idea of sending freed slaves back to Africa. To Allen, colonization was nothing more than a subtle attempt to remove blacks from America. What discouraged him was that it had its strong proponents. Numerous state legislatures approved of colonization, and the Presbyterian, Methodist,

Baptist, and Dutch Reformed churches all endorsed the movement.[12]

In December of 1816, the American Colonization Society held its first meeting. In attendance were James Monroe, Andrew Jackson, Francis Scott Key, and Henry Clay.[13] It was clear to Allen that the colonization movement must be fought immediately, and little more than two weeks after the Colonization Society met, a meeting was called at Bethel. Nearly three thousand free blacks crowded into the building.[14]

"Friends," Allen began, looking out on the packed assembly, "can we not discern the project of sending the free people of colour away from their country? Is it not for the interests of the slave-holders to select the free people of colour out of different states, and send them to Liberia?"[15] He paused, watching and listening for the effect of his words. A ripple of whispers passed through the crowd. "Our ancestors, though not of their own free will, were the first successful cultivators of the wilds of America, and we their descendants feel ourselves entitled to participate in the blessings of her luxuriant soil. The Colonization Society is planning our removal from this country. If the movement is allowed to run its course, the freed population will be removed from America. We must fight. We are Americans, and we should have the right to compete in a free society, socially and economically."[16]

Only a few weeks after the public meeting, the American Colonization Society sent a Reverend Finley to talk Allen and the other leaders of the anti-colonization movement out of their plans for opposition. John Forten, one of the black leaders in Philadelphia, and Allen, made it very clear that they strongly opposed the programs of the A.C.S. and were convinced that it would produce only unfortunate results for all blacks in America. In November 1827, Allen wrote in *Freedom's Journal*, the nation's first colored newspaper: "This land which we have watered with our tears and our blood is now our mother country."

Allen's fight against colonization was ultimately successful. Though President James Monroe passed legislation in 1821 purchasing property in Africa for the establishment of a colony of freed slaves known as Liberia, by 1830, of the nearly 200,000 freed blacks in America, only 2,638 emigrated back to Africa.[17]

When Allen died in 1831 at the age of 71, the great abolitionist, William Lloyd Garrison, wrote in his newspaper, *The Liberator*:

> When a good man dies, his country sustains a loss; but when not only a good but a great man has been summoned by the Angel of death to bid farewell to existence, humanity throughout the world becomes a mourner. In the death of RICHARD ALLEN, the first Bishop of the African Methodist Episcopal church, religion has lost one of her brightest, most talented, and distinguished ornaments; philanthropy one of her firmest and most practical advocates and supporters; and the cause of African Emancipation one of the purest friends and patriots that ever exerted his energies in favor of civil and religious liberty.[18]

Notes

1. Allen, *Life Experience*, 13.
2. Ibid, 6.
3. Ibid, 7.
4. George, *Segregated Sabbaths*, 32.
5. Allen, *Life Experience*, 12.
6. Ibid, 14-15.
7. Ibid, 16-17
8. Matthews, *Richard Allen*, 81.
9. Allen, *Life Experience*, 18-19.
10. Cannon, *A History of the African-American Methodist Episcopal Church*, 24.
11. Ibid, 9.
12. George, *Segregated Sabbaths*, 138-139.
13. *"The American Colonization Society,"* 2002. <http://webby.cc.denison.edu/~waite/liberia/history/acs.htm>.
14. George, *Segregated Sabbaths*, 139.
15. Ibid.
16. George, *Segregated Sabbaths*, 135; Matthews, *Richard Allen*, 110.
17. *"The American Colonization Society,"* 2002.
18. George, *Segregated Sabbaths*, 173.

Chapter 5

ADONIRAM JUDSON

"A life once spent is irrevocable.
It remains to be contemplated throughout eternity..."

It was early Tuesday evening, June 8, 1824, when the door of the Judsons' house crashed open and a Burmese official and a dozen armed soldiers rushed into the room. They were accompanied by another Burman, whose tattooed cheeks signified a king's executioner.

The missionary, Adoniram Judson, and his wife, Ann, looked up in surprise.

"Where is the teacher?" the official demanded. "Where is the teacher Yoodathan?"

"I am the teacher," Judson replied, rising from where he sat at his dinner table.

"You are called by the king," the official stated.

The executioner immediately seized Judson and threw him to the floor. Pinning Judson with a knee to the back, the executioner pulled out a thin, small cord, one of the Burmese's instruments of torture.

Ann Judson grabbed the executioner's arm. "Stay," she begged. "I will give you money."

The official looked at Ann. "Take her too. She also is a foreigner."

"Please," Judson gasped from where he lay on the floor. "Your orders were for me, not for her. Let her stay until further orders."

The official looked at Judson and shrugged. With a jerk of his head, he motioned for the executioner to move. Drawing the thin cord tightly around Judson's arms, the executioner roughly jerked Judson to his feet and dragged him through the door.

Outside the scene was chaotic. The masons who had been working on the Judsons' home threw down their tools and ran, while the children of the neighborhood began screaming and crying. The Judsons' Bengalese servants stood in the shadows of the doorway, frozen in fear, as the Burmese soldiers and executioner led Judson away.

Several weeks before, war had broken out between Burma and England. Now all foreigners in Ava, capital of Burma, were being rounded up and imprisoned on suspicion of being British spies.

Ann followed the Burmese and her husband a short way, begging the executioner to take some money and loosen Judson's cords. The executioner refused. Frantic, Ann gave the money to one of her servants and asked him to persuade the executioner to loosen the cords. Hurrying after the retreating forms of Judson and his captors, the servant begged them to loosen Judson's bindings. The executioner gave the servant a cold smile, then threw Judson to the ground and pulled the cords even tighter, so tight that Judson's breathing was nearly cut off.[1] By the time the procession arrived at the courthouse, Judson's arms were swelling and bleeding, and his breathing was coming in short gasps.

The judge ordered the cords loosened, then motioned for one of the court's officers to read the charges. "Mr. Yoodathan," the officer said, looking at Judson, "you have been arrested at the order of the king. You will be taken to Hand Shrink Not and held as long as the king so wills it."

Judson, dazed, still gasping for air, heard the words and realized what they meant. Hand Shrink Not was the Burmese term for their death prison, and many who entered never came out alive.

Dragged from the courtroom, Judson was led to prison and was met in the courtyard by the chief executioner. With a wicked smile, the man, his cheeks covered with spotted tattoos, his chest branded with the word *murderer*, looked at Judson.

"Greetings, my beloved child," he said. "I am your father now."[2] He ordered Judson led to the center of the courtyard, where three pairs of fetters were riveted on to Judson's legs. Forced onto his feet, Judson was led into a windowless room, which was covered with refuse and occupied by 50 prisoners. One of the prison guards motioned for him to lie in the corner and be quiet.

Lying there, Judson's eyes adjusted to the darkness, and he was able to see that he was not the only foreigner there. There were several Englishmen whom he knew, and a short while later, another Christian missionary, Dr. Price, was flung into the room.

That night, the chief executioner entered the room, accompanied by several assistants.

"Hello, my children," he said. "I have come to wish you a good night."

Lowering from the prison roof a long bamboo pole suspended by pulleys, the chief executioner and his assistants ran the bamboo pole through the prisoner's fetters, then hoisted the bamboo pole up until only the prisoners' shoulders and heads rested on the floor.

The chief executioner studied the height of the pole, then lowered it a bit. "I want to protect your lives," he assured the prisoners before leaving.[3]

Left in the darkness, surrounded by the stench of the prison, his legs suspended above his head for the night, his arms still throbbing from the brutal cords that had bound them, Judson was alone with his thoughts. Sixteen years before he had been a brash young graduate of Brown University, the valedictorian of his class, an avowed Deist who had rejected his conservative Congregationalist upbringing. Then one night an event took place that was to change his life forever and start him down the road that led to Ava and the death prison.

He had left home a month before, a 20-year-old graduate of college, declaring to his father that he could not believe in the God of the Bible or that Jesus was the Son of God. He traveled from Plymouth, Massachusetts, to New York City, intent on becoming an actor and playwright. But after several weeks of roaming the countryside outside New York City with a troupe of actors, Judson became disenchanted with the life of an actor, and one night he slipped away and headed north. Several nights later he found himself stopping at a small country inn.

"Do you have a room?" Judson asked the landlord.

"There is one left," the landlord replied.

As he led Judson to his room, the landlord looked over his shoulder.

"I hope you do not mind, but I have been obliged to place you next to the room of a young man who is very ill; I'm afraid he is dying," the landlord said. "I hope this will not cause you any uneasiness."

Judson shook his head. "I assure you, beyond pity for the sick man, I will have no other feelings of uneasiness."

Despite his brave words, Judson spent a very restless night at the inn. He could hear the sounds of activity in the dying man's room, the groans, the creaking of the floor as those tending the sick man moved in and out of the room. Thoughts began to cross Judson's mind. *The man is probably going to die, perhaps even tonight. But is he ready? Is he pre-pared to die?*

Judson sat up in bed, a faint smile on his face at those thoughts. *What would his friends say about him, an avowed Deist, having such worries?* He thought of his good friend from Brown, Jacob Eames, the one who had persuaded him of his Deist beliefs. *What would Jacob Eames—talented, witty, intellectual Eames—have to say?* Judson shook his head and lay back down. But again the thoughts came.

Is the dying man a Christian, calm and strong at the hope of immortality? Or is he afraid, fearful of what might lie over the brink of the dark unknown? Was he a "freethinker," raised and educated by Christian parents? Who was he?

But the light of the rising sun dispelled the doubts of the night, and rising from his fitful sleep, Judson gathered his few things and went downstairs to settle with the landlord. As he was paying his bill, Judson asked after the sick young man.

"How is he?" Judson asked.

"He is dead," the landlord replied.

"Dead?!"

"Yes, he is gone, poor fellow. The doctor said he would not last the night."

"Do you know who he was?"

"Oh, yes. A young man from Providence, a very fine fel-low. His name was Eames—Jacob Eames."

Stunned and speechless, Judson staggered to a nearby chair. For hours he sat there, staring straight ahead, unable to move. He eventually managed to leave the inn and continue on his journey. But he was still lost in thought over his friend

Jacob Eames. *Dead! Lost! Lost!* The words kept echoing and reverberating through his head. *Lost! Lost for eternity.*

Judson pulled his horse up short and sat there on the road, and then and there he knew. The Bible was true. He knew it. It had to be, and in his despair over Eames he was prepared to face his doubts over its truths. He pulled his horse's head about and quietly urged it back down the road toward Plymouth and home.[4]

One month later, Judson enrolled at Andover Theological Seminary, "but, having made no profession of religion, he could not be received as a member in full standing."[5] The next several months were spent wrestling with his doubts. A Professor Woods, able to discuss ideas at Judson's intellectual level, helped Judson along. Finally, in December, Judson wrote in his journal that he had dedicated himself to God. Dr. Francis Wayland, a friend and Judson's biographer, later wrote, "...gradually faith, trust in God, and finally hope through the merits of Christ, took possession of his soul, he scarcely knew how; and from the moment that he fully believed, I think he never doubted."[6]

In September of 1809, Judson came across a sermon entitled "A Star in the East." A Dr. Claudius Buchanan in Bristol, England, had given it, and it recounted Dr. Buchanan's work in India and how India was ready for the gospel. Judson became fascinated with the idea of the foreign mission field. He would recount, "For some days I was unable to attend to the studies of my class, and spent my time in wondering at my past stupidity, depicting the most romantic scenes in missionary life, and roving about the college rooms, declaiming on the subject of missions." He came across a book, entitled *Embassy to Burma*, and became enamored with the idea of going to Burma to preach the gospel. Then, during a walk in the woods behind the seminary, while meditating and praying about the subject, "the command of Christ, 'Go into all the world, and preach the gospel to every creature,' was presented to my mind with such clearness and power, that I came to a full decision, and though great difficulties appeared in my way, resolved to obey the commandment in all events." There was no foreign mission board in America at the time, and there were no other students at Andover interested in pursuing the idea of foreign missions. But Judson was determined. If necessary, he would sail to England and join the London Missionary Society.

Soon he rallied a handful of young men who also were intent upon foreign missions, and in June of 1810, Judson found himself addressing the General Association of the Congregational Church on the subject of foreign missions.

"The undersigned, members of the Divinity College, respectfully request the attention of their reverend fathers," Judson began, reading from the petition he and three others had written out and signed. "They beg leave to state that their minds have been long impressed with the duty and importance of personally attempting a mission to the heathen. After examining all the information that they can obtain, they consider themselves as devoted to this work for life, whenever God, in his providence, shall open the way." There was a gasp throughout the assembly, but Judson continued on. "The undersigned, feeling their youth and inexperience, look up to their fathers in the Church, and respectfully solicit their advice, direction and prayers." He paused, then read, "Signed by

Adoniram Judson, Jr., Samuel Nott, Jr., Samuel J. Mills, and Samuel Newell."[7]

Less than two years later, Judson was aboard the *Caravan*, sailing for India then to Burma, a missionary sent out under the auspices of the newly formed American Board of Missions. But, he was not alone. The day he had addressed the General Association, he had met a young woman by the name of Ann Hasseltine, and in several months' time, Judson asked Ann to marry him. She accepted. Now the two Judsons, joined by Samuel Newell and his wife, Harriet, stood at the railing of the *Caravan* on a cold, blustery February day, watching the port of Salem disappear over the horizon. They didn't know if they would ever return, and they had only the slightest idea of what lay in store for them.

During the four-month journey, Judson did something he had never dreamed of: He became a Baptist. Raised in a Congregational home by Congregational parents, he was a Congregational minister sent out by the Congregational mission board. In expectation of how his theological views might clash with the Baptist missionaries in India, Judson began studying the subject of baptism in detail. To his surprise, he realized that the Bible clearly taught that faith must always precede baptism, and that baptism is immersion. So Judson promptly told Ann that he was a Baptist and wrote the Baptist church in America that if they should form a mission board, he would be their first missionary.

When the Judsons and Newells landed in India, they were met with a series of discouraging news. William Carey, the renowned British missionary to India, shook his head when Judson stated he and the others were headed to Burma.

"My son, Felix, is there," Carey said. "I cannot say that your prospects there are good. The country is full of corruption. Your lives would depend on the whim of the ruling governor, and religious toleration is unknown. You could very well be killed if the Burmans suspect you are trying to convert them." Carey shook his head. "Besides, enemy raids from Siam and internal rebellion, thievery and robbery are so common that you never know if you will live until the next day."[8]

Taken aback by the news, the Judsons were even more discouraged by Carey's next words.

"I doubt the East India Company will let you stay here in India," Carey said.

"Why?" Judson asked.

"The Company does not want the preaching of the gospel to the Hindus. They fear the 'subversive ideas' of the gospel might create unrest," Carey replied. "But in all honesty, I fear the Company's real reason is that the Company is deriving large revenues directly from the toleration and protection of the Hindu religion. Whatever their reason, they are determined to resist the introduction of Christianity here."[9]

Ten days later, Judson and Newell were summoned to Calcutta, and the East India Company agent ordered them to immediately leave the country and return to America. Judson and Newell "petitioned for leave to reside in some other part of India, but were prohibited from settling in any part of the company's territory, or in any of its dependents."

The Newells obtained passage on a ship leaving for the Isle of France, an English-held island in the middle of the Indian Ocean. The Judsons remained in Calcutta for several more months, looking for passage to the Isle of France, when the Company ordered them to sail for England on one of the Company's ships. The Judsons were desperate not to be sent to England. There was war between America and England now, and who knew how long their forced stay in England might last. At the last minute a ship bound for the Isle of France was found, and under cover of darkness the Judsons slipped aboard the ship. The Company discovered the attempted escape, however, and prevented the ship's departure. Permission was eventually granted for the Judsons to sail, so long as they sailed away from any of the East India Company territories.

They arrived at the Isle of France, then sailed for Madras, intent upon finding someplace to land and begin their missionary work. Yet, their difficulties with the East India Company had not ended. Judson wrote:

> We arrived there [Madras] in June, and were immediately informed of the renewed hostility of the company's government towards missionaries…We were, of course, reported to the police, and an account of our arrival forwarded to the supreme government in Bengal. It became…a moral certainty that, as soon as an order could be received at Madras, we should be again arrested, and ordered to England. Our only safety appeared to consist in escaping from Madras before such an order arrived.[10]

Judson went down to the Madras harbor and found only one ship that would sail soon enough. It was a "crazy old" Portuguese vessel, the *Georgiana*, headed for Rangoon, Burma.

As Judson wrote, "A mission to Rangoon we had been accustomed to regard with feelings of horror. But it was now brought to a point. We must either venture there or be sent to England." With those their only choices, the Judsons boarded the ship and "commended themselves to the care of God."

After a voyage in which Ann endured a serious illness, and pirates, shipwreck, and cannibals were a very real possibility, the Judsons arrived in Rangoon, only to find it a very "disheartening place." It was "dark, and cheerless, and unpromising." Judson went ashore, and when he returned, he and Ann, "instead of rejoicing as we ought to have done, in having found a heathen land from which we were not immediately driven away, such were our weaknesses that we felt we had no portion left here below and found consolation only in looking beyond our pilgrimage, which we tried to flatter ourselves would be short, to that peaceful region where the wicked cease from troubling and the weary are at rest."[11]

Settling in Rangoon, the Judsons struggled in their work for the next six years. They threw themselves into learning the language, studying for 12 hours a day. It was a difficult process learning an eastern language written on dried palm leaves, the symbols written in unending succession without punctuation. But as soon as Judson mastered the language, he began translating the Bible into Burmese, as well as writing tracts; "There were only two channels through which the truths of the Gospel could be conveyed to the conscience of the Burman—the eyes and the ears." Millions of the Burmans could read, and Judson was determined to give them the Bible in their own language. A baby boy was born to the Judsons, but he soon died. Sickness and the threat of corrupt officials were constant, and to further add to their difficulties, after six years, not one Burman had converted to Christianity.

Then, in April of 1819, Judson built a *zayat*[12] on one of the busiest roads in Rangoon. He would spend days on the front porch of the *zayat*, reading out loud a tract he had written in Burmese, or from the catechism Ann had compiled, sometimes crying out to the passing Burmans, "Ho, every one that thirsteth, come ye to the waters! And he that hath no money, come ye, buy and eat!"

The prominence of the *zayat* brought with it increased hostility toward Judson, but it also brought in more Burmans curious about the message of this foreign missionary. On May of 1819, the first Burman, Maung Nau, converted to Christianity. In a quiet pond on the edge of Rangoon, underneath a giant statue of Buddha, Judson baptized Maung Nau and the native Baptist church in Burma was born.

But the hostility toward the Judsons grew, not only from the local officials, but from the Buddhist priests as well. The threat of persecution began scaring away interested Burmans, and Judson soon wrote, "I sometimes sit there [in the *zayat*] whole days without a single visitor." Judson finally felt the need to go to Ava, the capital of Burma, and petition the king. "Our business must be fairly laid before the emperor. If he frowns upon us, all missionary attempts within his dominion will be out of the question. If he favor us, none of our enemies…can touch a hair of our heads."

The day Judson and a fellow missionary came to petition the king, the king immediately noticed them.

"Who are these?" he asked, studying the two Americans.

"The teachers, great king," Judson replied.

"You speak Burmese?" the king asked, surprised. "Are you the priests I heard of last night?"

"Yes."

"You are teachers of religion?"

"Yes."

The king nodded, then seated himself on his elevated throne. He read the petition Judson had brought, seeking permission to preach in Burma, then took one of Judson's tracts. He read the first two sentences, then dropped the tract to the floor.

One of the king's counselors looked at Judson, shaking his head. "Why do you ask such permission? Have not the Portuguese, the English, the Mussulmans, and people of all other religions, full liberty to practice and worship according to their own customs? In regard to the objects of your petition, his majesty gives no order. In regard to your sacred books, his majesty has no use for them: take them away."[13]

With his petition denied, Judson returned to Rangoon. Then events led him back to Ava in the fall of 1822. Another American, Dr. Jonathan Price, had arrived in Rangoon, and news of his skill at removing cataracts soon reached the attention of the king in Ava. Needing someone to interpret for him, Dr. Price took Judson.

Shortly after their arrival in Ava, Judson, Dr. Price, and two Englishmen sat in the palace, awaiting an audience with the king. When the king entered, he saw them and approached.

He looked hard at Judson. "Have any Burmans embraced your religion?"

"Yes, a few," Judson replied.

"Are they real Burmans?" the king demanded.

"Yes.

The king grunted. "Do they dress like other Burmans?"

Judson nodded. "Yes, they are Burman in every way, and I preach to them every Sunday."

"What?!" the king exclaimed. "In Burmese?"

"Yes."

"Then let us hear how you preach," the king ordered.

The others gathered in the palace hall who had been listening to the discussion between the king and Judson now hushed and grew silent as Judson stood.

"Go ahead," one of the king's counselors urged after a few moments of silence.

"There is one Being who exists eternally, who is exempt from sickness, old age, and death; who was and is, and will be, without beginning and without end. His power and wisdom are infinite. He is pure and good, and full of everlasting kindness." Judson's voice filled the audience hall as the king looked on, listening intently. "Love God supremely. Love others as yourself. Set not your hearts on worldly riches or goods, but look forward to those riches which are free from defilement and eternal in the heavens. Love your enemies and pray for them. Be compassionate to the poor and needy, and give alms." He paused.

"Continue," urged one of the king's counselors.

Judson nodded. "Before this world was made, God remained happy, surrounded by pure and incorporeal sons of

Heaven. In order to display His perfections, and make creatures happy, God created the heavens, the sun, the moon, and all the stars, the earth, the various kinds of brute creatures and man."

"That is good," the king interrupted, holding up his hand to signify the end of Judson's sermon.

Shortly afterwards the king approached Judson again. "What do you think of Gaudama [Buddha]?"

"He is the son of King Thog-dau-dah-nah, and we regard him as a wise man and great teacher, but not as God," Judson replied, unsure of what his response might elicit from the king.

But another of the king's counselors, with whom Judson had shared the gospel a few days before, started in. "That is right," he declared to the king, and proceeded to share that God was indeed eternal and how He was three persons united in One. Another of the counselors, seeing the direction of the conversation, said to the king, "Nearly all the world, your majesty, believes in an eternal God. All except Burma and Siam, those little spots!"[14]

The king said nothing more on the subject, asked Judson a few "desultory questions," and then retired to his private chambers. Judson was so encouraged by the interview that he and Ann moved to Ava, acquired a plot of land and built a home.

But in the spring of 1824, war broke out between England and Burma, and soon the foreigners in Ava found themselves in Hand Shrink Not.

The circumstances Judson and the others found themselves in were nearly intolerable. Kept in a windowless room covered with filth, with little ventilation, their surroundings were the least of their concerns. Executions took place daily at

3 p.m. Judson witnessed the chief executioner stomp "with heavy wooden shoes on the face of a prisoner in the stocks until he was nearly dead, then finished him off with a club," and one night heard the horrifying screams of another prisoner as his back was slowly broken. Death was always present, and Judson feared his was likely at any moment.

On the outside, only one foreigner in all of Ava had not been arrested: Ann Judson. She worked tirelessly to save her husband and the others. Daily she petitioned the local governor, even members of the royal family, to release the prisoners. She succeeded in lessening the prisoners' suffering and managed to obtain a pass whereby she could visit her husband daily for several hours. She even was able to smuggle Judson's translation of the Burmese New Testament to him, wrapped in the lining of a lumpy pillow. But, she was not able to obtain her husband's release.

One night, as Judson lay there in the darkness, he heard the executioners just outside the cell, sharpening their knives on the whetstones, and the foreign prisoners began whispering amongst themselves that tonight was their night to die. Judson looked over at Henry Gouger, an Englishman and a friend of Judson's before their imprisonment.

"Henry, I've been here ten years preaching the gospel to timid listeners who wish to embrace the truth but dare not, beseeching the emperor to grant liberty of conscience to his people but without success." He paused, closing his eyes, thinking of Ann. She had just had another baby, a little girl named Maria. He felt a pang of regret that he was to leave them without even being able to say good-bye. He looked back to

Gouger. "When all human means seem at an end, God opens the way by leading a Christian nation to subdue the country. It is possible our lives will be spared tonight. If so, I will pursue my work here with renewed determination. If not—His will be done. The door will be opened for others to do the work better."[15]

Judson did not die that night, but two months later, all the foreign prisoners were hastily rounded up one morning, stripped of their shoes and outer clothing save shirts and trousers, and tied together in pairs. With spotted-faced executioners prodding them with spears, the men were marched out of the death prison. Judson, suffering from fever, felt the bottom of his feet blister, then go raw, and as they crossed over the Mootangai River, he looked back at Gouger. The riverbed was dry and full of rocks. The present pain and discouragement were almost more than Judson could handle, and a plunge over the side would quickly end his suffering

"Gouger," he whispered, "the parapet on this bridge is low. There can be no sin in our availing ourselves of this opportunity."[16]

But the man Judson was tied to, a Scotsman named Laird, refused to jump, and in Judson's heart, he knew he couldn't do it either. The next day, the prisoners arrived in Oung-pen-la, a small village eight miles outside of Ava. When they arrived at the local prison, the prisoners exchanged uneasy glances amongst themselves. It was "an old, shattered building, without a roof," on poles four or five feet above the ground. Underneath the building was stacked dry wood, from the ground to the bottom of the building, and the prisoners remembered the rumor they had heard in Ava: They were being taken to Oung-pen-la to be burned alive.

It quickly became clear that it was only a rumor. The wood had been stacked beneath to prevent the prisoners from escaping through the rotting floor. The next night, Ann, with baby Maria and a loyal servant, entered the village, looking for her husband. She found him, his hair matted to his head, his slender frame emaciated, lying half-dead on the floor of the prison.

"Why have you come?" he managed to ask. "I hoped you would not follow, for you cannot live here."[17]

But Ann was determined to stay, and for the next six months she lived in the grain room attached to the head jailer's home. She was able to lessen the suffering of the prisoners, cooking meals for Adoniram and the others. However, soon she was deathly ill and unable to feed Maria. For Judson, "his spirits had never been so low...His daughter was starving before his eyes; [Ann] was nearly dead; his translation was lost; he himself was marked for death." Judson didn't realize how close he was to death until Gouger revealed to him one day the reason they were in Oung-pen-la.

"The Pakan Wun, supreme commander of the Burmese forces, was born here," Gouger said. "Do you know what Oung-pen-la means?"

"Yes," Judson said, beginning to feel uneasy, "Field of Victory."

"The Pakan Wun has assembled one last great army to try and defeat the British; its headquarters will be in Oung-Pen-la," Gouger said. "When the army is ready to be moved against the British, we will be offered up to propitiate the spirits of war by being buried alive at the head of the army. Planting our bodies in the Field of Victory can result only in a harvest of victory," Gouger finished.

Three days before the sacrifice was to take place, the Pakan Wun was suddenly arrested on charges of treason and "trodden to death by elephants." Finally, in the fall of 1825, Judson and the others were released after nearly two years of imprisonment. England had won the war, and interpreters were needed to help with the negotiations. Judson was chosen by the king to help negotiate the treaty with England, and by early 1826, the war was officially ended.

At the end of the negotiations, the British held a dinner to celebrate the victory and to impress the Burmese negotiators. The guest of honor that night was Ann Judson, and when the British commander, General Campbell, sat her at his right hand, the Burmans began exchanging uneasy glances amongst themselves.

"I fancy these gentlemen must be old acquaintances of yours, Mrs. Judson," General Campbell remarked.

"What is the matter with that one with the pointed beard?" another Englishman asked. "He seems to be seized with an ague fit."

Ann looked at the trembling Burmese official. "I do not know, unless his memory may be too busy. He is an old acquaintance of mine, and may probably infer danger to himself from seeing me under your protection."

She then related how, when her husband had been in the death prison suffering from a fever, she had walked several miles to the man's house to ask a favor. He had roughly refused her request, and as she left, had taken her silk umbrella from her, laughing when Ann protested that she needed something to protect her from the blazing sun.

"Only stout people are in danger of sunstroke. The sun can't find such a skinny person like you," the man had laughed, then ordered her removed from his house.

The Englishmen hearing the story became indignant, and the Burmese official's face went pale, beads of sweat suddenly appearing on his brow. Ann looked at the man, then leaned toward him and said softly in Burmese, "You have nothing to fear." She told the Englishmen what she had said, and the conversation drifted on to other subjects.[18]

But soon after the war's end, tragedy struck. While Judson was away in Ava with the British envoy, Mr. Crawfurd, attempting to win a provision for religious toleration in Burma, Ann died of an acute fever. Grief-stricken, Judson wrote his sister:

> [someday]...she [Ann] will come again, and resume the form which now moulders in the grave. Then she will be bright as the sun, beautiful as an angel, immortal as the Saviour. And all of us who are entitled to immortality by a union to the same immortal Head will live together with her in the enjoyment of eternal life. We will not, then, mourn as those who have no hope; "for if we believe that Jesus died and rose again, even so them also that sleep in Jesus will God bring with him." Yet, notwithstanding the consolations of the gospel, grief claims its right, and tears their course....[19]

His daughter, Maria, shortly followed her mother to the grave, and Judson threw himself into his work for the next several years. He finished the New Testament translation; for in the midst of the chaos at the death prison when Judson and the others were being marched to Oung-pen-la, a faithful servant had retrieved Judson's Bible. It was also found that the few converts made in Rangoon before the war still held to their faith. He proceeded with revising the New Testament, and even began translating the Psalms. By 1828, "persons from all parts of the empire were earnestly desiring writings which would explain them the new religion."

But in the fall of 1828, discouraged and lonely, Judson wrote his mother and sister on the anniversary of Ann's death: "I have moved into a small cottage, which I have built in the woods, away from the haunts of men. It proves a stormy evening, and the desolation around me accords with the desolate state of my own mind, where grief for the dear departed combines with sorrow for the present sin, and my tears flow...."[20] He wrote them again, exactly one year later. He was still living alone in the same cottage. "Have either of you learned the art of real communion with God, and can you teach me the first principles? God is to me the Great Unknown. I believe in him, but find him not."[21]

Gradually, his grief lifted, and in 1830 he went to Prome, up the river from Rangoon, to begin a mission there. But after one week there, the Burmese government began suspecting that Judson was a British spy, and he was taken before the magistrates and questioned concerning his work in Burma. After several months, realizing the threat of persecution by the government was hindering inquiring Burmans, Judson returned to Rangoon, and there he threw himself into translating the Old Testament.

Holed up in an attic, Judson left the ministering to the native converts and quickly finished the Psalms, the Song of Solomon, and Daniel. One day, in the midst of his translating, he was visited by a traveling Englishwoman, a Miss Emma Roberts. Though Judson did not realize it, his work and story had become well known throughout the entire civilized world, and Miss Roberts was anxious to see this famous missionary. She and Judson spent the afternoon conversing, until "...the bats, which frequent the houses at Rangoon, began taking their evening round...the flap of the heavy wings so near us interrupting the conversation, we at length took our leave and parted. And this thought I, as I descended the dark ladder, is the solitary abode of Judson, whom after ages shall designate, most justly, the great and the good."[22]

By March of 1831, in a change of fortunes, Judson and his fellow missionaries, many of whom had come to Burma after the war, found their work flourishing. Judson wrote that during one of the large Buddhist festivals, he had distributed:

> ...nearly 10,000 tracts, giving to none but those who ask. I presume there have been six thousand applications as the house. Some come two or three months' journey, from the borders of Siam and China—"Sir, we hear that there is an eternal hell. We are afraid of it. Do give us a writing that will tell us how to escape it." Others come from the frontiers of Kathay, a hundred miles north of Ava—"Sir, we have seen writings that tell about an eternal God. Are you the man that gives away such writings? If so, pray give us one, for we want to know the truth before we die." Others came from the interior of the country, where the name of Jesus Christ is little known—"Are

you Jesus Christ's man? Give us a writing that tells about Jesus Christ."[23]

By 1831, 373 native Burmans had been baptized; it was a small number, but considering that Judson had baptized only 9 in his first 18 years in Burma, the number was encouraging. Judson continued with his translation of the Old Testament, attempting to do 25 to 30 verses a day. He married again, this time to a widowed missionary, Sarah Boardman. They started a family together, and it seemed to Judson that the sun had returned again to his life. He finished the Old Testament translation in 1835, then revised the New Testament again. He and Sarah had eight children together, six of whom lived to adulthood. In 1840, Judson sent the last sheet of the Burman Bible to the printing house. He promptly began work on an English-Burmese dictionary and began preaching seven days a week, meeting with the native Christians every morning "to keep track of their work and make suggestions to improve their preaching."

But in 1845, Sarah became seriously ill, and the doctor ordered a sea voyage to restore her to health. It was decided a visit to a cooler climate was what was really needed, and so Judson and his family, save the two youngest boys, boarded a ship and began the voyage back to America. When the ship reached St. Helena, Sarah took a turn for the worse, and before Judson continued his journey home, he buried Sarah "in a beautifully shaded spot" beneath a banyan tree on St. Helena.

When Judson entered Boston Harbor six weeks later, he expected few to be there to welcome him. Many of his old friends were dead, and his father, mother, and younger brother had passed away. Besides his sister and those he corresponded with, Judson was sure no one would know him. What he didn't realize was that in the 33 years that he had been gone, the name of Adoniram Judson had become a household word. He " had been the subject of thousands of sermons, the theme of hundreds of thousands of prayers. Thousands had named their children for him. The country was full of men and women who had been hearing all their lives about the great missionary, Adoniram Judson, the saint of Burma."[24]

Hundreds came to the harbor that day to greet Judson, giving him a hero's welcome. The Friday after his return a meeting was held at the Bowdoin Square Church in Boston to celebrate his return home. Judson made a few comments, then took a seat while a pastor began to review Judson's career to the crowd.

The pastor was interrupted, however, by an elderly man who began working his way up the crowded aisle until he stood at Judson's side. Judson gave the man a quizzical look, and then recognition dawned on his face. It was Samuel Nott, one of the four who had signed the petition before the General Association requesting a foreign mission board so many years before. Judson rose and embraced him. He had thought Nott dead, but Nott, after several years in India, had been forced home by ill health and was now the pastor of the Congregational Church in Wareham. Nott was introduced to the crowd, then asked to address it.

"There were five of us that went to India; three have died, and soon the remaining two will also be gone. But what we went for, the word of God, will stand fast and prevail," Nott said. "We were mere boys, but with God's blessings, those boys began an influence which is spreading across the world."[25]

More meetings followed, and Judson was praised everywhere he went. But Burma was calling him, and his "thoughts began to turn once more to his duty in the East—not only to his children, but to the unfinished dictionary."[26] Before he left for Burma, however, Judson fell in love again, this time with Emily Chubbock, an accomplished writer who had desired to be a missionary from the day she'd read the story of another female missionary: Ann Judson. When Judson asked her to marry him, she said yes.

Shortly before his return to Burma, Judson agreed to address Emily's home congregation. He gave his sermon and afterwards spoke of "'the precious Savior,' and what he has done for us, and what we owe him." As he and Emily traveled home, she began sharing with Judson what some people had said to her after the sermon.

"There were some people who inquired as to why you did not tell some stories of your times in Burma," she began. "I could tell there were many who were disappointed."

"Well, what did they want?" Judson asked. "I presented to them the most interesting subject in the world, to the best of my ability."

"But they wanted something different—a story," Emily replied.

"Well, I am sure that I gave them a story, the most thrilling one that ever can be conceived of."

"But they have heard it all before. They wanted something new of a man who had just come from the antipodes."

"Then I am glad they have it to say, that a man coming from the antipodes had nothing better to tell them than the wondrous story of Jesus' dying love," Judson replied. "My business is to preach the gospel of Christ, and when I speak at all, I dare not trifle with my commission." He shook his head. "When I looked upon those people today, and realized that I will not likely see them again in this life, how could I stand up and furnish food to vain curiosity and tickle their fancies with amusing stories, however decently strung together on a thread of religion? That is not what Christ meant by preaching the gospel. How could I hereafter meet the fearful charge, 'I gave you one opportunity to tell them of me, and you spent it in describing your own adventures!' "

In July of 1846, having been in America less than a year, Judson and Emily boarded a ship and sailed for Burma. Desiring a good American education for his older children, he left them in the care of his sister and friends. He never saw them again, nor did he ever return to America.

The Judsons arrived in Burma in late November. They were greeted joyously by the Burmese Christians. Emily described their arrival in a letter to her sister:

> We were scarcely anchored this morning when a boat of six or seven men came bounding towards us...Adoniram, who for some time had been silently watching them from the side of the vessel, leaned over for a moment gazing at them intently, and then sent forth a glad wild hail. In a moment the glancing of oars ceased, a half dozen men sprang to their feet...and a wilder, longer, and if possible more joyous cry showed that the voice of salutation was recognized....in a few moments the men had brought the vessel alongside and were scrambling up the side of the

vessel....How the black eyes danced beneath their grave brows, and the rough lips curled with smiles beneath bristling beards! Then came a quick grasping of hands, and half-choked words of salutation....[27]

Judson settled his new wife and family into a house in Rangoon, a place that Emily dubbed the "Bat Castle" for the thousands of bats residing in the upper story of the house. He launched back into his work on the Burmese-English dictionary, but the threat of the new vice-governor of Rangoon, a man Judson described as a "ferocious, blood-thristy monster," and his underlings oncemore limited the missionary work amongst the natives. Judson's son, Edward, later wrote that "Nothing but a wholesome fear of the British Government kept these bloodthirsty wretches from the throat of the missionary [Judson] himself."[28] The native church in Rangoon began meeting in secret, in small groups in private homes, and Judson moved his family to Moulmein in British-held territory.

Then, in November of 1849, Judson was struck with a congestive fever, and his health rapidly declined. It was feared he was dying, and the doctor's orders were an immediate sea journey, in hopes that the fresh air would somehow help Judson regain his strength.

Several days before he set sail he told Emily, "It is not because I shrink from death that I wish to live, neither is it because the ties that bind me here, bear any comparisons with the drawings I at times feel towards heaven." He paused, and tears began streaming down his face. "But a few years would not be missed from my eternity of bliss, and I can well afford to spare them, both for your sake and the sake of the poor Burmans. I am not tired of my work, nor am I tired of this world; yet when Christ calls me home, I shall go with the gladness of a boy bounding away from his school."

"Then death will not take you by surprise, even if it should come before you should get on board ship?" Emily asked.

"Oh, no," Judson replied, "death will never take me by surprise—do not be afraid of that—I feel so strong in Christ. I leave myself entirely in the hands of God, to be disposed of according to his holy will."[29]

Shortly after that, in great pain, Judson was carried aboard the *Aristide Marie*, and after a few days' delay, the ship set sail. But, a recovery was not for Judson. On the afternoon of April 12, 1850, Judson murmured to his Burmese servant, "It is done, I am going."

Many years before, on New Year's Eve of 1810, Judson had written Ann: "A few days and our work will be done. And when it is once done, it is done to all eternity. A life once spent is irrevocable. It will remain to be contemplated throughout eternity."[30] His work done, Judson slipped away quietly, and his death was described as though he were "falling asleep." A plank coffin was made, and at 8 o'clock that same evening, Judson was buried at sea, only three days out of sight of Burma.

Emily wrote his sister, "Neither could he have a more fitting monument than the blue waves which visit every coast; for his warm sympathies went forth to the ends of the earth, and included the whole family of man. It is all as God would have it, and our duty is but to bend meekly to his will, and wait, in faith and patience, till we also shall be summoned home."[31]

★   ★   ★

When Judson died, the number of native Christians who had been publicly baptized after their confession of faith numbered over 7,000, and there were 63 churches throughout Burma. Today, the Baptist church in Burma numbers in the hundreds of thousands.

Notes

1. This incident taken from Wayland, *A Memoir of the Life*, Vol. 1, 338-39.

2. Ibid, 376.

3. Judson, *The Life of Adoniram Judson*, 221.

4. This incident taken from Wayland, *A Memoir of the Life*, Vol. 1, 24-25.

5. Ibid, 27.

6. Ibid, 28.

7. Ibid, 55.

8. Anderson, *To the Golden Shore*, 134.

9. Ibid, 134-35.

10. Wayland, *A Memoir of the Life*, Vol. 1, 119.

11. Ibid, 120-21

12. A shelter where men could gather and talk and where Buddhist lay teachers could teach.

13. Wayland, *A Memoir of the Life*, Vol. 1, 254-56.

14. Ibid, 313-14.

15. Anderson, *To the Golden Shore*, 333-34.

16. Ibid, 341.

17. Wayland, *A Memoir of the Life*, Vol. 1, 355.

18. Judson, *The Life of Adoniram Judson*, 278-79.

19 Wayland, *A Memoir of the Life*, Vol. 1, 415.

20. Ibid, 482-83.

21. Ibid, 483.

22. Anderson, *To the Golden Shore*, 398.

23. Ibid, 528.

24. Anderson, *To the Golden Shore*, 445-46.

25. Wayland, *A Memoir of the Life, Vol. II*, 219-20.

26. Anderson, *To the Golden Shore*, 451.

27. Ibid, 468-69.

28. Judson, *The Life of Adoniram Judson*, 505.

29. Ibid, 539-40

30. Wayland, *A Memoir of the Life*, Vol. 1, 33.

31. Judson, *The Life of Adoniram Judson*, 542.

Chapter 6

ELIJAH LOVEJOY

"In Defense of Freedom"

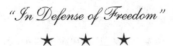

The night of November 7, 1837, was a cold and blustery one in Alton, Illinois. On the streets near the warehouse of Godfrey & Gilman, a mob had begun to form, stooping to gather stones while others concealed rifles and pistols under their coats. Torches lit their way as they surged toward the warehouse, a tall, imposing three-storied structure. As the mob approached, a man appeared in one of the upper windows.

"What do you want?" the man called. It was Winthrop Gilman, one of the wealthiest men in Alton and an owner of the building.

"The press!" came the shouted reply.

Gilman glanced over his shoulder at the men inside and then back down to the crowd below. There were 20 other men in the warehouse with Gilman, and the crowd below far outnumbered them.

"Tell them to come and get it," came a voice from behind Gilman. Gilman did not have to turn to see who it was. He knew. Elijah Lovejoy, Presbyterian minister and editor of the Alton *Observer*, an abolitionist paper, had already had three of his presses destroyed by pro-slavery mobs like the one below. He was not about to lose another.

"We have no ill feelings toward any of you and should regret to do any injury; but we are authorized by the Mayor to defend our property with force if necessary, and we will do so!" Gilman yelled to the mob below.

A rock whizzed past his head and struck the side of the building in reply as one of the mob drew his pistol and aimed it at Gilman. As the mob began hurling rocks at the building, shattering the windows, Gilman quickly retreated inside. A pistol shot rang out, then another.

As Gilman moved to the back wall of the warehouse, his fellow defenders began creeping to the windows to return fire. Within minutes, a sharp gunfight had broken out. Several men in the crowd fell, struck by the bullets fired from above. One man lay twitching on the ground, mortally wounded.

"Burn them out!" someone screamed. "Shoot every abolitionist that tries to escape!" One of the attackers, a 15-year-old boy named Okeh, was persuaded to try and set the roof on fire.

Inside, the defenders looked to Lovejoy. If the mob succeeded in firing the roof, they had nowhere to go except right into the guns of the mob. "We must fight it out, if necessary, to the bitter end," Lovejoy said, his voice shaking with emotion. "I, for one, am willing and ready to lay down my life."[1]

In the spring of 1836, on a street several blocks from the St. Louis jail, Elijah Lovejoy stood before a horrific sight. There, chained to the locust tree a few feet in front of him, was the mutilated body of a freedman by the name of Francis McIntosh.

The day before, McIntosh, a cook on a steamboat docked in St. Louis, had been arrested for interfering with the duties of two policemen. As they led him away, fearing a whipping and jail time, McIntosh resisted. Drawing a knife, he wounded one officer and killed the other before fleeing. He was immediately apprehended and jailed. That night, a mob stormed the jail and dragged McIntosh out. Wrestling him down the street, the mob chained him to the locust tree and stacked lumber around him. As McIntosh sang hymns and prayed, begging for someone to shoot him, the mob burned him alive.

Now, as the April breeze kicked up the dust on the streets, Lovejoy stood there, his mind a whirl of emotions. For three years now he'd been the editor for the St. Louis *Observer*, a religious newspaper. However, editorials that stated "slavery as it now exists among us must cease to exist. There can be no doubt on this subject; God and man...alike forbid its perpetuity"[3] earned him few friends in St. Louis. Despite living in the slave state of Missouri, he felt it his duty to speak out against the practice of slavery. He'd been warned to desist from the subject by the very men who financed the *Observer*,[4] even threatened with violence by others. But, he'd refused to stop his antislavery editorials.

After a few more minutes of quietly studying the scene before him, Lovejoy walked back to the office of the *Observer* and wrote the editorial for the next day's paper.

> Our hand trembles as we record the story...we may all see...the legitimate result of the spirit of mobism, and whither, unless arrested in its first outbreakings, it is sure to carry us....in St. Louis it forces a man—a hardened wretch certainly, and one that deserved to die, but not thus to die—it forces him from beneath the aegis of our constitution and laws, and hurries him to the stake and burns him alive....we make our appeal to the citizens of this community, and wherever else our voice can be heard, and ask, and ask with the most heart-felt anxiety, is it not time to STOP?...We must stand by the constitution and laws, or ALL IS GONE! We visited the scene of the burning on the day following, about noon. We stood and gazed for a moment or two, upon the blackened and mutilated trunk—for that was all which remained—of McIntosh before us, and as we turned away in bitterness of heart, we prayed that we might not live.[5]

These words were not favorably received by the St. Louis public. He was threatened again with violence, and later that month, the *Observer* was broken into and $700 worth of materials destroyed. After three years of constant abuse and threats, and fearing for the safety of his wife and newborn son, Lovejoy felt it wiser to move the paper across the Mississippi to Alton, Illinois. He did so in July of 1836. The first night he was in Alton, men from St. Louis followed him over and, while Lovejoy slept, knocked his press to pieces and pushed it into the Mississippi.

The citizens of Alton welcomed Lovejoy at first, even moving to replace the destroyed press. But their acceptance quickly turned to dismay, then anger, when they realized Lovejoy would not cease his arguments against slavery. Though in a free state, many of Alton's citizens were originally from the South and did not take kindly to Lovejoy's attacks on slavery.

Despite the difficulties facing him, Lovejoy refused to back down in his fight against slavery. He wrote his mother in August of 1836:

> ...you ask, Are you discouraged? I answer promptly, no. I have opened my mouth for the dumb, I have plead the cause of the poor and oppressed I have maintained the rights of humanity...For these things I have seen my family scattered, my office broken up...have been loaded with execrations, had all manner of evil spoken falsely against me, and finally had my life threatened...Yet none of these things moves me from my purpose; by the grace of God I will not, I will not forsake my principles; and I will maintain, and propagate them with all the means He puts into my hands. The cry of the oppressed has entered not only into my ears, but into my soul, so that while I live I cannot hold my peace...such as I have, I give freely—my time, my energy, the best years of my life, some little ability, and a good deal of zeal—these I give, and bless God for the opportunity, to so holy a cause. I may not live to see its success—I may even die—though most unworthy—its victim and its martyr, yet it will ultimately succeed, and that too at no distant day, I am as

well assured as I am that there is a God in Heaven, who sits on a Throne of Righteousness.[6]

Once the new press was in place, Lovejoy continued his fight against slavery. "Two million and a half of our fellow creatures are groaning in bondage, crushed to the earth, deprived of the rights which their Maker gave them," he wrote in February of 1837. A target of his editorials quickly became his fellow clergymen. In Lovejoy's estimation, those who did not fight slavery were fighting against God. He condemned those ministers who "preach against intemperance and Sabbath breaking, against covetousness and murder, yet pass over slavery in silence." Lovejoy added, "I have lived about eight years in a slave state and except in one or two instances, I do not recall ever having heard slaveholders, whether in or out of church, criticized for neglecting or abusing their slaves."

When a reader complained that there was too much anti-slavery material in the *Observer*, Lovejoy replied, "If I could hold my peace on this subject with a clear conscience, I would most assuredly do it. My course has cost me many a valued friend. But I cannot, and I am sure you do not ask or wish a Christian to connive at what he believes to be a sin, for the sake of popularity."

On the night of August 21, 1837, twelve of Alton's leading citizens, four of them doctors, decided that Lovejoy needed to be taught a lesson. It was decided that they would tar and feather him, then set him adrift in the Mississippi. As Lovejoy left the apothecary's that night, having retrieved some medicine for his sick wife, he stepped onto the nearly deserted streets. Pulling his hat low and placing the package under his arm, he began walking home.

Just as he was about to turn off of the main street, a mob of men approached him. Ducking his head, Lovejoy walked past them, knowing they were likely looking for him. He was nearly past the men when suddenly one of them called out, "Ain't that Lovejoy?"

Immediately the mob turned about and surrounded Lovejoy. They began throwing clods of dirt at him, and one of the men approached Lovejoy and knocked his hat off with a club. "It's that abolitionist!" he yelled.

"Tar and feather him! Rail him out of town!" the mobsters yelled as they crowded around Lovejoy.

Lovejoy looked calmly about at the men. "You had better let me go home. You have no right to detain me. I have never injured you."

The mob continued to swear and curse him. "I am in your hands, and you must do with me whatever God permits," Lovejoy said. After a few more minutes, the mob parted and let Lovejoy go home. But later that night, they broke into the Observer and destroyed the printing press.[7]

When Lovejoy visited St. Charles, Missouri, the next month to preach at the Presbyterian church, he again met violence. As he sat in his mother-in-law's home in St. Charles that Sunday night, two men knocked at the door. When asked what they wanted, the men replied, "We want to see Mr. Lovejoy, is he in?"

"Yes," replied Lovejoy.

Immediately the men burst into the room and grabbed hold of him. When Lovejoy asked them what they wanted, they replied, "We want you downstairs!"

Lovejoy resisted, and joined by his wife, who also fought the attackers, managed to push the men out of the house. The men returned with others, and soon a mob had formed in the yard. Torches lit drunken faces, and knives and guns gleamed in the flickering light. From where he stood inside, Lovejoy could hear them swearing at him. "The infernal scoundrel, the amalgamating abolitionist, we'll have his heart out yet!"

The mob rushed the house several times, but Lovejoy escaped their clutches and managed to sneak out the back of the house to safety. When he returned to Alton, he recounted the events to his brother Leviatt, and added that, as he wrote the letter, "A loaded musket is standing by my bedside, while my two brothers, in an adjoining room, have three others, together with pistols, cartridges, etc. And this is the way we live in Alton!"[8]

At this juncture, again fearing for his wife and young son, Lovejoy was willing to step down as editor of the *Observer*. His friends would have none of it. Edward Beecher, brother of Harriet Beecher Stowe, and Winthrop Gilman, who'd befriended Lovejoy from the moment he'd arrived in Alton, were among those who persuaded Lovejoy to stay on as editor of the paper. It was decided that a new press would be bought and that the paper would continue as before. Lovejoy and his friends would not have their actions dictated to them by a mob.

The new press was scheduled to arrive in Alton on November 7. As the day approached, tensions began building. A meeting was called by the leading citizens of Alton, and a committee formed in hopes of reaching a compromise and avoiding bloodshed. As men filed into the Reverend Hogan's merchandise store on the night of November 2, the head of the committee, Samuel Baily, called the meeting to order.

"Gentlemen, we've assembled to see if there can't be some peaceful resolution to what is increasingly becoming a very bitter conflict. The committee is considering a motion asking Mr. Lovejoy to desist from publishing the *Observer* and to leave Alton," Baily began.

Winthrop Gilman, the only Lovejoy supporter on the committee, stood abruptly. "I for one did not, and will not, condone such a resolution! It is preposterous, an outright abuse of Mr. Lovejoy's basic rights as a citizen!"

"We on the committee realize this resolution might sound drastic," Baily replied. "But it is necessary in the interest of peace and harmony in the community."

"Surely you can see that the opposing parties are arming themselves for a conflict. It may terminate in a train of mournful consequences!" Cyrus Edwards, an Illinois state legislator, added. From where he sat quietly in the front of the room, Elijah Lovejoy said nothing as his fate was argued.

Usher Linder, the State Attorney of Illinois, now spoke. "Mr. Gilman, it cannot be denied that Mr. Lovejoy is an agitator. Wouldn't it be better to sacrifice one man's right to agitate than for an entire community to be embroiled in violence and bloodshed?"

"We are not here tonight to debate the sentiments or character of Mr. Lovejoy!" Gilman said. "We are here to discuss the principle of free speech and Mr. Lovejoy's right to it!"

"As Attorney General of Illinois, I think in the best interest of peace, Mr. Lovejoy should retire from Alton and take the *Observer* with him," Linder replied.

"Mr. Lovejoy has a right, a God-given right, to speak on whatever subject he would like, be it slavery or otherwise. It is the law that he have this right, and to acquiesce to the demands of the mob is to put the power of the mob over our Constitution and the basis for every law in this land!" Gilman said. "We are called upon to defend the rights of free speech, especially in the case of unpopular persons of sentiments."

Baily leaned over toward Gilman. "Perhaps we should mutually sacrifice our prejudices and seek some compromise for the sake of tranquility."

"I am not speaking of prejudices!" Gilman replied. "I am speaking of the freedom of speech and Mr. Lovejoy's right to it!"[9]

The room burst into shouting as Gilman and Lovejoy were roundly cursed. There was an attempt by Baily to regain order, but it was only when Lovejoy stood and moved to the front of the room that a semblance of order was regained.

Looking at the committee members, then at those gathered, Lovejoy began quietly. "Let me beg of you all before I proceed that you construe nothing as being disrespectful to this assembly."

Taking a deep breath, Lovejoy began. "This committee has no right to decide whether I can publish a newspaper in this city. I have a right to do this, given to me by my Maker and guaranteed by the Constitution. There are not two parties involved here. I have planted myself down on my unquestionable rights. It is simply a matter now of whether a mob can trample with impunity the rights of an innocent individual."

Lovejoy looked at the members of the committee. "My rights have been shamefully, wickedly outraged! I cannot go home at nights without fear of being tarred and feathered, even killed. My wife lives in constant fear, spending nights in the garret to avoid the violence of the mobs!" With the mention of his wife, Lovejoy paused as tears began to stream down his face. There was a hush on the room now as every eye was on Lovejoy.

"Forgive me. I fear for my family," he said after a moment. "You speak of compromise. But if by a compromise you mean for me to stop what duty requires of me, I will not do it!" His voice rose as he stared out on the hard faces in front of him. "The reason is that I fear God more than men! I will not step down at the demand of a mob! You have come together to drive out an innocent man because he dares to think and speak as his conscience and God dictate," Lovejoy continued, looking at Baily, then at the members of the committee. "You cannot drive me from Alton, nor can you disgrace me. I, and I alone, can disgrace myself. The deepest disgrace would be at a time like this to deny my Master by forsaking His cause. He died for me, and I were most unworthy, if I refused, if need be, to die for Him. I will not leave Alton. The contest was begun here, and here it will be finished!"[10]

Lovejoy wiped away the tears that still flowed from his eyes and moved once more to his seat. The hush that had fallen upon the room remained, and it seemed that perhaps Lovejoy had persuaded the assembly of the rightness of his cause. But the silence was broken when Reverend Hogan stood.

"I cannot help but think that all things that are right are not expedient. Why should we risk the peace of our city for some abstract ideas?" Hogan asked.

"Because it is a right!" Gilman shot back.

"I am interested to see whether the citizens of Alton will be consulted as to their rights, or if they will have the rights of another shoved down their throats by foreigners!" Linder interjected. "Mr. Lovejoy is not from here! Are we really going to sit here and take Mr. Lovejoy's self-righteous cant? I propose that the Mr. Lovejoy and the *Observer* are destructive to the peace and harmony of the citizens of Alton, and the paper cannot, and should not, be reestablished!"

From the back of the room, Judge Hawley cleared his throat. "Mr. Linder, we all agree that abolitionists and their words are nonsense. We can all see that. Yet they do have the right to voice their opinions. We cannot use violence to take away Mr. Lovejoy's rights."

Despite the Judge's words and the eloquent defenses of Gilman and Lovejoy, those assembled had already made up their minds. With only Gilman dissenting, the committee passed resolutions banning the *Observer* and Lovejoy from Alton. As Baily sounded the gavel to signal the end of the meeting, Lovejoy, Gilman, and their few friends walked into the night. As Lovejoy moved passed him, Linder muttered, "Lovejoy will be dead in two weeks time."

Already ostracized by many in Alton, now condemned by the leading citizens of the city, Lovejoy and his supporters refused to be cowed. The press, which had already been ordered and shipped, arrived in Alton early on the morning of November 7. While his enemies slept, Lovejoy and his band of friends moved the new press into the warehouse of Godfrey & Gilman. There was no initial outcry, but by that evening, word had spread through Alton that Lovejoy had stored his new press in the warehouse. A mob quickly formed, determined to destroy the abolitionist press. Soon 150 men had gathered outside the warehouse, screaming for blood.

Inside the warehouse, its defenders could hear the thump of a wooden ladder being placed against the side of the building.

"They're trying to fire the roof!" Gilman shouted.

Quickly, Lovejoy threw down his rifle. "Royal, Amos!" he yelled as he ran for the staircase. Royal Weller, the owner of the local shoe store, clattered down the stairs, followed by Amos Roff.

Hiding in the shadows of the warehouse, Lovejoy, Roff, and Weller crept toward the front of the building. The noise of the mob was deafening. Bursting from the shadows, the three men surprised the mob, grabbed the ladder, and threw it to the ground. Jumping through the front door of the warehouse, they dove to the floor as bullets whizzed around them.

Another one of the mob, James Rock, now offered to try and set the roof on fire. Two of Alton's leading citizens, Dr. Beal and Dr. Jennings, with rifles in hand, assured Rock that they would cover him, and they hid themselves behind a pile of wood a stone's throw away from the warehouse's entrance.[11]

As Lovejoy and his friends lay in the darkness, a thump told them that the ladder had been replaced. Fortified by drink and wearing top hat and tails, Rock began climbing the ladder thrown up against the side of the warehouse, a pot of burning pitch in tow.

Without a word, Lovejoy jumped to his feet and threw the door open again with Roff and Weller close on his heels. However, this time the mob was ready for them. Dr. Beal and Dr. Jennings, and the others hiding behind the pile of wood no more than 20 yards away, could hardly miss. As Lovejoy moved toward the ladder, there were rifle shots. Five bullets hit him almost simultaneously, three in the chest, one in the abdomen, and one in his left arm.[12]

With a grunt, Lovejoy staggered backwards into the warehouse. Beside him, Weller cried out as a bullet passed through his calf, and Roff gasped in pain, shot in the arm. Lovejoy struggled to his feet and staggered up the flight of stairs to the landing on the second floor of the warehouse. By the time he reached the landing, Lovejoy was crawling, clutching his chest as though to stop the bleeding.

"My God, I am shot," he gasped as another friend, Thaddeus Hurlbut, raced down the stairs toward him.

"Elijah!" Hurlbut cried as he fell to his knees by his friend's side.

"I'm shot," Lovejoy said weakly.

Scooping him up in his arms, Hurlbut held Lovejoy, and a few moments later heard Lovejoy give one last gasp.

Weeping in sorrow and from the pain of their own wounds, Roff and Weller heard an ominous crackling above them. The mob had succeeded in setting fire to the roof. Moments later Winthrop Gilman and the others rushed down the stairs. Dragging Lovejoy's body deeper into the shadows, the men turned and ran from the building. As they fled into the night, the mob opened fire on them, but no one was hit.

Surging into the warehouse, the mob made for the press. They did no harm to Hurlbut, Roff, and Weller, who alone had stayed to guard the body of Lovejoy. The mob threw the press out of the third-story window, then smashed it to pieces before throwing it into the Mississippi.[13]

The next day the friends of Elijah Lovejoy returned to find his body undisturbed. As they moved the body to Lovejoy's home, members from the mob laughed and jeered as the wagon carried the body down the street. Dr. Beal danced a little jig in front of the wagon, and as the spectators laughed, he cried out, "If I had a fife, I would play a death march for him!"[14]

The next day, in the cold and rain, Elijah Lovejoy was buried just outside of Alton. His wife wasn't there, having collapsed at the news of his death, and only a few courageous friends attended. A short prayer was said, and, in the distance, the bell of the First Presbyterian tolled. It was November 9, 1837, Elijah Lovejoy's thirty-fifth birthday.[15]

The death of Lovejoy stunned the nation. John Quincy Adams wrote that Lovejoy's death was "a shock as of an earthquake throughout the continent."[16] Yet, out of this seeming defeat came victory. His death helped awaken American abolitionism, and it has been said that along with the publishing of *Uncle Tom's Cabin*, Lovejoy's death became one of the greatest boosts for the antislavery movement in the years leading up to the Civil War.[17]

Notes

1. Based upon an account from the *Alton Observer*, November 7, 1837; Joseph and Owen Lovejoy, *Memoir*, 284-90.

2. Dillion, *Elijah P. Lovejoy*, 80.

3. Ibid, 53.

4. Joseph and Owen Lovejoy, *Memoir*, 137.

5. Ibid, 173-73.

6. Ibid, 185-86.

7. Ibid, 233-34.

8. Ibid, 253-58.

9. Tanner, *The Martyrdom of Lovejoy*, 138-42.

10. Beecher, *Narrative of the Riots*, 85-91, and Tanner, *The Martyrdom of Lovejoy*, 145-47.

11. Simon, *Freedom's Champion*, 129-30.

12. Ibid.

13. Based upon an account from the *Alton Observer*, November 7, 1837; Joseph and Owen Lovejoy, *Memoir*, 291-92; and Tanner, *The Martyrdom of Lovejoy*, 150-51.

14. Jospch and Owen Lovejoy, *Memoir*, 291-92.

15. Ibid, 292-93.

16. Ibid, 12.

17. Simon, *Freedom's Champion*, 154.

Chapter 7

ANGELINA GRIMKÉ

"Forsaking All"

★ ★ ★

On the morning of February 21, 1838, a young woman from South Carolina stood before the legislature of the State of Massachusetts, nervously studying the faces before her. Angelina Grimké and her older sister, Sarah, were in the midst of an extremely successful New England lecture series concerning the evils of slavery. After weeks of touring and speaking, their appeal for immediate abolition was beginning to win support.

Yet, today was different from all the other speaking engagements. Angelina was not standing before a small crowd of friendly listeners. She was standing before the legislature of Massachusetts, ready to address it on the subject of slavery in a day when the abolition movement was considered to be a radical one.

Her heart pounding, her hands shaking, Angelina later recounted to a friend, "My heart never quailed before, but it almost died within me at that tremendous hour."[1] To her future husband, Theodore Weld, Angelina wrote:

> I wrote you word that Sister was to speak today and I tomorrow, but she took a violent cold and will not be able to speak at all. She could not even go to the meeting, but Jesus was there. His arm was underneath and round about me, He sustained me and brought me through. But I never was so near fainting under the tremendous pressure of feeling. My heart almost died within me...I well nigh despaired, but our Lord and Master gave me His arm to lean upon and in great weakness, my limbs trembling under me, I stood up and spoke nearly two hours....[2]

It was not just the highly controversial subject matter that brought nearly every prominent citizen of Boston to hear Angelina Grimké. It was the very fact that a woman was addressing the legislature. This was the America where women did not have the right to vote, and had no political voice, and where no woman had ever before addressed a legislative body. Putting her fears behind her, Angelina lifted her eyes to study the audience before her and began.

> Mr. Chairman—More than 2000 years have rolled their dark and bloody waters down the rocky, winding channel of Time into the broad ocean of Eternity, since woman's voice was heard in the palace of an eastern monarch, and woman's petition achieved the salvation of millions of

her race from the edge of the sword...I feel that if you are to be reached at all, it will not be by me, but by the truths I shall endeavor to present to your understandings and your hearts....I stand before you as a southerner, exiled from the land of my birth, by the sound of the lash, and the piteous cry of the slave. I stand before you as a repentant slaveholder. I stand before you as a moral being, endowed with precious and inalienable rights, which are correlative with solemn duties and high responsibilities; and as a moral being I feel that I owe it to the suffering slave, and to the deluded master, to my country and the world, to do all that I can to overturn a system of complicated crimes, built up upon the broken hearts and prostrate bodies of my countrymen in chains, and cemented by the blood and sweat and tears of my sisters in bonds.[3]

Less than eight years before, Angelina, horrified by slavery and its brutality, had left Charleston, South Carolina, in protest. The lifestyle that turned men into beasts and others into cruel despots sickened her. She recounted one incident when her brother Henry had punished his slave John within Angelina's hearing: "I know not how the boy must have felt, but I know that night was one of agony to me; for it was not only dreadful to hear the blows, but the oaths and curses H. uttered went like daggers to my heart. And this was done, too, in the house of one who is regarded as a light in the church."

The next morning over breakfast, Angelina spoke with her brother.

"Henry, I heard what you did to John last night," Angelina said. "You treated him worse than you would treat your horse."

"Maybe because my horse is better than John!" Henry replied.

"How could you say that? John is a human being, infinitely more valuable than any horse could ever be!" Angelina cried.

Henry grew agitated, but said nothing.

"Can you not see that John is a human being?"

Henry admitted that he felt somewhat ashamed and wretched for what he'd done. But that ended the discussion.[4]

Incidents like this were normal in the South in Angelina's day. The father of one of the girls in the Bible school Angelina taught at was the workhouse master in Charleston. Masters who did not wish to dirty their hands punishing slaves sent them to the workhouse, where whippings were administered upon the naked backs of both men and women. There was also the treadmill at the workhouse, an instrument of punishment that could cripple a slave for days.[5]

Angelina wrote, "These are not things I have heard; no my own eyes have looked upon them and wept over them."[6] It was a mystery to Angelina how a Christian could tolerate such things, much less approve of them. She broached the subject of slavery and its injustices many times with family members and friends. One night, the subject came up again as Angelina and some guests sat in the Grimké parlor.

"I cannot believe what depraved beings those blacks are," one of the female guests declared. "Those who think they are as intelligent and capable as we are quite mistaken. The blacks are fitted perfectly for what they do; they can do nothing else."

"What is it that makes them so depraved?" Angelina asked. "Is it not their degraded situations? Is it not the white people who have placed and kept them in this state of depravity? Are we not to blame for it?"

The guest was taken aback by Angelina's words. "I wish that you would never again speak on the subject!" she declared.

"Why?" Angelina asked.

"Because you speak in such a serious way," the other said.

"Truth cuts deep into the heart," Angelina replied. "Slavery is an institution contrary to the spirit of the Gospel, and is a system that nourishes the worst passions of the human heart."[7]

There was no further response as the other guests shifted uncomfortably in their chairs and changed the topic of conversation.

In November of 1829, frustrated by the indifference of those around her, Angelina left Charleston. She was never to return. Moving north to Philadelphia, Angelina joined her sister Sarah, who had left Charleston some years before and joined the Society of Friends.[8] In 1831, Angelina became an official member of the Society and settled into her life in the North.

It wasn't until 1835 that Angelina became involved in the antislavery movement. Then one night in March, Angelina attended the lecture of the British abolitionist, George Thompson, who stressed the need for women to participate in the antislavery movement.[9] The lecture sparked something within Angelina. Though she was adamantly opposed to slavery, she had never associated herself with the antislavery movement in an active way. However, in the spring of 1835, Angelina joined the Philadelphia Anti-Slavery Society.

The abolition movement in the 1830s was a despised one. Seen as radicals and rabble-rousers, abolitionists were often the objects of derision and physical violence. The primary target of the anti-abolitionists in the Northeast was William Lloyd Garrison, editor of the Boston abolitionist paper, *The Liberator*. Constantly in physical danger, mocked and ridiculed, Garrison refused to be quiet. When abolitionists were having difficulty holding meetings in Boston, Garrison wrote an appeal to the citizens of Boston. A copy of this appeal reached Angelina, and, touched by it, she wrote Garrison a letter of encouragement.

> Respected Friend: It seems as if I was compelled at this time to address thee, notwithstanding all my reasoning against intruding on thy valuable time, and the uselessness of so insignificant a person as myself offering thee the sentiments of sympathy at this alarming crisis....Although I expected opposition, I was not prepared for it so soon—it took me by surprise—and I greatly feared abolitionists would be driven back in the first onset, and thrown into confusion. Under these feelings I was urged to read thy Appeal to the citizens of Boston. Judge, then, what were my feelings on finding that my fears were utterly groundless, and that thou stoodest firm in the midst of the storm, determined to suffer and to die, rather than yield one inch...The ground upon which you stand is holy ground; never, never surrender it....If persecution is the means which God has ordained for the accomplishment of this great end, Emancipation; then in the dependence upon Him for strength to bear it, I feel as if I

could say, Let It Come! For it is my deep and solemn conviction that this is a cause worth dying for. I say so, from what I have seen, heard and known in a land of slavery, where rests the darkness of Egypt, and where is found the sin of Sodom. Yes! Let it come—let us suffer, rather than insurrections should arise....[10]

Garrison was so moved by Angelina's 36-page letter that he printed it in its entirety in *The Liberator*. With one letter, Angelina publicly renounced her upbringing and committed herself to a despised cause. For her, there would be no turning back. The Quakers denounced her, and even Sarah disapproved of Angelina's actions. Unswayed by any of the opposition, Angelina felt burdened to be even more outspoken in her fight against slavery. Yet, she was at a loss as to what to do. Then one morning in 1836 it came to her.

It has all come to me; God has shown me what I can do; I can write an appeal to Southern women, one which, thus inspired, will touch their hearts, and lead them to use their influence with their husbands and brothers. I will speak to them in such tones that they must hear me, and, through me, the voice of justice and humanity....I intend to take up the subject of abolitionism, and endeavor to undeceive the South...to close with as feeling an appeal as possible to them as women, as Christian women, setting before them the awful responsibility resting on them in this crisis; for if the women of the South do not rise in the strength of the Lord to appeal to their fathers, husbands, brothers and sons, that country must witness the most dreadful scenes of murder and blood.[11]

She began writing her appeal that morning. Later that very day, she received a letter from Elizur Wright, the secretary of the American Anti-Slavery Society, inviting Angelina to come to New York to meet with Christian women in private settings to discuss slavery. Angelina replied that she would be willing to come to New York and speak, but first she must complete her appeal.

She finished writing in the fall of 1836, and titled her work *An Appeal to the Christian Women of the South*. It was a unique appeal, written by a Southern woman for Southern women, and Angelina hoped that the spirit in which it was written would touch the hearts of those who read it. In her opening address to the women of the South, Angelina wrote:

> …I know you do not make the laws, but I also know that you are the wives and mothers, the sisters and daughters of those who do; and if you really suppose you can do nothing to overthrow slavery, you are greatly mistaken. You can do much in every way…1st. You can read on this subject. 2d. You can pray over this subject. 3d. You can speak on this subject. 4th. You can act on this sub-ject….Above all, try to persuade your husbands, fathers, brothers and sons, that slavery is a crime against God and man….[12]

The *Appeal* raised a firestorm among friends and foes alike. Close friends rebuked her for writing the pamphlet, while others praised it as a superb piece of antislavery litera-ture. The Quakers denounced her, and there was talk of dis-ownment. However, all this was just a shadow of what occurred in Charleston. Theodore Weld wrote of what took place when the *Appeal* reached the city.

> When it [the *Appeal*] came out, a large number of copies were sent by mail to South Carolina. Most of them were publicly burned by postmasters. Not long after this, the city authorities of Charleston learned that Miss Grimké

was intending to visit her mother and sisters and pass the winter with them. Thereupon the mayor called upon Mrs. Grimké and desired to inform her daughter that the police had been instructed to prevent her landing while the steamer remained in port, and to see to it that she could not communicate, by letter or otherwise, with any persons in the city; and, further, that if she should elude their vigilance and go on shore, she would be arrested and imprisoned until the return of the vessel. Her friends at once conveyed to her the message of the mayor, and added that the people of Charleston were so incensed against her, that if she should go there despite the mayor's threat of pain and penalties, she could not escape personal violence at the hands of the mob.[13]

Despite the condemnation of her and her appeal, Angelina was not to be dissuaded in what she felt was her duty. She would not be silent on the subject of slavery, and if friends disowned her, she would continue on. She and Sarah traveled to New York shortly after the printing of the *Appeal* and promptly became agents of the American Anti-Slavery Society. In a short time, Angelina and Sarah began a series of parlor talks to women concerning the evils of slavery.

The talks became so popular that parlors could not hold the gatherings, and almost immediately the talks began being held in churches. Some were shocked that women would be holding lectures in a church, but Theodore Weld encouraged the sisters to continue on, and soon there was a demand for Angelina to speak regularly. Now not only women attended, but men as well, and crowds of three and four hundred would come to hear Angelina speak.

As the lectures continued in the New England region, the opposition grew. Clergymen began denouncing Angelina and Sarah, and the New England Yearly Meeting of the Quakers advised "the closing of meeting house doors to all anti-slavery lecturers, and the disownment the sisters had long expected became imminent." The sisters took the opposition in stride. Angelina wrote a friend, "...thou wilt want to know how we feel about all these things. Well, dear, poor enough in ourselves, and defenseless; but rich and strong in the help which our Master is pleased to give from time to time, making perfect his strength in our weakness...how good it is to cast all our burdens upon the Lord." Sarah wrote another friend, "They think to frighten us from the field of duty; but they do not move us. God is our shield, and we do not fear what man can do to us....Is really amusing to see how the clergy are arrayed against two women who are telling the story of the slave's wrongs."[14]

Their speaking would eventually lead them to the Legislature of Massachusetts, where in February of 1838, Angelina and Sarah addressed the legislators three times. Though the press mocked the sisters, the legislators and public praised Angelina's eloquent arguments against slavery. It was even agreed by pro-slavery and abolitionists alike "that Angelina's lectures before the legislature had done more for the abolition cause in Massachusetts than any or all other measures together for the whole season."[15] Angelina wrote Theodore Weld, "So far as intellect and power of language was concerned, I did not excel—it was not one of my happiest efforts; but my heart broke over the wrongs of the slave, the deep fountains of sympathy were broken up, and many were melted to tears."[16]

Shortly after this, Angelina and Theodore Weld, himself a noted abolitionist, were married. Though both worried that their marriage might take away from their duties, Weld assured Angelina that it did not have to be so.

> We marry, Angelina, not merely nor mainly nor at all comparatively to ENJOY, but together to do and to dare, together to toil and to testify and suffer, together to crucify the flesh with its affections and lusts and to keep ourselves and each other unspotted from the world, to live a life of faith in the son of God, pilgrims and strangers ready yea rejoicing, called to it and each other, together to lie upon the rack or clasp the faggot or walk with steady tread the scaffold looking to Jesus, together condescending to men of low estate, the poor and despised our companions, rejoicing always to share each others burdens, looking not each on his own things, but each on the things of the other, in honor preferring one another, and happy beyond expression, happy if we may lie down at last together and fall asleep in Jesus—and if it be in a martyr's grave, amen. Alleluia! Good night, my hope, and may Jesus' banner float gently over thee.[17]

In the days following the wedding, the Quakers finally disowned the sisters—Angelina for marrying somebody outside the Society of Friends, and Sarah for attending the wedding. Some of the Welds' Philadelphia friends were offended by the idea of them marrying, saying they were "public property," and some even mentioned that now that Angelina was married, she would be good for nothing to the cause.

As if to prove them wrong, Angelina spoke two days after her marriage at the Anti-Slavery Convention of American Women, being held at Pennsylvania Hall in Philadelphia.[18] That night, as Angelina moved to the front of the hall to speak, a mob that had gathered outside began yelling, throwing stones through the windows, and cursing the abolitionists.

Moving to the podium, Angelina looked out over the crowd, which was growing anxious as the mob grew louder.

"What is a mob?" she began, then stopped as a rock shattered a window near her. Looking at the broken glass, Angelina continued. "What would the breaking of every window be?" she asked as she looked back to the assembly. "Any evidence that we are wrong, or that slavery is a good and wholesome institution? What if that mob should now burst in upon us, break up our meeting, and commit violence upon our persons—would this be anything to what the slaves endure? No, no: and we do not remember them, as bound with them, if we shrink in the time of peril, or feel unwilling to sacrifice ourselves, if need be, for their sake."

The mob's yells grew in volume. "Abolitionists!" they screamed.

Refusing to be drowned out by the mob, Angelina raised her voice. "I thank the Lord that there is yet life enough left to feel the truth, even though it rages at it—that conscience is not so completely seared as to be unmoved by the truth of the living God!"[19]

As she and the others left the convention that night, they were forced to walk the gauntlet of the screaming crowd arrayed outside the hall. As the angry faces of the mobsters leered at her, swearing at her and her friends, Angelina marched resolutely forward. No harm was done to any person, but later that night, Pennsylvania Hall, having been opened only a week, was burned to the ground.

Her speech before the convention was to be Angelina's last public appearance for nearly 25 years, but her work was not done. In 1839, she and Sarah helped Theodore write and edit a book entitled *American Slavery As It Is*. Angelina and Sarah compiled articles from more than 20,000 newspapers, articles that authenticated the facts concerning the atrocities of slavery. Many of the accounts were from slaveholders themselves. Though little known today, *American Slavery As It Is* sold over 100,000 copies in its first year and was widely distributed and read in Great Britain, and Harriet Beecher Stowe, influenced by the book, was to partially base *Uncle Tom's Cabin* on information from the Welds' book.[20]

Perhaps the most intriguing part is that Angelina's family in Charleston never once disputed any of the facts in the book. When one of Angelina's family wrote, calling the book "an infamous work," Angelina replied, "We wrote them [the testimonies] to show the awful havoc which arbitrary power makes in human hearts, and to excite a holy indignation against an institution which degrades the oppressor as well as the oppressed."[21]

As Angelina and Theodore began a family together, Angelina drifted away from the front lines of the abolition movement. When she and Theodore were asked if they should not fight the error of slavery for as long as it existed, they replied, "There is a fighting era in everyone's life. While you feel it so, fight on; it is your duty, and the best thing you can possibly do.

But when your work in that line is done, you will reach another and higher view."[22] For Theodore and Angelina, that new and higher work was the raising and teaching of their own family.

However, they did not entirely remove themselves from the abolition movement. In 1862, Theodore, at the encouragement of William Lloyd Garrison, began speaking again on the subject of slavery. He did an extended tour of 18 weeks, lecturing to crowds that were far more receptive than they had been 25 years before. Even Angelina was persuaded to make another public appearance, and in the spring of 1863 spoke before a national convention of women. In the speech, she encouraged the North to fight on and never abandon the principles that it had adopted and believed in.

When Angelina died in October of 1879, her old friends from the antislavery movement came to see her laid to rest. The last person to address the gathering that day was Wendell Phillips, who had known Angelina since the 1830s.

> This life carries us back to the first chapter of that great movement with which her name is associated to 1835, '36, '37, '38, when our cities roared with riot, when William Lloyd Garrison was dragged through the streets, when Dresser was mobbed in Nashville, and Macintosh [sic] burned in St. Louis....we were but a handful, and our words beat against the stony public as powerless as if against the north wind....At this time a young woman came from the proudest State in the slave-holding section. She came to lay on the altar of this despised cause, this seemingly hopeless crusade, both family and friends, the best social position, a high place in the church, genius, and many gifts....no man who remembers 1837 and its lowering clouds will deny that there was hardly any contribution to the anti-slavery movement greater or

more impressive than the crusade of the Grimké sisters through the New England States....This is no place for tears...It was not the dust which surrounded her that we loved. It was not the form which encompassed her that we revere; but it was the soul. We linger a little while, her old comrades....Farewell for a little while. God keep us fit to join thee in that broader service on which thou hast joined.[23]

Notes

1. Birney, *The Grimké Sisters*, 228.
2. Barnes and Dumond. eds., *Letters*, Vol. 2, 564.
3. Lerner, *The Grimké Sisters*, 371-74.
4. Birney, 76-77.
5. Lerner, *The Grimké Sisters*, 77.
6. Birney, 75.
7. Ibid, 85.
8. More commonly known as the Quakers.
9. Lerner, *The Grimké Sisters*, 120.
10. Birney, 125-26.
11. Ibid, 138, 140.
12. Grimké, *Appeal to the Christian Women*, 16-18.
13. Birney, 150.
14. Ibid, 183-84.
15. Lerner, *The Grimké Sisters*, 231.
16. Barnes and Dumond, eds., *Letters,* Vol. 2, 564.
17. Ibid, 601.
18. Pennsylvania Hall was unique in that the abolitionists, being denied the use of the churches and lecture halls in Philadelphia, raised $40,000 and built their own meetinghouse.
19. Birney, 239.
20. Thomas, *Theodore Weld: Crusader for Freedom*, 222-23.
21. Barnes and Dumond, eds., *Letters,* Vol. 2, 789.
22. Lerner, *The Grimké Sisters*, 314.
23. Birney, 317-18.

Chapter 8

FATHER DAMIEN
DE VEUSTER

"To be dissolved and be with Christ…"

★　★　★

For being a part of paradise on earth, Molokai was a foreboding place. The natives called it "The Land of Many Precipices" for its torn and twisted landscape fashioned by the volcanic activity that had formed the Hawaiian islands. On the northern end of the 260-square-mile island was a promontory. There, with the sea surrounding it on three sides, sat the leper colony of Kalawao, overshadowed from behind by a mountain of rock called the Pali.

It was here that the Board of Health in Honolulu shipped the first 140 lepers in 1866, quarantining them from society. In the 60 years since the disease first came to the tropical islands, the very word *leprosy* struck fear into the hearts of the listeners. Considered incurable, the disease caused discolored patches to appear on the face, created loss of feeling in affected areas, ate away the flesh, and eventually killed its victim with a slow, tortuous death. As in ancient times, the lepers of Hawaii were ostracized and made outcasts of society.

Now, on a stormy day in November of 1884, a lone figure struggled to climb the Pali. He was a stout man, clothed in the soutain of a priest. Breathing heavily, he rested, leaning on his staff. Below him was the leper colony of Kalawao, the small, whitewashed huts gleaming in the darkness that surrounded them. With a soft grunt, Father Damien de Veuster continued his journey up the Pali, reflecting on the "personal rule" he had written for himself years before: *Keep always in mind your three vows...You have no personal possessions...Be dead to the pleasures of the flesh...be dead to your own will...Remember always the unchangeableness of God, and try to imitate Him by continual perseverance. Think of His long-suffering and imitate His patience.*[1]

"Imitate His patience," Damien whispered as he walked.

Life had not been easy from the day a young and impetuous Damien arrived in Hawaii. A member of the Catholic order of the Congregation of the Sacred Hearts, he had been given the district of Puna on the Big Island. Many times capsized in his canoe while traveling around the district, or lost, stranded in the mountains, Damien was often alone. When his friend and fellow priest, Father Clement, collapsed from over-work, his district was exchanged with Damien's. The district of Kohala-Hamakua covered almost one quarter of the Big Island—one thousand square miles. Damien's days and weeks were filled with priestly duties—offering Mass, preaching, bap-tizing, and hiking long distances to share a meal with his parish-ioners. Always the avid carpenter, Damien also built eight chapels with his own hands and often surprised the native Hawaiians by carrying huge trees across his broad shoulders.

Now he was struggling to even lift the walking stick he held in his hand. Ignoring the pain in his left leg, Damien smiled as he walked, the memories of his first months on the Big Island flooding over him. Not only had he often surprised the natives with his abundance of energy, but once, in his youthful exuberance, he heard of a Protestant minister who had scaled the 2,000-foot cliff on Kohala in two hours. Not to be outdone, Damien scaled the cliff in 45 minutes.

Feeling a stab of pain shoot up his left leg, Damien winced and sat for a moment, stretching his legs out in front of him and leaning against the tree behind him. He chuckled in spite of the pain. He would never scale any cliffs that fast again. As he sat, he closed his eyes, smelling the tang of the tropical soil newly rained upon. It was different from the soil he had grown up tilling on his family's farm in Belgium. When it rained at home, the smell was heavy and earthy. Here it was....*Alive, yes, alive is the word*, Damien thought, his mind drifting back to the memories of years before.

He was sitting in his brother's sickroom at the Sacred Hearts' house in Louvain, Belgium.

"Jef," his brother, Pamphille, whispered, using his family nickname, "Are you sure?"

Damien, wiping his brother's sweaty and hot brow, nodded silently.

"I have already written the Father General," he replied. "He has granted me permission to take your place. Rejoice with me!"

"What did you tell him?" Pamphille asked weakly, the effects of typhus creasing his face.

"That I should take your place just as Pauline took Eugenie's." Both brothers grew silent at the mention of their sister's death and of the younger one who took her place at the Ursuline convent.

"I am convinced it is God's will for me to take your place. And I told the Father General that my taking your place would avoid wasting the price of your ticket aboard the ship. No one seems to be giving refunds these days." Pamphille chuckled at his brother's words. "Just like you, Jef. Always practical." At his words, both brothers laughed out loud.

As he thought of his older brother, a smile creased Damien's round face. In spite of Damien's pleas, Pamphille never made the journey to the Sandwich Islands, preferring to remain at the Sacred Hearts monastery in Louvain as a scholar.

Damien opened his eyes to see the sun breaking through the clouds, its fingers of light playing on the turquoise sea far below. As he rose and began walking once more, he again was lost in thought. His brother's illness had intially brought him to the Sandwich Islands. His bishop's request had brought him to Molokai 11 long years ago.

"Brother Bertrand has just returned from the colony. He says that patients have sent word that it is not enough for them to see a priest once a year." The Bishop paused for a moment. "They say it is not enough because there is so much time to die between visits."[2]

It was May 4, 1873. Bishop Maigret, the vicar apostolic of Hawaii, had summoned six of the Sacred Heart Fathers to the Island of Maui to dedicate the new church there. After celebrating Mass together and talking about their territories and the need for even more churches, the conversation drifted to the leper colony on Molokai.

Bishop Maigret paused again to look at the priests gathered with him. Solid men of the cloth, they braved tropical storms, traveled over impossible terrain, and endured illness and solitude like the soldiers of Christ they were. But, what he was to ask of them now was beyond what any of them had ever experienced.

"In all good conscience, I cannot ask any of you to go on a permanent basis. However, if we were to rotate every two to three months, the other districts would not be left without a priest and the lepers would have someone with them year round."

He was startled, but not surprised, when Father Damien leapt to his feet.

"I want to go!" the Flemish priest exclaimed. "I desire nothing more than to share in the lives of these unfortunates."[3]

In later years, Damien confided to a friend. "I volunteered because I knew Maigret would never send one of us into such an ordeal." He also knew that, though it was to be a rotation of service, his volunteering for the district likely meant once he was there, he would never leave. For a priest to volunteer on the island of the lepers meant that he himself might become one. Once a leper, there was no leaving Molokai.

Only the year before he wrote to his sister Pauline, "Let us be in the hands of God as tools in the hands of a skilfull [sic] workman. Whether in life or death, we belong to Jesus." Girded by this knowledge, Damien's transition from his district to the island of Molokai was a rapid one. On May 10, a steamer left the harbor of Maui and set course for Molokai. On board were Bishop Maigret and Father Damien. With them were 50 lepers and numerous heads of cattle. When they arrived, Bishop Maigret addressed the lepers who appeared at their arrival.

"Hitherto, you have been alone and abandoned, but that is all over and done with. Here is someone who will be a father to you. He loves you so intensely that he does not hesitate to become one of you and wishes to live and die with you."[5]

In spite of his exterior smile, Damien's stomach churned at the specters before him. They hardly appeared human, so ravaged were they by the disease of leprosy. Some of the lepers before him were missing limbs, others noses, eyes, and lips. Damien forced the smile to stay on his face and said good-bye to his bishop.

Scared to share a leper's hut for fear of the contagious disease, Damien's first night was spent sleeping under a giant pandanus tree. He quickly fired off a letter to his superior, "I am sleeping under a tree until you send me some wood to build a house."[6] However, it was several weeks before the wood arrived, and during that time he slept under the tree.

Six months later, he wrote his brother, Pamphille, from the solitude of the one-room hut he built for himself when the wood finally arrived from Honolulu. "It is six months since I came here and all the time I have been surrounded by lepers...Leprosy appears to be incurable. It eats away the flesh and as the flesh rots, it gives off a horrible smell."

Leaning back in his chair, Damien scanned the words he had written as he puffed on his pipe. He smiled ruefully as the heavy smell of tobacco pervaded the small hut. It was his one small concession, this pipe. He smoked it as often as possible in hopes that the smell of the tobacco would cling to his clothes and at least neutralize the stench of leprosy. Keeping it clenched between his teeth, he continued writing. "It has almost been impossible for me to get used to the stench, and at Mass one Sunday I felt I should have to leave the altar and go into the fresh air, but I managed to control myself by thinking of Our Lord when he ordered them to open the grave of Lazarus in spite of Martha's words, 'Lord, by now he will smell.' But now I can go into the leper's huts without reluctance...."[7]

Without reluctance. Through Damien's mind flashed the image of the two lepers he had ministered to during his first week at the leper colony. Lying on filthy mats, covered with decay, blood, and pus, their rotting bodies covered with maggots, they looked up at him, eyes pleading for his care. The smell was too much for him. His stomach churned and Damien fled, gasping, retching on his hands and knees. The words he had written to his sister screamed through his mind as he clutched the dirt path beneath him—*Let us be in the hands of God as tools in the hands of a skilful* [sic] *workman. Whether in life or death, we belong to Jesus.* Still shaking, tears in his eyes, Damien forced himself to return. He knelt beside the men, washing them, bandaging their open wounds, speaking softly to them. For months on end, the scene would replay itself—Damien tending to the needs of the lepers, rushing outside to get sick, then staggering back into the dark huts to care for them.

Tears began to form in Damien's eyes as he continued to write. He set his pen down to wipe them away. The tears were becoming a nightly occurrence as Damien sat alone in his hut. He was alone, and he felt the loneliness. He was amidst a colony of lepers, whose needs, both medical and spiritual, were often beyond him. The longer he stayed with them, the greater the chances grew that he would contract the disease— and he knew it. Wiping his eyes, he finally set his pen down. He would finish the letter to Pamphille tomorrow. Leaning over, he snuffed out the candle.

"Lord," he whispered in the darkness, "give me strength."

In time, the loneliness would dissipate and the revulsion for the leprosy was replaced with love. Damien began to refer to himself and his flock as "we lepers." He spent his days sweeping the floors of the lepers' huts, washing patients, disinfecting the sores caused by leprosy, and even amputating certain parts of the body that were in the last stages of leprosy. In later years, a visitor would write of Damien, "[He] bandaged the most revolting sores as if he were handling lovely flowers."[8]

As befitted the son of a Flemish farmer, Damien was also a practical man. He realized within his first week on Molokai that it would not be enough to simply visit the lepers and give them comfort. When he first arrived at Kalawao, there were only a few wooden huts for the lepers. The remainder lived in simple huts made of entwined branches, thatched with straw. Shortly after Damien's arrival, a hurricane destroyed many of the huts. Damien requested that lumber be sent, and soon he, and as many of the lepers who could still work, built small wooden huts and whitewashed them. When he was told there was no fresh water nearby and that the lepers had to walk a considerable distance for it, Damien hiked the surrounding region. He found a deep pool of fresh water at the end of the valley. He requested water pipes. No engineers came with the pipes, however, so Damien and the lepers carried them inland and laid them out so that, in time, every hut in the leper colony of Kalawao had a tap nearby it.

In time the Board of Health in Honolulu would recognize his work. In late autumn of 1877, he was offered the post of deputy superintendent of Molokai with a salary of $10,000 per year. For a man who was often penniless and constantly requesting supplies and funds, the offer was tempting. Or, at least, it appeared so.

Damien wrote back to the Board. "If you were to offer me one hundred thousand dollars for doing what I am doing, I would not stay here for five minutes. God and the salvation of souls are the only reasons why I remain. If I accept a salary for my work, my mother would no longer accept me as her son."[9]

Damien did accept the post, however, but only upon the insistence that he receive no salary and that he fill the post only until a permanent deputy was appointed. It was a trying time for him. His manners were rough, he was a stubborn man, and administration was simply not his calling. After three months, his successor was named.

"And now I am free again!"[10] he exclaimed to his friends—free again to minister to the dying souls around him. For his work, the Board of Health insisted he take money. Realizing that needs of the colony were beyond his resources, Damien accepted $134, all of which he spent on his flock.

As word of Damien's work at Kalawao spread, his hopes of anonymity vanished.

Here was a single man, in the prime of his life, living among hundreds of people sick with the most contagious disease of his day—and he was doing it in the name of Christ.

"We care not what this man's theology may be," wrote the editor of the *Nuhou* in Honolulu only days after Damien landed on Molokai, "he surely is a Christian hero."[11] In future years, the *Commercial Advertiser* in Honolulu wrote of Damien:

> This young priest, Father Damien, is the glory of Hawaii. In him we see the heroism of the martyrs in the bloody arenas of the ancient world. His heroism is even greater, for would it not be a greater favor to be thrown to savage beasts than be condemned to spend one's life in a leper settlement? And Damien, Damien, the soldier of Christ, has already lived several years among the exiles of Molokai…Such a love for these unhappy people can only be inspired by the love of God, and it is God alone who can reward him fittingly.[12]

Everyone in Hawaii, however, did not glory in Damien's service to the leper colony at Kalawao. For the general public, and even among some of the medical community, there was the belief that leprosy was the fourth stage of syphilis—the just desserts for a life of sin. It was a theory dismissed easily by scientific medicine. The idea, however, of leprosy being caused by syphilis remained.

To address the problem, 48 Protestant ministers gathered at the Hawaiian Evangelical Association a month after Damien's arrival at Kalawao. They addressed the topic of leprosy and issued a statement at the end of their meeting.

> While striving to comfort and strengthen with the love of Jesus the afflicted hearts of the lepers and their friends...we must also teach and persuade all the people to obey the law of God and segregate the lepers from among us...and teach every leper who cleaves to his people and refuses to go away, that he is sinning against the lives of men and against the law of God.

The Association did not produce one volunteer from among the ministers gathered. Instead there was found a Hawaiian Protestant, a minister and a leper, to be sent to Kalawao. He went. But never in Damien's lifetime did a white, Protestant, healthy minister ever live on Kalawao.[13]

Even his fellow priests were hesitant to join him. In the 16 years Damien spent at Kalawao, he was without a fellow priest or assistant for nine of them. The priests who were sent to him, for the most part, were a source of great distress to Damien. First came Father Andrew Burgermann, a fellow member of the Sacred Hearts fellowship. Suffering from elephantiasis contracted in Tahiti, Burgermann was a talented medical practitioner whose dream was to help the lepers on Molokai. He, like Damien, was a straightforward, stubborn man. Though their relationship began well, soon Damien refused to make his confessions to Burgermann and Burgermann retaliated by not talking to Damien for days. When Burgermann was finally transfered from Kalawao, Damien's greatest source of distress would come—Father Albert Motiton.

Given that leprosy was considered the fourth stage of syphilis, Damien's superiors in Honolulu were afraid that Damien was surrounded by sin and debauchery and feared he might fall prey to it, if indeed he had already not done so. Motiton's sole purpose was to be Damien's spiritual and moral guardian. As Damien listened to the accusations, he was stunned. For some time, their relationship was like the one Damien had had with Burgermann, so much so that Damien fired off two letters to his superiors in Honolulu. "Please send Motiton somewhere else," he pleaded. His request was ignored. He sent a second letter, saying he would leave Molokai if Motiton was not removed. It too was ignored as his suspicious superiors sided with Motiton. Finally, in desperation, Damien wrote a third letter to his superior, Bishop Koeckemann. "If my conduct, badly viewed by Father Albert here, displeases you, I will willingly leave Molokai...If you do not work to soften Father Albert's insupportable temper, you will soon see me, even with out obedience."[14]

After two-and-a-half years on Molokai, Father Motiton's physical health became so bad that he was sent to Honolulu for treatment. There, with his forceful ways and harsh temper, he drove his superiors and fellow priests almost to madness, shedding light on Damien's ordeal with him on Molokai.

The next priest sent to Damien was Father Gregory Archambaux, a leper in the last stages of the disease. A kind, mild man, Archambaux was also an asthmatic, and many nights Damien would spend by his side so that if he ever had trouble breathing, Damien would be there for him. Realizing he was a burden to Damien, he asked to be sent back to Honolulu, where he died shortly after leaving Molokai. And so Damien worked alone, constantly asking that a compatible priest be sent to him.

In the midst of the struggle came the news in December of 1884 that Damien had been expecting for so long. Upon a return trip from visiting his superiors in Honolulu, the sea was too rough for Damien's boat to land. Tucking his soutane around him, he jumped into the ocean and swam to shore. Returning to his hut, he heated water to plunge his feet into to warm himself. Unaware that he boiled instead of heated the water, Damien watched as his feet began to burn and blister—and he felt nothing. His fears were realized. The internal pain he had been experiencing in his left leg and foot was more than strain and weariness. He was a leper. The words he had written to his friends so long ago were realized: "As for me, I make myself a leper among the lepers, to gain all to Jesus Christ."[15]

For a time, the news stayed within the Sacred Hearts family. To them he wrote that his leprosy was "anticipated from my first arrival into this leper asylum...and voluntarily accepted before hand, and [I] hope that, helped by the prayers of many, our Lord will grant me the necessary graces—to carry my cross behind him on our peculiar Golgotha of Kalawao."

However, the loneliness he had struggled with in the past returned full force. Alone in a leper colony, its only priest, overburdened with caring for lepers in worse condition than he, Damien began to slip into despair. Kalawao became a living tomb for him. He wrote to his superiors—could he come to Honolulu, to the Kakaako hospital, and spend a few days to confess? He received a simple reply—no. Although in time he would be allowed to visit Honolulu, the answer to his prayers and pleas for a companion came on July 29, 1886.

"Kamiano! Kamiano!"

In spite of despair and leprosy, Damien was atop the church roof, repairing its recent storm damage. He squinted down at the boys running up the path from the ocean, yelling his Hawaiian nickname.

"Kamiano, a boat is coming!"

Clambering down from the church roof, Damien set his hammer down and hitched his horse, Daisy, to his two-wheeled buggy. The harbor of Kalaupapa was two miles away—too far to walk these days. As he rode in the buggy, he turned to Paul, one of the Hawaiian boys who had become a faithful helper to him.

"I have a feeling that something special will happen today—perhaps a surprise."

As Damien and Paul watched the small steamer creep closer to the dock, Damien scanned the ship's deck. There were new patients and animals. As was his practice, Damien slowly climbed out of his buggy to meet each of the new patients as they walked off the gangplank. Even without having met him, the lepers knew Father Damien. When the last of the lepers had disembarked, Damien turned to go.

"Father Damien?"

Damien turned to see the man at the top of the gangplank, his dark brown hair ruffled by the wind, his gray-blue eyes twinkling.

"Yes, I am Father Damien. And you?"

"I am Ira Dutton. I have come to join you in your work. Where would you have me start?" A smile split Dutton's face as he reached for Damien's hand, seemingly unperturbed by the sores that the leprosy had left on the priest's hands.

"I cannot pay you," Damien said, grasping Dutton's hand in his own.

"Even if you could, I would not accept it."

Damien nearly wept for joy. This was the surprise he felt would come today.

As the days and weeks passed, Dutton told his story to Damien. A veteran of the Civil War, he had fought on the side of the Union. After the war, he married, only to have his wife run away with another man. He then turned to whiskey for solace. Wandering for years as a drunk, in 1876 he took a vow of sobriety and joined the Catholic Church in 1883. In later years, after spending 18 months at a Trappist monastery, he read of Damien's work on Molokai. Right then and there, he knew what his calling in life was.

"And now I am here," he would say, clapping Damien on his broad shoulders. Although not a priest, he and Damien became fast friends from the moment they met, his easy-going style softening Damien's rough edges. With Brother Joseph, as Damien called Ira, running the orphanage for the leper children, Damien's load became more bearable. And then, to add to the blessing of Dutton, another man appeared at Kalawao.

An Irishman by birth, a wanderer and drunken brawler and with no real life history to speak of, James Sinnett was just as mysterious as his arrival at Kalawao. Having appeared at the Board of Health in Honolulu, with no credentials, he asked to be sent to Kalawao. Strangely enough, the Board agreed, even paying his fare to Molokai. Upon his arrival, he became a changed man, working side by side with Damien in the infirmary.

Upon the heels of Sinnett came another helper for Damien, another Belgian and a priest, Father Lambert Conrady, and then another priest, Father Wendelin. After years of laboring alone, of seeking a fellow worker with whom he was of the same mind, Damien was blessed with four such men as the leprosy in his body began to take its toll.

There were days Damien was the Damien of old, clambering atop the church to give it a new steeple, building a one-room hut for Brother Joseph, and taking care of the day-to-day affairs of the colony. Other days, the leprosy gripped him. In early October of 1888, while saying Mass, he collapsed, whispering, "Holy, Holy, Holy Lord God of Hosts."

Confiding in Father Motiton, with whom in a strange turn of events he had become fast friends, Damien wrote of his own leprosy:

> The terrible disease…is making alarming progress. My great dread is that I may soon not be able to celebrate Mass regularly—or not even at all.…Sickness and suffering

cannot discourage me—quite the contrary. Until now I am happy and contented and if it were possible to be restored to health by living here, I would say, without hesitation, "I will remain with the lepers until the end of my days."[17]

To the surprise of those around him, he gathered his strength one last time. Visiting Kalawao, a fellow priest saw Damien atop the church, directing workers in his effort to remodel the church.

"Is that not Father Damien?" the priest asked.

"Yes," Father Conrady replied. "I fear one day we will find him dead, with that hammer in his hand. He refuses to be slowed by the leprosy. He says there is too much to be done."

But, the leprosy would not allow the work to continue. On March 31, 1889, confined to his bed, too weak to move, Damien whispered to Father Wendelin, "Look at my hands. The sores are healing and the crust is turning black. Death is near...God is calling me to celebrate the Feast of Easter with Him."

"Will you leave me your mantle," Father Wendelin pleaded, "that I might inherit your great heart?"

Damien smiled in spite of the weariness and pain. "What would you do with it? It is full of leprosy."

"Then give me your blessing."[18]

Placing his hand on Father Wendelin's head, Damien blessed him. Days later, the end came. Receiving communion for the last time, Damien died in the arms of James Sinnett, who, in his last weeks, had become Damien's faithful nurse.

Damien left behind him a leper colony dramatically changed from the day he had arrived 16 years before. And his fellow laborers? Father Conrady stayed at Kalawao for six more years before departing for China, imitating Damien's life and work in a leper colony there. Father Wendelin stayed on Molokai until 1902. Ira Dutton, "Brother Joseph," continued Damien's work on Molokai, dying in 1931, having left the island only once since the day he arrived in July 1886. As for James Sinnett, just as mysteriously as he arrived, he disappeared from Kalawao three months after Damien's death. And Damien? He left behind a life's work of love, sacrifice, and devotion for his Master. In his "personal rule," written in 1880, he wrote:

Have a scrupulous attitude for everything regarding God; that is to say, in prayer, meditation, the holy service, the administration of the sacraments. Unite your heart with God…May passion lead you to whisper these words continually, "Cupio dissolvi et esse cum Christo." I wish to be dissolved and be with Christ.[19]

Notes

1. DeBroey, *Father Damien*, 77.
2. Beevers, *A Man for Now*, 62.
3. Ibid.
4. Letter from Father Damien to his sister Pauline, July 14, 1872, *Damien of Molokai*, 64.
5. Beevers, *A Man for Now*, 63.
6. Ibid, 64.
7. A letter from Father Damien to his brother, found in Stoddard, *Diary*, 47-50.
8. Beevers, *A Man for Now*, 67.
9. Ibid, 83.
10. Ibid, 84.
11. Daws, *Holy Man*, 61.
12. Beevers, *A Man for Now*, 86.
13. Daws, *Holy Man*, 64.
14. Ibid, 105.
15. Stoddard, *Diary*, 51.
16. Daws, *Holy Man*, 149.
17. DeBroey, *Father Damien*, 120.
18. Conversation taken from Beevers, *A Man for Now*, 139.
19. DeBroey, *Father Damien*, 77.

Chapter 9

PETER MUHLENBERG

"There is a time for war."

★ ★ ★

It was a crisp spring day in the year 1775 when Peter Muhlenberg rode into Richmond, Virginia. The unrest that threatened to boil over into armed rebellion against the mother country of Great Britain seethed in the American colonies.

The year before, on May 28, 1774, Lord Dunmore, royal governor of Virginia, dissolved the Virginian Assembly only days before its appointed June 1 day of fasting and praying. The Assembly had sought to gather to seek divine intervention in hopes of averting the "heavy calamity which threatens the civil right of America."[1] Tensions had reached such a state in the colony of New York that, when the king's tax collectors came to colonist doors, many were thrown out. One tax collector wrote to the Board of Trade in England saying: "If you ask an American, who is his master? He will tell you he has none, nor any governor but Jesus Christ."[2]

For Peter Muhlenberg, his trip was the next step in a public career that had seen him become not only a spiritual leader, but a civic one as well. Three years before, word arrived from Williamsburg that a minister was needed in the local Lutheran Church located in Woodstock, Virginia.

Sensing God's call there, Muhlenberg went. Now Chairman of the Committee of Correspondence and Safety for Dunmore County, Muhlenberg was in Richmond for a gathering of the Virginia Assembly at St. John's Church.

As Muhlenberg sat with his fellow delegates, a fiery, red-haired man stood to speak. Everyone knew Patrick Henry. He was an orator and a member of the Sons of Liberty. His voice was often the loudest and clearest in enunciating the colonies' grievances against the mother country of Great Britain.

Rising to stand before the convention, Henry began to speak:

> This is no time for ceremony. The question before the house is one of awful moment to this country. For my part, I consider it as nothing less than a question of freedom or slavery…we are not weak, if we make proper use of the those means which the God of nature hath placed in our power…we shall not fight our battles alone. There is a just God who presides over the destinies of nations, and who will raise up friends to fight our battles for us. There is no retreat but in submission and slavery. Our chains are forged. Their clanking may be heard on the

plains of Boston. The war is inevitable. And let it come!
I repeat it, sir; let it come!

A murmur rippled through the men seated in St. John's as
Henry continued.

> It is in vain to extenuate the matter. Gentlemen may cry
> peace, peace, but there is no peace. The war is actually
> begun! The next gale that sweeps from the north will
> bring to our ears the clash of resounding arms! Our
> brethren are already in the field! Why stand we idle
> here?…Is life so dear, or peace so sweet, as to be pur-
> chased at the price of chains and slavery? Forbid it
> almighty God!

Henry struck his hand upon the speaker's dais. His eyes
were flashing as he thundered, "I know not what course others
may take, but as for me, give me liberty or give me death!"[3]

The men in the sanctuary erupted in a cacophony of
sound, some applauding Henry; others crying out that cooler
heads must prevail.

In the midst of it sat a quiet and meditative Peter Muhlenberg. For a man who was torn between his ministry and the
growing strife between the colonies and England, between a
father and a brother who cried for peace and his conscience,
Peter Muhlenberg's answer to the question that had hounded
him was answered by Henry's words. He would join forces
with the patriots—whether as soldier or chaplain—he did not
know.

He wrote to his brother Frederick, telling him of his duties as Chairman of the Committee and of Henry's speech. The
patriot rhetoric was not lost upon his brother, who fired a brisk
reply back to his brother.

"You have become too much involved," he wrote, "in matters with which, as a preacher, you have nothing whatsoever to do and which do not belong to your office....Nothing can excuse you."[4]

But if Frederick thought his older brother was already too involved in the cause for independence, he and the rest of Peter's family could not have fully expected the events of January 21, 1776.

It was Sunday morning. As the parishioners at Peter Muhlenberg's church in Woodstock listened, Muhlenberg preached from Ecclesiastes 3. In a manner unusual for him, Muhlenberg read through his sermon quickly, scarcely glancing up at his congregation.

A change came over him as he finished his sermon.

"In the language of the holy writ, there was a time for all things, a time to preach and a time to pray, but those times have passed away. There was also a time to fight," he said.[5] He looked up from his text, his eyes scanning the congregation. He took a deep breath. "And that time has now come," he said. With one swift motion, he threw off his clerical robes, revealing a Peter Muhlenberg dressed in the uniform of a colonel in the Continental Army.

An audible gasp was heard though the congregation. Many of the men in the congregation were part of the militia, but this turn of events was something entirely different. Before them now, eyes blazing, jaw clenched, was their minister in the uniform of George Washington's army.

Strapping on his sword, Muhlenberg led his congregation in singing "A Mighty Fortress Is Our God." When the church fell silent, he pronounced the benediction. Looking up, he asked, "Who among you is with me?"

He stepped down from his pulpit and strode down the center aisle. All eyes were on him as he neared the church's doors. There he turned and asked again, "Who among you is with me?" His eyes scanned the church.

The shock of his actions was written on every face. Slowly, near the front of the church, a man rose. He looked at Muhlenberg and gave a slow nod. Around him, more men stood, slowly, one by one. It is recorded that over 300 of the men from Muhlenberg's congregation joined him that cold day in January.

"Follow me," Muhlenberg said.

The drummer boy he had placed at the door snapped out a quick march as Muhlenberg exited his church for the last time.

It was a year later now. After enduring seemingly endless defeats in New Jersey and New York at the hands of the British, Muhlenberg, now a brigadier general in Washington's army, sat astride his horse on the edges of Brandywine Creek.

In front of him was the British Army under Sir William Howe. Behind him was the city of Philadelphia. It was clear that Howe, if he could not destroy Washington and his army, wanted to cut the Americans off from their supply base in nearby Reading, Pennsylvania. All Washington wanted to do was escape annihilation and survive to fight another day.

One wonders, in times such as these, when Muhlenberg took position with his brigade in General Nathanael Greene's division at Chad's Ford, if Muhlenberg reflected on the conflict within his family at his decision to put aside his clerical robes in favor of the army uniform he now wore.

He had replied, in time, to his brother Frederick's rebuke at his involvement in the war. Denouncing Frederick as a Tory, Peter's letter was passionate and suspicious. "You say as a clergyman nothing can excuse my conduct," Peter wrote. "This excellent Doctrine is certainly a Production of that excellent City N.Y. which must be purged with fire, before it is ever cleansed from Toryism; may there be none to pity it...."

For Frederick, this was too much. He did not mind Peter's patriotism; he minded that he blended pastor with soldier.

"Purged with fire," Frederick spat back, "Toryism...I am convinced the majority here are as strong for the American cause as the Virginians, if not stronger....None to pity it! Good God!....Brother, brother, the rough soldier peeps out from behind the black hat....That is contrary to the teaching of Jesus, which you formerly preached. None to pity it...Heathenish."

Peter's reply was equally as strong:

I am a Clergyman it is true, but I am a member of Society as well as the poorest Layman, and my Liberty is as dear to me as any man, shall I then sit still and enjoy myself at Home when the best Blood of the Continent is spilling? Heaven forbid it....I am called by my country in its defence [sic]—the cause is just and noble—were I a Bishop, even a Lutheran one I should obey without hesitation, and so far am I from thinking that I act wrong, I am convinced it is my duty to do so and duty I owe to God and my country.[6]

In time, when the British would shell New York in late summer of 1775, Frederick would join the patriot cause and move his wife and family to Philadelphia, the city Peter now sought to defend.

On the morning of September 10, 1777, Peter peered into the early morning mists that hovered along the shores of Brandywine Creek. It was rumored that across the ford, the Hessians would lead the enemy attack.

Feared and loathed in the same breath, the mercenaries from the German province of Hesse had been hired by George III to augment his troops in North America. With their tall hats, waxed mustaches, and ponytails, the Hessians' reputation was for giving—and expecting—no mercy. It was the Hessians whom Washington had smashed at Trenton. In the near future, however, it was the Hessians who would lead the charge of the British at the Battle of Long Island, bayoneting surrendering American troops without mercy.

Now Muhlenberg sat with his troops, awaiting their arrival. With a roar, the enemy cannons opened fire, breaking the stillness of the morning. Out of the heavy mist, drums rolling, bayonets fixed, came the Hessians. Supported by two British brigades, the Hessians charged across the ford. American Revolution folklore has it as legend that these same Hessian troops knew of Peter Muhlenberg, and upon seeing him astride his horse in the distance, were heard to cry out, "Heir kommt Teufel Pete—Here comes Devil Pete!"[7] Clearly, Muhlenberg's reputation as a warrior preceded him.

Officers from both sides barked commands at their men. From the American forces, General Maxwell's light infantry charged to meet the enemy. However, the attack was only a feint by the British and their allies.

In a well-executed move, General Cornwallis took the majority of the British army 17 miles north of Chad's Ford and crossed at Jeffries Ford. While the Hessians under General Knyphausen engaged the Americans at Chad's Ford, Cornwallis and the bulk of the British army curled around the American flank commanded by General Sullivan. Before Sullivan knew it, Cornwallis and his troops were behind him.

Had it not been for a warning carried by a local Quaker, the Americans would have been annihilated. Washington moved quickly. Ordering General Anthony Wayne and his brigade to hold Chad's Ford, he swung Greene's division, composed of Muhlenberg and Weedon's brigades, to assist Sullivan. Badly surprised, Sullivan and his men were fighting for their lives. In the act of swinging around to face the enemy, Sullivan's troops became disorganized. Within the hour the Americans were retreating. With Weedon's brigade placed in a narrow defile to provide a place for the Americans to retreat to and rally, Muhlenberg and his brigade advanced into action.

According to one account, "The contest here was terrific. The troops were engaged at the point of bayonet, and charge followed charge with the utmost desperation."[8]

With only his brigade against a vastly superior British force, Muhlenberg and his men attacked again and again, breaking the advance of Cornwallis's army.

The engagement was fierce, hand-to-hand fighting, with men stabbing and slashing with their bayonets, swinging clubbed muskets, and firing their muskets at point-blank range. In the middle of it all was Peter Muhlenberg.

Behind him and his men, the rest of the American army retreated to safety behind Weedon's brigade. Muhlenberg's brigade was the last of the American troops to retire from the field. However, Muhlenberg's day was not finished. General Wayne and his brigade were hard pressed by the Hessians. Again, Weedon and Muhlenberg's brigades came to the rescue. Two combined factors saved the American army that day—the fall of darkness and the actions of Weedon and Muhlenberg's brigades. Because of their actions, the American army would survive to fight another day.

Of the two brigades, even the British wrote, "They exhibited a degree of firmness, order and resolution and preserved such a countenance in extremely sharp service, as would not have discredited veterans."[9]

By September 25, however, the British were in control of Philadelphia and the surrounding countryside. The Americans retreated and by December were in winter quarters at Valley Forge.

Caught between Valley Forge and the British in Pennsylvania was Peter's boyhood home, the Trappe, a German community seven miles north of Valley Forge. For Peter it was a trying time.

"I wish sincerely that Pappa and his family were removed from the Trappe," he wrote to Frederick. "Should he be taken and escape murder by those villains [local Tories], yet he would perhaps perish in the ruins of Philadelphia. I beg you would once more try to have him removed, spare no costs and I will repay."[10]

Peter's mother was too ill to be moved, though, and her husband would not leave her side. So Peter spent as much time as he could spare riding to visit his mother and father. Constant rumors abounded that the British and their German allies were keen to find the older Muhlenberg and hang him. On the night of February 18, 1778, Peter's father, Henry Muhlenberg, wrote in his journal: "The British calvary is coming nearer and nearer and is taking captive former officers of the American militia. Toward evening came a report that they were nearby and going to take me. I cannot flee, much less leave my sick wife behind, so I must await whatever God's holy providence and governace, which doeth all things well, has ordained for me and commit it to him, the Lord of Lords, in humble prayer."[11]

The raiders did not come that night, or any other night. It appears the hand of God that so miraculously spared Peter Muhlenberg again and again in battle rested over his family as well.

For Peter Muhlenberg, the remainder of the American War for Independence was filled with action. At Monmouth, he was nearly killed. "I lost two fine officers by their cannon, Major Dickinson and Capt. Fauntlroy, who was killed very near me,"[12] he wrote to his brother-in-law. When Anthony Wayne made his daring bayonet attack to capture the British fort at Stony Point, it was Muhlenberg and his brigade who covered his flank in case the attack went poorly.

In 1780, when the Americans needed more troops, it was to Muhlenberg whom George Washington wrote: "I have now only to entreat that you will use every possible exertion to collect and form the Drafts and to have them disciplined....The crisis is a most interesting One, and on your and their exertions, and the discipline and bravery of the Troops, great and early events depend."[13]

Again, Muhlenberg came through for the Continental Army, keeping a steady stream of men pouring south into the areas of conflict. However, on October 22 of that same year, Peter Muhlenberg was back in action. Virginia was being invaded.

The British, with 60 ships, had begun landing troops near Portsmouth on the James River. Under the command of General Leslie, three thousand British troops prepared to move from the coast and invade Virginia. With only eight hundred regulars under his command, Peter Muhlenberg stepped into the breach. His bold move was enough, and without a major battle, the British re-embarked less than a month later. However, the threat was far from over.

Only two months later, British troops under the command of the turncoat Benedict Arnold sailed up the James River. With his 1,600 troops, his aim was to destroy the American base in Virginia. In a frantic letter, Baron Steuben, the drill master of Valley Forge, sent for Peter Muhlenberg. In a race against time, Muhlenberg, outnumbered and with only poorly armed militia making up his command, paralleled Arnold's movement, careful not to engage, yet careful not to let Arnold move freely. The objective of the British was Petersburg.

"You must govern your movements," Steuben wrote Muhlenberg, "so as to prevent their reaching Petersburg before you."[14] On April 25, with nowhere else to go and the enemy approaching rapidly, Muhlenberg made his stand at Blanford, a mile east of Petersburg.

The day after the battle, Peter wrote his brother Frederick:

> Yesterday, about one o'clock, p.m., the enemy approached the town in two columns, and were met by our light infantry about a mile from the town, where the skirmish commenced, and every inch of ground to the bridge was warmly disputed. The dispute was very hot at the bridge for some time, but at length they cannonaded us so severely, that we broke up the bridge and retreated in the greatest regularity, after maintaining the fight for two hours. I have the pleasure to assure you that the militia behaved with spirit and resolution which would have done honor to veterans.[15]

In his General Orders, Steuben begged "General Muhlenberg to accept his very particular thanks for his gallantry and good dispatches." To Congress, Steuben boasted that Muhlenberg "possessed the rare faculty of making soldiers out of militia." Determined to make Muhlenberg the hero of the Tidewater Campaign, Steuben also wrote to General Greene. His letter must have carried the same tone as his one to Congress, for Greene responded that "Your report on the good conduct of General Muhlenberg and the troops under his command, affords me great pleasure."[16]

As for Benedict Arnold and his troops, their advance stopped at Petersburg as they waited to join forces with Cornwallis, who was moving up from his campaign in the south.

For his gallantry at Petersburg, Muhlenberg was given command of one thousand Continental light infantry, dubbed the "flower of Washington's army."

Eager to fight, Peter and his troops snapped constantly at the British. It is reported that General Wayne, dubbed "Mad Anthony" Wayne for his own eagerness to fight, was worried at the daring and boldness of Muhlenberg. Yet, Muhlenberg made no mistakes, and again he came to Wayne's rescue on July 6, 1781, as Wayne fell into a trap set for him by Cornwallis.

Believing the British to have crossed the James River and to be heading for Yorktown, Wayne had pressed forward, thinking that the British would have left only a small rearguard behind. He soon discovered that he was not taking on the rearguard; he was fighting the whole British army under Cornwallis.

Hearing an unexpected volume of gunfire, Muhlenberg did not wait for orders.

He mustered his men and charged to Wayne's rescue just as the British were about to surround Wayne and his troops. By his bold and daring actions, Muhlenberg again saved the day for the Americans.

Under orders from his superior, General Clinton, Cornwallis retreated to Yorktown, not because he faced a superior American force but because Clinton needed his men for the northern campaign in New York. It was a colossal error of judgment on the part of the British. Assuming their fleet was superior, they did not fear the French fleet under Admiral De-Grasse. The annals of history tell otherwise.

Just off Chesapeake Bay, at Cape Henry, the two fleets met. After four days, the French were victorious. Invigorated by his allies' success, Washington, coordinating two armies, including that of the French general, Count Rochambeau, pinned Cornwallis in Yorktown. With the British fleet beaten, Cornwallis was trapped.

The end of the siege of Yorktown came on October 14, 1781. The American and French siege works were within three hundred yards of the British lines. Only Redoubt 10 and its mate stood between the Americans and victory. The French were to assault the latter, the Americans the former. Commanding the American assault on Redoubt 10 was Peter Muhlenberg.

The image etched in American history is that of Alexander Hamilton leading his men over Redoubt 10. Perhaps this is due in part to the fact that he had the honor of writing the report to Lafayette after the redoubt was taken. But Peter Muhlenberg, even while suffering from a fever, is reported to have been wounded in the assault as he led his men over the redoubt. Why he never received the attention Hamilton did has left many questions. Did he think writing the report was unnecessary? Could it be that Hamilton, eager for publicity, asked to write the report? It is more likely that the combination of fever and wound left him incapacitated the next day, and so history remains silent in laying the laurels at Muhlenberg's feet for the part he played at Redoubt 10.

However, it is Muhlenberg, not Hamilton, who is immortalized not only by a statue in the United States Capitol, but also in the famous painting that hangs in the Rotunda of the United States Capitol depicting the surrender of the British at Yorktown on October 19, 1781. As one of the escorts of General Lincoln, whom Washington sent to accept Cornwallis's sword, Muhlenberg can still be seen today, sitting astride his horse, the tallest figure in the painting.

Whether or not he received the praise he so richly deserved, Muhlenberg himself did not seem to mind. With the war all but over, and still fighting the fever that had threatened to leave him bedridden at Yorktown, Muhlenberg sought and received permission from Washington himself to go home. He quietly disappeared over the mountains to his home and family in Woodstock.

For the veteran of Brandywine, Germantown, Stony Point, and Yorktown, his career in the public eye was not yet completed. Moving from the ranks of soldier to politician, Peter was elected to the U.S. House of Representatives three times and to the Senate once in 1801. In an odd twist of events, his brother Frederick, once so emphatically opposed to Peter's mixing of minister and soldier, joined Peter as a Representative, twice being elected Speaker of the House, both as members of the Anti-Federalist Party.[17]

On October 1, 1807, almost a year after his wife had died, 61 years to the day that he was born, Peter Muhlenberg died. He is buried alongside his wife and parents beside the north wall of Augustus Church in the Trappe. His tombstone reads:

> He was Brave in the field, Faithful
> in the Cabinet, Honorable in
> all his transactions, a Sincere Friend
> and an Honest Man.

Notes

1. Hocker, *The Fighting Parson*, 51.
2. Barton, "The Myth of Separation."
3. Patrick Henry's speech taken from Wallace, *The Muhlenbergs*, 113-14.
4. Ibid, 115.
5. Wright, "A Sketch," and Wallace, *The Muhlenbergs*, 118.
6. Exchange between Peter and Frederick Muhlenberg taken from Wallace, *The Muhlenbergs*, 120-21.
7. Hocker, *The Fighting Parson*, 80.
8. Muhlenberg, *The Life*, 96.
9. Quotes and the Battle of Brandywine taken from Wallace, *The Muhlenbergs*, 131-42; Hocker, *The Fighting Parson*, 78; and Muhlenberg, *The Life*, 91-101.
10. Wallace, *The Muhlenbergs*, 155.
11. Tappert and Doberstein, *The Journals of Henry Muhlenberg*, 133.
12. Wallace, *The Muhlenbergs*, 167.
13. Muhlenberg, *The Life*, 197.
14. Ibid, 232.
15. Ibid, 250.
16. Quotes from Steuben and Greene taken from Muhlenberg, *The Life*, 250-52.
17. Hocker, *The Fighting Parson*, 139-40.

Chapter 10

EDITH CAVELL

"Offer up thyself to the honour of My name..."

★ ★ ★

It was 5 a.m.

On a clear day, the first rays of dawn would be lighting the eastern sky. But on this cold, overcast morning of October 12, 1915, the splendor of the rising sun was hidden from the rain-slicked streets of Brussels, Belgium.

Two women dressed in nurses' uniforms walked along these streets, the few words spoken between them soft and hurried. After several kilometers, their destination loomed in front of them—St. Gilles prison. It was an imposing structure of thick walls and high towers, its windows covered with sturdy bars of iron. For nearly two hours the two nurses stood on the street, and were soon joined by other nurses from their clinic.

Their hushed conversations fell silent as the large, iron gates of the prison swung open. With muffled roars, two black sedans exited the prison. In the backseat of the first was a frail, gray-haired woman, nestled tightly between two German soldiers.

"Beatrice," the first nurse gasped, "she has seen us!"

"Can you be sure?" Beatrice Smith asked, her hand half raised to wave at the woman in the car.

"Yes," Elisabeth Wilkins replied. "She did. She did."

The small woman in the car had indeed seen her two nurses. They had come to say good-bye to her, and though they had not spoken, their presence had been enough. As the car wound through the dark streets of Brussels, she became lost in thought.

It was a strange place for a woman like Edith Cavell to be in. The Directing Matron of the *École Belge Infirmières Diplômées*, she was a nurse, a teacher, and overseer of nurses. To have spent ten weeks in prison, to have been court-martialed, to have been sentenced to death, was not the fate of most nurses.

A small, sad smile played across the lips of Edith Cavell. She was far from her childhood home in England, far from her father's vicarage. She glanced down at the small edition of Thomas à Kempis' *The Imitation of Christ* clasped in her hands. Quietly, she quoted from it.

Thou must pass through fire and water before thou comest to a place of refreshing....Then, with full resignation and with thy entire will, offer up thyself to the honour of My name, on the altar of thy heart a whole burnt offering even body and soul, faithfully committing them unto Me.[1]

One of the soldiers beside her grunted a warning, and she fell silent. At the rifle range of Tir National, she and the man in the second car, Philippe Baucq, were marched along the cold stone corridors. Just before they reached the courtyard, Edith Cavell stopped.

"May I sign my book?" she asked her guards.

It was a strange request, but it was granted. Quickly she penned in the front of her *Imitation of Christ* the dates of her arrest, her internment, her trial, and her sentence. She signed her name and paused, then wrote again. "With love to E.D. Cavell." Closing the book, she held it to her lips. The times she had spent with Eddy Cavell, her second cousin, flashed through her mind. She had loved him, and he had loved her.[2]

The hands that grabbed her jolted her from her reverie. Her moment was up. Gripped tightly by the elbow, she was forcibly led outside and toward the rifle range.

It seemed inconceivable that the events of June 28, 1914 would affect the life of an inconspicuous nurse as dramatically as they did. Yet, when Archduke Ferdinand of Austria-Hungary was assassinated in the small town of Sarajevo on that summer day, his death launched Europe into a war that would extinguish the lives of millions.

Austria accused Serbia of playing a part in Ferdinand's death. Russia, in alliance with Serbia, rushed to defend its ally.

German, in alliance with Austria, decried Russia's actions. By the beginning of August, Austria had declared war on Serbia; Germany declared war on Russia; and France, Russia's ally, declared war on Germany. As the European nations fell into war like a series of dominoes, Great Britain joined the struggle on the side of Russia and France, and on August 23, the British Expeditionary Force under Sir John French collided with the German First Army under General Alexander von Kluck outside the Belgian village of Mons.

Outnumbered 70,000 to 160,000, the British were forced back to the River Marne and, at the village of La Cateau, fought a rear guard action to slow the German advance. In the midst of their retreat, the Allied British and French armies left thousands of wounded soldiers behind enemy lines.

In Brussels, Belgium, the citizens waited anxiously for news from the battlefront. It was not good news. First Liege fell in the face of the German advance, then Namur. In the small clinic on the Rue de la Culture in Brussels, the nurses, many of them English, waited as well. The Matron of the clinic, a petite, stoic nurse named Edith Cavell, urged her fellow English nurses to leave. They would not hear of it, and in late August, the German Army moved into Brussels.

"The sun shone in mockery of our fallen hopes," Cavell wrote to her mother. "In the afternoon, the German troops marched in....At least 20,000 men entered the city that day, and camped there for the night."[3]

Gathering her nurses, Cavell spoke to them. "It is our duty to nurse all the wounded," she said, her words hanging in the small room, "of any nation."[4] She looked around at her young nurses, some of whom were Belgian. Disgust was evident on their faces. No one wanted to care for the wounded of the enemy, but all nodded and silently filed out of the room. Soon the occupying German forces sent out an edict—all English nurses in Belgium were to be sent home. Sixty left immediately, but the small band of English nurses who worked at the clinic refused to go, and for a time nothing changed in the daily routine at the clinic. Nurse Cavell still walked her dogs, still checked on the nurses she had trained who were working at the St. Gilles hospital, and still made plans to move the clinic from its present small building to a larger one.

This continuity of living, though, was to change with the arrival of three men at the clinic on the evening of November 1, 1914. The loud rapping at the door of the clinic at 149 Rue de la Culture was answered by Sister Millicent White, assistant matron of the clinic. Outside, in the rapidly approaching darkness of evening, stood three men. The first she recognized. He was Herman Capiau, an engineer from the nearby town of Wasmes. The other two she did not recognize, though it was evident both were wounded and suffering from malnutrition.

The door behind her that led to Sister Cavell's office quickly opened. With barely a word of greeting to Sister White, the three men walked past her into the Matron's office. A moment later, Capiau exited and rushed out the door, obviously hoping to make it home before the German-imposed curfew found him on the streets.

A moment later, Cavell's door opened, and she, with the two men in tow, exited.

"My dear," Cavell said cheerily, "this is Colonel Boger and Sergeant Meachin—they both have been wounded. You will look after them, won't you, and give them a meal?"[5]

And as quickly as Herman Capiau had entered and exited, Edith Cavell found herself, and her clinic, involved in one of the great clandestine events of World War I.

Numerous British and French officers and soldiers had been stranded behind enemy lines after the battles of Mons, Chaleroi, and Le Cateau. To add to their difficulties, the Belgian Army had opened dam sluice gates in its retreat, flooding the countryside, which slowed the German advance, yet left no way of escape for the stranded soldiers. As the Germans began a systematic search of the countryside for the Allied soldiers, peasants, priests, and nuns found themselves feeding and sheltering those men and helping them escape from enemy-held territory.

Though the Germans threatened death to those who gave aid to the stranded soldiers, the people of the Belgian and French countryside were undeterred and continued to help the soldiers escape. In time, the operation became more organized and split into two territories, one serving the area of Borinage around Mons, the other working in the north of France. It was there, in the region of Borinage, that much of the secret activity involving Edith Cavell and her clinic took place.

Only a few miles from Mons was the castle of Belligenes, home of the de Croys, an ancient family linked by marriage to more than half the aristocracy of Europe. At the time of World War I, a brother and sister, Reginald and Marie de Croy, lived at the castle.

"It was one day, as we were walking round the lawn, that two girls, who were standing near the gate, came and asked to speak to Reginald," writes Princess Marie de Croy. "They had come to ask what they should do with several English soldiers they had nursed for slight wounds, and kept hidden...."[6]

The "girls," as Princess de Croy called them, were Mlle. Moriam, the sister of the local brewer, and Louise Thuliez, a schoolteacher, who became an integral part of the secret operation. Gathering French and English soldiers, Louise Thuliez had begun secreting them out from behind German lines to an escape route to the Dutch border. When she began finding more and more soldiers behind enemy lines, she knew she needed help, and she went to the de Croys. Their chateau, with its medieval tower and hidden staircases, was the perfect place to hide large numbers of soldiers. In time, an engineer, Herman Capiau, and a lawyer, Albert Libiez, joined the effort to save as many Allied soldiers as possible.

Thus began the pattern. Louise Thuliez would locate the soldiers and bring them to the safe haven of the de Croy chateau. There, Capiau would provide counterfeit identity cards, which a local pharmacist by the name of Derveau would stamp. The Princess de Croy would take photographs for the cards, and, when the soldiers were able to travel, Capiau and other guides would take them to Erquennes to Angela Quidon's cottage. From there Capiau would smuggle them into Brussels and to Edith Cavell. Her first two "visitors" were Colonel Bogers and Sergeant Meachen. Outside of Sister White, none of Cavell's nurses initially knew of the two Englishmen hidden within the confines of the clinic. That is, until one probationer, Paula von Bockstaele, was walking down to the cellar early one morning.

Seeing a shadowy figure, she gasped. "It is a ghost!" she exclaimed.

"Hallo, nursie," rang out an English voice.[7]

Now the game was afoot, and the several dozen nurses and probationers in the clinic knew of the deadly enterprise their Matron was undertaking. By keeping her secret, they too faced the threat of being shot for aiding German enemies. But, it seemed the game would be brief. Within a week of their arrival, Edith Cavell approached one of her nurses, Jacqueline van Til.

"Will you wake me at four tomorrow morning?" Cavell said quietly. As she turned to go, she spun on her heel. "And please tell José to have enough bread and coffee made for two."

The next morning, van Til, White, and Bockstaele awoke to find Cavell and the two Englishmen already dressed and waiting.

"I will return shortly," was all Cavell said as she and the two Englishmen slipped out into the predawn darkness. Three hours later, Cavell returned without the Englishmen. She never mentioned where she had taken them or who she had left them with. The less her nurses knew, the better.[8]

After her first predawn adventure, Cavell gathered her nurses to discuss the details of the day. As she ended, she said, "There will be no further mention of our houseguests." She paused for a moment, her gray eyes scanning the faces of her nurses. "However, we will be expecting nine more tomorrow night. Sister Wilkins, will you please see to it that nine beds are made ready? That will be all."

The next morning, in broad daylight, Louise Thuliez appeared at the clinic's door. In tow were one Frenchman and eight Englishmen. The pattern continued for months. Thuliez or another guide would appear at the door with soldiers. Cavell would assimilate them into the civilian patients already being treated at the hospital. Then, when they were healthy enough to travel, she would disappear with a handful in the early morning hours, always returning before the 6 a.m. breakfast. But, word began to spread through the neighborhood: The clinic in the Rue de la Culture was hiding French and English soldiers.

"We began to realize keenly the danger we were incurring in harboring them," writes Jacqueline van Til. "Notwithstanding, we probationers endeavored to assure ourselves that there was nothing to fear, that perhaps our imaginations were getting the best of us."[9]

It seemed for a while that her assumption was correct, and life continued in its semi-normal way at the clinic. With a boldness tinged with naïveté, the soldiers housed at the clinic played the piano, their English and French songs wafting out onto the streets. They played raucous games of cards and walked to the local pub for drinks with their Belgian neighbors.

"Can't you keep them hidden, more quiet?" Herman Capiau exclaimed during one visit to the clinic.

Cavell fixed her eyes on him. "They are not animals to be caged. What can I do about it?"

"But your life is in danger!"

Cavell shrugged. "All of our lives are in danger." And that was the end of the conversation.[10]

And so the routine at the clinic at 149 Rue de la Culture continued with one exception. It was felt that Cavell was risking too much by continuing to guide the soldiers from the clinic. Soon, native Belgians began appearing at the clinic, leading groups of four or five soldiers to the tram. There, dressed as workmen with the papers forged by Capiau and de Croy, they would take the tram, one by one, from Brussels to Haecht. At Haecht, other members of the organization would house them and send them to Turnhout on the Dutch border. From there, the soldiers were guided through treacherous, high voltage, barbwire fences, avoiding German snipers and machine gun nests, and then across the border to safety.

Back at the clinic in Brussels, the fear that the Germans were onto the events inside the clinic was more than just imagination. It was reality.

In May of 1915, a Polish soldier appeared with a group of other Allied soldiers. Nursed back to health, he left the clinic three weeks later. He left behind a cryptic note.

"This house is a nice one. I can do nothing required of me."

Later that month, Nurse Elisabeth Wilkins, tending to four Belgian soldiers, heard the doorbell ring. Leaving her patients, she walked down the stairs and opened the door. The guest had already entered.

"Have you any more?" the man asked.

Nurse Wilkins, thinking he referred to the nurses from the clinic, many of whom were spread throughout Brussels in either private or public hospitals, answered, "No, none." As there were many requests for nurses trained at the clinic, their numbers were sadly depleted.

The man's eyes narrowed. "What, no more Tommies?"

Nurse Wilkins froze, unable to speak. She simply shook her head. The man, his eyes boring into Wilkins, pulled out his badge. German secret police. Gathering herself, she said, "Would you like to see my papers?"

Guiding him to her office, she let the man search her desk.

"Where are the patients?" he asked when his search revealed nothing.

"This way."

As she entered the patients' ward, she caught another nurse's eye. With a nod at the man, she raised her eyes to the ceiling. Get the soldiers out of here, she pleaded silently. Without even a pause, the other nurse smiled and nodded at both Wilkins and the policeman. Leaving the man to interrogate the patients, all of whom were civilians, Wilkins rushed to Cavell's office. Pulling incriminating papers from the Matron's desk, she rushed to the bathroom and stuffed them inside the water closet cistern. Returning to the ward, she found the policeman waiting for her.

"Come with me," he said. In the hours that she spent at police headquarters, Wilkins denied again and again that she knew of any soldiers being hidden at the clinic. When the policeman dropped her off at the clinic, his only words were, "Be careful."[11]

Frightened and speechless, Wilkins nodded and quickly walked inside and headed straight for Edith Cavell's office.

There she found Cavell, recently returned from the new clinic building. With her were two more secret policemen.

"Ah, there you are my dear," Cavell said, without the slightest trace of worry. Wilkins glanced at the papers strewn all over Cavell's desk. The policemen had evidently already been through them.

"These men want to know if we are hiding any soldiers," Cavell said with a slight smile and a wink.

"Soldiers?" Wilkins gasped softly, her heart pounding.

"Yes, soldiers. And with all those *Verboten* signs hanging in the streets."

The rest of the conversation was a blur for Wilkins as she listened to her Matron answer the questions fired at her by the policemen.

Suddenly, both men rose. "We are watching you," the one said. With a slight smile and a nod, Cavell turned to Wilkins.

"Will you show these men to the door?"

When she returned to the office, Wilkins found Cavell re-sorting and stacking her papers. Behind Wilkins came José, Cavell's house boy.

"Where are my papers?" Cavell asked with a smile.

"I hid them in the water closet cistern. Will you not burn them? Please, this is becoming too dangerous," Wilkins burst out.

Cavell ignored her for the moment. "José, where are the soldiers?"

"I got them out to safe houses when the first policeman came."

"Well done. As for the papers, yes, I think you are right, Miss Wilkins, I will destroy them. That will be all. Thank you for your good work today."

A moment later, Cavell looked up to see Wilkins still standing there.

"Yes, my dear?"

"We must stop this. You are in grave danger."

The look on Cavell's face softened from a smile to sadness. "Yes, I know."

"Will you go into hiding? Or go to Holland? I'm sure one of our guides will take you."

Cavell shook her head. "If I give up now and go into hiding, think of how many men will lose their lives. My leaving now is not an option."[12]

For a time, the influx of soldiers stopped at the clinic. It was too dangerous. Cavell knew she was being watched, and, at strange hours, the secret police would visit the clinic, always looking. But on July 7, nine English soldiers arrived during the night. This time Cavell treated them as caged animals. There was to be silence and no going out of doors. They were housed in the room behind Cavell's office.

Two days later, the German secret police visited again. This time, there were four of them. Again, Cavell's young nurses came to her aid. While two of the German policemen interrogated Cavell, the other two lounged just outside the strong door of the clinic. Two nurses went outside to talk with them while three others crept through the basement and up the back stairs to the room behind Cavell's office. There Nurse Wilkins found the soldiers reading and talking, oblivious to what was occurring in the room next to them.

"Hel-"

The look on Wilkins's face and her finger to her lips hushed the soldier's greeting. Without a word, she motioned for them to follow her. Quietly creeping down the basement stairs, the soldiers climbed out the window, into the garden, and leaped over the walls, running to safe houses. Inside, Cavell was keeping her interrogators occupied while Wilkins and the other nurses cleaned up the magazines the soldiers had left behind. As they left the room, the policemen, having ransacked Cavell's office, burst into the room where the Englishmen had been. They found nothing. When they had left, the nurses rushed into Cavell's office.

She was sitting there, pale, quiet, her back straight.

"When we saw her calmly seated there, so small and frail," Jacqueline van Til wrote, "we almost felt as if we could fall down and worship her...we were so impressed by her stoic English nature that we felt ashamed in her presence."

Later that evening, Cavell joined her nurses for dinner. They ate in silence until she spoke.

"I want to thank you for all the help you have given me in these troublesome times."

The trouble for the day, however, was not over. One German policeman had stayed behind, sleeping in the front room of 147, and the English soldiers were bound to return at any moment. They did, at midnight. But, Cavell's nurses again came to her aid. Quietly sneaking past the German guard, a nurse signaled for the soldiers to remove their shoes. Once inside, she and the others hid them in a large linen closet, and van Til went to get Cavell. She found her kneeling in prayer by her bed.

"The soldiers have returned," Jacqueline whispered. Cavell nodded and rose and began dressing. "Can you get the men out of the house again, through the garden?"

"Yes."

"I will meet them on the street. I must take them to a safe place."

"But the curfew?"

"If they stay here, all may be lost."[14]

So Cavell departed into the night with the soldiers behind her. Her nurses waited anxiously. At 6 a.m. they heard footsteps at the front door. The door swung open to reveal Edith Cavell. She had returned safely.

In late July, the clinic received an unexpected visitor— the Princess de Croy herself.

When she and Cavell were alone, Cavell spoke first.

"I wish you had not come. I am suspected."

"So are we."

Cavell sat quietly for a moment, then said, "Yesterday I received another visit from the police. I barely had time to throw my papers in the grate, pour alcohol on them, and burn them."

The Princess spoke. "This shows we must stop."

Suddenly Cavell asked, "Are there any more hidden men?"

"Thirty more men, my dear Edith, have been found in the woods and fields near Cambrai. Louise Thuliez found them."

Cavell knew what was being asked of her. She rose and went to the window that looked out on the street in front of the clinic.

"Do you see those laborers over there?"

"Yes," said the Princess, walking to stand by her.

"They are not laborers. They are German secret police, monitoring the clinic day and night. They have been there for days."

The Princess returned to her seat.

"We too are being watched. We cannot bring anymore men to the chateau."

"In that case, we cannot stop here because if one of those men gets shot, it will be our fault."[15]

However, Edith Cavell never got a chance to help the 30 men. On August 5, three men entered the clinic. What the nurses had feared so long was now a reality. Cavell was upstairs in the pantry, arranging flowers, when the secret police found her. She and Nurse Wilkins were dragged outside and into a car.

As she passed her disconsolate nurses, Edith said, "Don't be sad, my children. Everything will be all right. I'll be back soon."[16]

But, she was not back soon. Wilkins was released after hours of interrogation. She had denied knowing anything about any soldiers at the clinic.

Edith Cavell, though, was taken from the police station to the Prison of the Kommandantur. After a few days there, she was taken to the Prison of St. Gilles. There she spent almost two months in solitary confinement.

She was not the only one of the organization arrested for her activities. Philippe Baucq, Louise Thuliez, Hermann Caipau, the Princess de Croy, and others, 35 in all, were arrested and thrown into prison.

The German secret police had effectively broken the back of the underground organization.

On October 6, 1915, the trial began. The accused were not to stand trial before a civil court, but before a military tribunal. On the way to the trial, Cavell rode with three others, one of whom was Georges Hostelet, an engineer and a scholar. Hostelet, not knowing who she was, struck up a conversation with her.

"Good God, I am frightened," Cavell said, her usual stoicism gone.

"What have you done?" Hostelet asked.

"I lodged some Englishmen."

"Nothing else?"

"No."

"Then don't be frightened. You will not be shot."

"Are you sure?"

"Quite sure, and in these days, that is all that matters, isn't it?"

"That is true," Cavell replied, some of her exterior calm returning.[17]

Their German military prosecutor, Herr Stoeber, opened the proceedings by reading the charges in German. All the accused were charged with assisting escaping Allied soldiers and helping them return to Allied lines.

Edith Cavell was tried first. To the surprise of all, she did not lie and answered every question truthfully.

"From November 1914 to July 1915, you have lodged English, French and Belgian soldiers, all of who were in civilian clothes?" Stoeber asked.

"Yes," Cavell replied.

"With whom did you collaborate?"

"M. Capiau, Mlle. Thuliez, M. Derveau and M. Libiez."

"Who was the chief of your organization?"

"We had no chief."

On and on the questions came in rapid succession. Cavell answered them all.

"Do you realize," Stoeber asked, "that in recruiting men you have hindered the German cause and helped our enemies?"

"My aim has not been to assist your enemies but to help these men gain the frontier. Once across they were free to do as they liked."

"How many men have you helped to get to the frontier?"

"About two hundred."

"What do you have to say in your defense?"

"Nothing."[18]

Next on the stand was Thuliez, followed by Philippe Baucq, then others. It was finally the Princess de Croy's turn on the stand. Before the trial, she had asked a friend to sit in the balcony. If her brother was safe, out of German-held territory, the man was to stroke his face. When she took the stand, she glanced briefly at the friend. He stroked his face.

Without waiting for Stoeber to ask any questions, de Croy addressed the judges.

"My lords, be merciful. My brother and I are the real culprits. It is we who in the undertaking of the evacuation of French and English soldiers led them into this affair."

"Do you not know what danger you ran in doing so?" Stoeber snapped. Eyes blazing, the Princess turned on him. "One must do one's duty without thinking of the consequences!"[19]

The trial lasted for days. During the nights of solitary confinement, Cavell reached for her copy of the *Imitation of Christ* and began reading, underlining and dating the passages she read. The passage dated for the last day of the trial read:

> Thou that rulest the power of the sea, and stillest the violent motion of its waves, arise and help me! Scatter the nations that desire war; crush Thou them in Thy might. Display Thy wonderful works, I beseech Thee, and let Thy right hand be glorified. For there is no other hope or refuge for me, save in Thee, O Lord my God.[20]

The next day the court's findings were read.

> The court is of the opinion...that de Croy, Baucq, Thuliez, Cavell, Belleville and Severin were the chief organizers of two seditious groups, one in northern France, and one in the Borinage, which helped English and French fugitive soldiers and French and Belgians of military age to escape into Holland whence they might join the Allied armies.[21]

Then the accused were gathered for the reading of their individual sentences. Herr Stoeber began reading. "Philippe Baucq—death by firing squad. Louise Thuliez—death by firing squad. Edith Cavell—death by firing squad..."

On and on his voice droned. In all, 5 were sentenced to death; 5 were sentenced to 15 years hard labor; 1, the Princess de Croy, to 10 years hard labor; 17 were sentenced to 2 to 8 years imprisonment or hard labor; and the final 8 were acquitted.

Georges Hostelet, Cavell's companion on the first day of the trial, wrote: "Baucq, his cheeks flushed and knees bent, cried out. Though he had been so courageous in his patriotic work he now clung to life in an appeal for mercy which he had written in advance. Miss Cavell stood leaning against the wall, cold and impassive. I went to her. 'Madame, make an appeal for mercy.' 'It is useless,' she answered placidly. 'They want my life.'"[22]

Louise Thuliez, who had already asked for mercy, approached Cavell.

"Will you not ask for mercy?"

"No. I am English. It is useless. They want my life."[23]

That night, Stirling Gahan, an Irish chaplain in Brussels, was allowed to see Cavell. He found a calm, resigned Edith Cavell. She sat upon her cot, he in a chair. She spoke first, as if to reassure herself.

"I have no fear or shirking. I have seen death so often it is not strange or fearful to me. I expected it would end thus. I believe my sentence is just."

For a moment Cavell stared straight in front of her at the opposite wall. Gahan sat in silence, and then she spoke again.

"I thank God for this ten weeks' quiet before the end. Life has always been so hurried and full of difficulty. This time of rest has been a great mercy. I would say this. Standing as I do in the sight of God and Eternity, I realize patriotism is not enough. I must have no hatred or bitterness towards anyone."

Gahan later wrote to a friend. "It was like a solemn fasting, free of all earthly or ordinary distractions of any kind…no visitors, perfect quiet, perfect solitude with God. It was of His mercy and goodness to prepare for the end."

To Gahan, it seemed Cavell's greatest concern was the nearness of eternity.

"How can I be sure?" she asked.

Gahan began quietly to tell her again of the story she knew so well of the thief on the cross next to Christ.

"Do you remember Jesus' words to him?"

"Yes. 'Today you shall be with Me in Paradise.' "

"Do you believe in Christ?" he asked quietly.

"I do."

"Do you believe in His finished work on the cross for your salvation?"

"I do."

"Then you need not fear," Gahan said.

Using the small table in her cell, Gahan placed the communion vessels. When they had partaken of the bread and the wine, Gahan fell on his knees beside her bed, opening his prayer book. Cavell knelt next to him.

"Our Father, who art in Heaven," Gahan began. Cavell quietly joined him.

When they had finished praying, they continued kneeling in silence until Gahan, and then Cavell, began to softly repeat the words of the hymn, "Abide With Me." As the hymn finished, Gahan turned to her.

"Perhaps I had better go now, as you will want some rest."

Cavell smiled. "Yes, I have to be up at 5 a.m."

As he rose, Gahan said, "We will always remember you as a heroine and a martyr."

"Don't think of me like that," Cavell responded. "Only as a nurse who tried to do her duty."

At the door, Gahan paused one last time. He grasped Cavell's hands in his, at a loss for words.

She gripped his hands. "We shall meet again."

Gahan finally found his voice. "Yes, we shall. God go with you."[24]

The next morning, the guards found Cavell dressed and ready. Outside the prison, unable to stand the strain any longer, were Cavell's young nurses, come to say good-bye.

At Tir National, Cavell handed her prayer book and copy of the Imitation of Christ to the German chaplain. Then she and Philippe Baucq were led to individual posts. The German chaplain offered her a bottle of smelling salts. She refused it. At the post, she spoke briefly to the chaplain.

"Ask Mr. Gahan to tell my loved ones that my soul I believe is safe, and I am glad to die for my country."

The chaplain nodded, noticing the tears in her eyes.

The end came quickly. One sharp command, and the firing squad did its duty. By her side, Philippe Baucq shouted, "Vive la Belique!"

Cavell said nothing as the four bullets hit her. She died instantly. She was 49.[25]

Notes

1. Ryder, *Edith Cavell*, 188.
2. Clarke-Kennedy, *Edith Cavell*, 211.
3. Ibid, 103.
4. Ibid.
5. Ibid, 114-17.
6. Ryder, *Edith Cavell*, 112-13.
7. Hoehling, *A Whisper of Eternity*, 58.
8. Ibid, 59.
9. van Til, *With Edith Cavell*, as cited by Hoehling, *A Whisper of Eternity*, 65.
10. Hoehling, *A Whisper of Eternity*, 70.
11. Clark-Kennedy, *Edith Cavell*, 143-44.
12. Ibid.
13. van Til, as cited by Clark-Kennedy, *Edith Cavell*, 147.
14. Ibid, 148.
15. Gray, *Friend Within the Gates*, 146-47.
16. Hoehling, *A Whisper of Eternity*, 96.
17. Conversation taken from Hoehling, *A Whisper of Eternity*, 118-19.
18. Cavell's interrogation taken from Clark-Kennedy, *Edith Cavell*, 181-82.
19. Ibid, 186-87.
20. Ibid, 200.
21. Ibid, 201.
22. Judson, *Edith Cavell*, 261.
23. Clark-Kennedy, *Edith Cavell*, 208.
24. Account of Gahan and Cavell's meeting taken from Gray, *Friends Within the Gates*, 180-81; Ryder, *Edith Cavell*, 213-15; Clark-Kennedy, *Edith Cavell*, 220-22; Hoehling, *A Whisper of Eternity*, 140-42.
25. Clark-Kennedy, *Edith Cavell*, 224; Ryder, *Edith Cavell*, 223.

Chapter 11

SAMUEL RUTHERFORD

"The Law Is King"

In the year of 1644, a small Scottish minister sat in his London residence. The only sound in his room was that of his quill pen quietly scratching its way across the parchment on his desk. He had come to London as one of the five Scottish commissioners for the Westminster Assembly, but now his attention lay elsewhere. John Maxwell, the excommunicated Bishop of Ross, had recently published a treatise entitled *Sacro-Sancta Regum Majestas*, in which Maxwell attempted to prove that "the royal prerogative of kingly authority is alone from God, and it demands an absolute and passive obedience of the subject to the sovereign." Samuel Rutherford, the small Scotsman, immediately sat down to refute "the wild and absurd" notions in Maxwell's work.

"Every man is by nature a freeman born," Rutherford wrote. "No man cometh out of the womb under any civil subjection to king, prince or judge. No man bringeth out of the womb with him a sceptre, and a crown upon his head. King and beggar spring out of one clay."[1] For Rutherford, it was quite clear—all men were created equal, and since God's law governed humanity, all forms of civil government must be in accordance with the laws of the "King of Heaven." As governments were a covenant between a king and the people, a king held power by the will of God moving through the people—the ruler governs by the consent of the governed.

When Rutherford finished his book, he titled it *Lex Rex, The Law and the Prince*, or loosely translated, "The Law is King." Over 450 pages long, it "caused great sensation on its appearance." The ideas of limited government and the limitations on the divine right of kings as spelled out by Rutherford were radical ones for his day. But Samuel Rutherford was hardly one to be afraid of being thought radical.[2]

Born in 1600 to a respectable farmer and his wife in Nisbet in Roxburghshire, Scotland, Samuel had two brothers, George and James. Little is known of his formative years except an incident that happened when he was still very young.

While playing around the village well, young Samuel slipped and fell headlong into the deep well. His friends, unable to save him, ran for help. When they returned, they found Samuel chilled and shaking, sitting by the well.

When asked how he had gotten out of the well, he replied, "A bonnie white man came and drew me out of the well."

His friends, and the adults who had come to help, looked around. There was no "bonnie white man" in the village, nor had any of them seen one. But young Samuel refused to change his story.[3]

Other than his miraculous rescue from the well, the rest of Samuel Rutherford's childhood remains a mystery. What is known is that his pastor in the parish of Crailing during his formative years was David Calderwood. A Covenanter, Calderwood firmly believed in the doctrine that called for the nation of Scotland to return to a covenant with God. His influence on Rutherford's early years impacted Rutherford for the rest of his life.

In 1617, Samuel matriculated to Edinburgh College after he passed the stringent Latin exam required to enter the college. To do that, Samuel had to translate Scottish texts into Latin and then read the translations out loud before a board of regents and professors. It was no small feat for a 17-year-old boy. But Samuel, a precocious learner, tackled the curriculum at Edinburgh with vigor.

While at Edinburgh College, Rutherford was involved in far more than education. Through David Calderwood, he became linked with the conservative Presbyterian group that protested the Five Articles of Perth passed by the General Assembly in 1618.[4] They were, however, the final part of the king of England's plan to complete the union between his two kingdoms of England and Scotland.

When he ascended the English throne, James I knew that in order to unite his two kingdoms, he must de-Presbyterianize Scotland. He began the process in 1600 with the appointing of three parliamentary bishops in Scotland. In 1606, he threw Andrew Melville, the Presbyterian leader, into the Tower of London. In 1609 he restored the courts of High Commission[5] and had three Scottish bishops ordained in London, thus returning diocesan episcopacy to Scotland.

Shortly after his triumph, James I stood before the English Parliament.

"This I may say for Scotland, and may truly vaunt it, " he said. "Here I sit and govern it with my pen. I write and it is done, and by the Clerk of the Council I govern Scotland now—which others could not do by the sword."

He continued his state governance of the Church in Scotland. In 1616, under pressure from him, the General Assembly created a new Confession of Faith, a new catechism, a new liturgy, and a book of canons. Then followed the despised Articles of Perth in 1618.

However, it was more than a struggle between Presbyterians and James I. It was the collision of two political ideologies. For the English, especially James I, a Stuart, kings ruled by divine right through heredity. For the Scottish, directly influenced by their Presbyterianism, kings ruled because God appointed them. They did not rule by heredity; nor were they above the law. They were answerable both to God and the people whom they governed.

In the midst of this religious and political upheaval, events that would forever change the life of Samuel Rutherford were set in motion. Made regent of humanity at Edinburgh upon his graduation at the age of 23, Samuel was asked to resign in 1626 from the college because he had "fallen into fornication with Euphame Hamiltoun, and has committed a great scandal in the college."[6] Humiliated, Rutherford resigned. It appears, however, that this incident had a transforming and jarring affect on young Rutherford. He married Euphame and a child was born to them in April 1626.

Rutherford's life became more than that of an academic theologian. It became one of zealous faith, combining in Rutherford his classical education with his newfound faith of the heart. As he wrote to his friend Robert Stuart, "I suffered my sun to be high in the heaven and near afternoon before ever I [accepted the mercies of Christ]."[7]

A new chapter began in the life of Samuel Rutherford that would see him rise from the disgrace at Edinburgh to become the voice of the Covenanter movement. As Rutherford would preach in later years, "We may learn here that it is God's way of the Gospel, to ride upon the weakest, poorest, basest...in the world, and to cause the news of mercy to sound effectually to those who seem most lost in the world."[8]

From the politically charged theology of Edinburgh, Rutherford sought, and received, the ministership of the parish in the small rural village of Anwoth in 1627. It was here that Euphame died, along with two of their children, all from illness. Grief stricken, Rutherford threw himself into the duties of a pastor. He rose at 3 a.m. every morning. It was said of him that he was "always praying, always preaching, always visiting the sick, always catechizing, always writing and studying."[9] Those who knew him best said he would often fall to sleep at night speaking of Christ, even talking of Him during his sleep.

Aside from his duties to the small parish in Anwoth, Rutherford began to write. His words were read across Scotland, and the influence of David Calderwood and the Convenanters was clearly seen. Slowly, but surely, he began to turn Anwoth into a stronghold for opposition against the religious dominance of England. He spoke out and wrote against Armmanism, disseminated political information, and wrote his own catechism. Most of all, he began to speak of Scotland's need to return to a covenant with God.

In a letter to his friend, Lady Kenmure, Rutherford wrote, "We are in great fears of a great and fearful trial to come upon the kirk of God....Our prelates assure us that for such as will not conform, there is nothing but imprisonment and deprivation....All sorts of crying sins without controlment abound in our land; the glory of the Lord is departing from Israel, and the Lord is looking back over his shoulder, to see if any will say, 'Lord, tarry,' and no man requesteth him to stay."[10]

Redoubling his efforts, Rutherford preached even more strongly on Covenant theology. He preached and spoke in defense of private worship. He circulated his own writings, directing his ire toward the Scottish bishops appointed by the English throne.

In 1629, he was part of a group of ministers called Nonconformists who gathered and wrote, "Grievances and Petitions concerning the Disordered State of the Reformed Church of

Scotland." His words both written and spoken from the pulpit at Anwoth, a place he likened to a "wilderness," did not go unnoticed. In June of 1630, he was summoned before the High Commission. They dispatched him back to Anwoth with a stern rebuke.

The conflict between Rutherford and the English-appointed bishops intensified in 1634 when James I's son, Charles I, ascended the throne. In his drive for religious uniformity, Charles I appointed Thomas Sydserff as Bishop of Galloway. A Scottish Canterburian, Sydserff was firmly in the camp of the Church of England and was intent upon squelching any dissension in the church. Later that year, Charles I issued new orders—English liturgy was to be used in Scottish cathedrals and universities. He then declared the need for a new Scottish prayer book and a new book of canons to totally revise the liturgy and organization of the Scottish Presbyterian Kirk. Rutherford wrote to his friend Marion McKnaught, "I am in care and fear for this work of our Lord's now near approaching, because of the danger of the time; and I dare not for my soul to be silent, to see my Lord's house burning and not cry 'Fire! Fire!'"[11]

As the year of 1636 unfolded, Rutherford knew his non-conformity was leading him again into danger, and he wrote a friend, "I expect our new prelate shall try my sitting. I hang by a thread, but it is (if I may speak so) of Christ's spinning."[12]

In spite of his own personal danger, Rutherford published in that year his book *Exercitationes Apolegeticase pro Divna Gratia*, an attack on the Church of England's Scottish bishops and their theology. In retaliation, Sydserff had him dragged to

Wington, then to Edinburgh, to stand before the High Commission. The trial lasted for three days.

Standing before the Commission, Rutherford answered the charges before him, especially that of his book.

"My newly printed book against the Armenians was one challenge; not lording the prelates of another."[13]

Rutherford's friends in the Scottish aristocracy came to his rescue. Young Lord Lorne rose, speaking fervently on his friend's behalf.

As the Commission seemed to be swayed by Lorne's speech, Sydserff spoke.

"If we do not condemn Rutherford here and now, I will bring this matter before the king." His words sliced through the crowd gathered to hear the proceedings. Silence reigned in the chamber. No one wanted the matter brought before Charles I.[14]

When the Commission assembled again to pronounce judgment, the influence of Sydserff was evident. Because of his refusal to be silent and challenging of the Church of England and Charles I, Rutherford was condemned into exile to the north of Scotland to Aberdeen. If his enemies hoped to silence Rutherford, their efforts did not have the desired affect.

To a friend, Rutherford was exultant. "Welcome, welcome, sweet, sweet cross of Christ!"[15] To another he wrote with joy of being "a prisoner of Christ in Aberdeen." If the Scottish bishops had hoped to conform Rutherford to their standard and silence him, exile renewed Rutherford's zeal for turning Scotland toward a spiritual renewal.

While in Aberdeen, he wrote hundreds of letters to friends, rebuking the bishops for their tyranny and bemoaning what he called his "dumb Sabbaths," for as part of his exile, he was not allowed to preach. To his friend Alexander Gordon, he wrote, "As for myself, I am here in good care, well feasted with my King....Blessed be His high name, who hath kept sap in this dry tree."[17]

The exile breathed new life into Rutherford. He sought out and debated the liberal Scottish theologians of Aberdeen, the very men whom the bishops in Edinburgh had hoped would transform Rutherford's conservative theology and ideology. The ministers in Aberdeen openly preached against him.[18]

Rutherford was undeterred. His debating of the theologians and his refusal to be silenced were so influential, the ministers of Aberdeen tried to exile him even further north. He refused to go. He continued to write letters to the Scottish nobles, lairds, burgesses, and ministers all over Scotland, condemning the new book of canons and the new prayer book.

In a letter dated July 13, 1637, the general theme of his letters was poured out to his parishioners in Anwoth.

"Hate and keep yourselves from idols....You owe no obedience to the bastard canons; they are unlawful, blasphemous and superstitious."[18]

The fiery little Scotsman was just beginning. It was at this crux in his life in exile that the complexity of Rutherford's life came into focus.

He fought for a purity of worship without the overbearing structure of the episcopacy while remaining a firm believer in ecclesiastical form. As a political theorist, he argued for the dichotomy of church and state. Although he spoke and wrote often of "King Jesus," his was not a vision of a theocracy. In a letter written in later years, he wrote of his "detestation of that Episcopal disease of authoritative meddling with civil affairs."[20]

If he was not considered a leader of the Covenanting movement before, the events of July 23, 1637, would throw Rutherford into the forefront of the Covenant movement.

It was well known that the conservative Presbyterians despised the new prayer book that Charles I dictated be used in Scotland. When the new prayer book was read at St. Giles Cathedral in Edinburgh, a riot broke out. News of it spread like wildfire. The Covenanting Revolution had begun. The outwardly spontaneous riot had been planned, and it is well known that Rutherford at least knew of the plans for the riot.

In October of 1637, hundreds of nobles, lairds, burgesses, and ministers met in Edinburgh and signed a national supplication to Charles I. The king's response was to withdraw his representatives from Edinburgh. His actions merely strengthened their resolve, and Tables were formed.[21] Charles I continued to ignore them, and, in February of 1638, the Covenanters began to solidify themselves into a provisional government in open rebellion against Charles I and England. Their final act of defiance came with the National Covenant first signed on February 28, 1638.

Outlining the grievances of the Scottish church and nation against not only Charles I but his father as well, it pledged the maintenance of "true religion." The signers pledged to "join such a life and conversation as beseemth [sic] Christians who have renewed their covenant with God." They decried the Five Articles of Perth and the government of the Scottish church by English-appointed bishops. Calling upon God as their witness, Jesus Christ to whom they would answer, and the Holy Sprit to strengthen them, the supplicants signed the Covenant. Hundreds signed the Covenant in Edinburgh while copies were made and spread throughout Scotland. Three hundred thousand more Scotsmen signed.

Samuel Rutherford left Aberdeen when news came of the uprising and returned to his parish in Anwoth. In June of 1638, he made a triumphant return to Edinburgh, preaching there against the Scottish bishops and the ceremonies of the Church of England. In Glasgow in that same year, the General Assembly held by the Covenanters, who for all intents and purposes governed Scotland, swept aside and abolished the Service Book, the book of canons, the episcopacy, and the Five Articles of Perth. It was a resounding victory for the Covenanters. As to be expected, their actions were an insult to Charles I, and he considered them in open rebellion, not only against his ecclesiastical authority, but against his political authority as well.

In 1639, the armies of England and Wales were mobilized against Scotland. They were quickly beaten by the Covenanters' army under their little general, Alexander Leslie. At the negotiating table, the Covenanters' demands were simple—the preservation of the laws and religion of Scotland. If these were not met, then they would fight again. Charles I agreed to their terms, but in June of 1640, he again mobilized his troops, still smarting over his defeat.[22]

It was the beginning of the end of his reign. Charles I, after ten years of not doing so, was forced to summon Parliament, hoping they would acquiesce to his demands for financing the new war. The Parliament immediately wanted to discuss grievances against the government of Charles I and voiced strong opposition to a second war. Charles I promptly dissolved Parliament on May 5, 1640. Now, instead of facing only the Scottish Covenanters, he also was faced with a Parliament in open rebellion. He was again beaten by the Covenanters, and by 1642 the tension between the king and the Parliament boiled into civil war. As a result, Charles I was forced to leave London.

In 1643, Parliament established an alliance with the Covenanters called the Solemn League and Covenant. The Scots would provide troops; the Parliament would uphold Scotland's religious reform.

In that same year, Rutherford was asked to meet in London with an Assembly of Divines to discuss the articles laid out in the Solemn League and Covenants. It was here in London, from 1643–1647, that the theorist in Rutherford found voice in the form of his political tome, *Lex Rex*.

Over 450 pages in length, *Lex Rex* gave a lucid defense of the Covenanters' rebellion against Charles I. Its biblical ideology made the book so popular that by 1645 every member of the Scottish General Assembly had a copy.

The book was in the form of questions and answers—44 questions, 44 answers. Questions 1-14 dealt with the origins of government, questions 15-21 with the relation of the king and the people, 22-27 with the king and the law, firmly placing *rex*, the king, under *lex*, the law. Questions 28-37 were a defense of the Scottish armies defending Scotland against Charles I's armies, and in 38-44 he concluded with how his political theory fit the history of Scotland.

In *Lex Rex*, Rutherford laid the foundation for the theory that any power a ruler might have was given to him by the people. It was radical political theory for his day. Intermingling biblical stories and natural law, Rutherford argued that governments were founded upon a covenant between the king and the people. Thus, Rutherford limited the king's power and provided a basis for resistance to ungodly government. The king was placed there by the will of God moving through the people: "God "moved and boweth the wills of a great multitude to promote such a man, who, by nature, cometh no more out of the womb a crowned king, than the poorer shepherd in the land."[23] For Rutherford, tyrannical government was immoral, and he wrote, "a power ethical, politic, or moral, to oppress, is not from God, and is not a power, but a licentious deviation of a power, and is no more from God, but from sinful nature...."[24]

Continuing to fuse natural law with biblical analogies, Rutherford cited the stories of David, Elijah, Jehu, and others for a biblical defense of his theory of resistance to tyranny. Clearly, for Rutherford, Scripture not only gave credence to resistance, but also demanded it.

The years of 1644–47 were the crowning pinnacle of Rutherford's life. All he had dreamed of and fought for was becoming reality. As a member of the Westminster Assembly, he helped write the Westminster Shorter Catechism and helped create a biblical form of government based on God's law. The tyrant Charles I had been deposed, and Covenanters ruled in Scotland. But, Rutherford expressed doubts. Writing to a friend, he wrote, "it may be thought the land is near deliverance. But I rather desire it than believe it."[25]

The ecclesiastical and political highs that Rutherford was experiencing were not to last for long.

In 1645, the Parliament's army, dubbed the New Model Army, crushed Charles I and the royalists at the battles of Naseby and Langport. Surprisingly, Charles I fled north, to Scotland, to seek refuge. He was held hostage there until Parliament paid his ransom. Holding Charles I at Holmby House outside of London, Parliament gathered to attempt to reform government and began to disband its army. However, the army refused to be disbanded and marched on Holmby House and kidnapped the king. He escaped to the Isle of Wight and from there negotiated a new agreement with the Scottish Covenanters, promising church reform.

It seemed Rutherford's world was collapsing into chaos. In 1648, in an ill-advised attack, Scotland invaded England. The New Model Army defeated the Scottish forces easily. With the army now in control of England, and Charles I held captive by them, England began an uneasy military regime. On January 30, 1649, Charles I was executed and Oliver Cromwell came to power. In 1650, Charles II was made "king-like" Protector of Scotland, promising, like his father, that he would uphold Scotland's Covenant when he came to power. In September 1650, Charles II and the Scottish army, fighting under the banner "No Kings and No Bishops," marched again on England and were soundly defeated by Cromwell at Dunbar.

It was clear now that the Covenanters had overstepped even the boundaries they had set for themselves. Defensive resistance to a tyrant had evolved into offensive attacks on a government they had had an alliance with.

Distressed with the turn of events, Rutherford left London in 1647, retreating to St. Andrews. There he became a Protestor, a group which condemed the hasty agreements with Charles I and Charles II. His actions were too late.

The church and government in Scotland were beginning to fracture. On one side were the Resolutioners, those who supported Charles I and his son. On the other were the Protestors, intent on preserving the National Covenant of 1638. In 1650, when Charles II visited St. Andrews, it was Rutherford who lectured him on the duty of kings, reminding him that it was his duty to keep the covenants.

However, Rutherford's days as a political maven were numbered. As a Protestor, he was among the minority, and no one was more aware of this fact more than he. Yet, still he refused to be silent. When the General Assembly gathered at St. Andrews in 1651, he attended and handed in a protest against the lawfulness of the Assembly of which the Resolutioners were the majority. It was the last time he would ever attend a General Assembly, and Rutherford began to remove himself from political circles, choosing rather to teach theology at St. Andrews and preach before thousands.

It was during these later years that Rutherford expressed some regret at his political machinations. When asked of his political activities, and his seemingly lost cause in Scotland, he replied, "When the head is filled with topicks [sic], and none of the flamings of Christ's love in the heart, how dry are all disputes? For too often, fervour of dispute in the head weakens love in the heart. And what can our Paper-industry add to the spotless truth of our Lord Jesus?"[26]

In 1660, after nine years of exile, Charles II returned to England, welcomed by a country tired of Parliamentary rule. That same year, he was crowned King of Scotland in Edinburgh, welcomed with open arms by the Resolutioners. When he assumed power, Charles II turned on his former Scottish allies, imposing Episcopal rule, appointing bishops, and throwing 350 Scottish ministers from their pulpits. At the top of the most wanted list in this purge of the Scottish church was Samuel Rutherford.

In September of 1660, the Committee of Estates, the ruling body under Charles II, declared that every person with a copy of *Lex Rex* who did not return it to the king's solicitor by October 16 would be declared an enemy of the king. The following month, *Lex Rex* was burnt at the cross of Edinburgh and at the gates of the new college of St. Andrews. In early 1661, Rutherford was removed from his position at St. Andrews as well as from his pulpit and confined to his house. When asked about *Lex Rex*, he responded, "[I] would willingly die on the scaffold for that book with a good conscience."[27]

Struck by a sudden illness, Rutherford lay dying when news came that his fellow Protestor and Covenanters, James Guthrie, Archibald Campbell, and Archibald Johnson, had been executed. Death held no fear for him, though. He told those gathered about his bed, "My blessed Master, He is a Kingly King. And soon I shall shine—I shall see Him as He is—I shall see Him reign, and all his fair company with Him."

Several days later, summons came for him to stand before Parliament on the grounds of high treason. Lying there,

Rutherford calmly looked at the messenger. "Tell them I have summons before a Superior Judge. I behoove to answer my first summons; and ere your day arrive, I will be where few kings and great folks come."

To his friends gathered by his bed, he said, "My Lord and Master is chief of ten thousands of thousands. None is comparable to Him, in heaven or in earth." He turned to his friend, James McGill, and said, "It may seem presumptuous in me, a particular man, to send a commission to a presbytery..." his words trailed off.

"No, friend, it is no presumption," McGill answered.

"Then will you take a commission from me, a dying man? Tell them to adhere to the doctrine of the covenant, and have a care of the flock committed to their charge. Tell them to feed the flock out of love. Tell them to pray for Christ. Preach for Christ. Do all for Christ; beware of men-pleasing."

Just before breathing his last, he whispered, "I close with it! Let Him be so. He is my all in all." He gasped, his eyes fixed beyond his friends. "Glory, glory dwelleth in Immanual's [sic] lands."[28]

And with that, the great Scottish minister and political theorist died. It was March 30, 1661.

Yet, his work lived on. The themes of Rutherford's *Lex Rex* are woven throughout the political theory of John Locke, the man credited with greatly influencing the Founding Fathers of the United States and their political theory. As one author wrote, "Jefferson...and others knew they stood in the stream of John Locke, and while Locke had secularized *Lex Rex*, he had drawn heavily from it."[29] And at least one Founding

Father, John Witherspoon, was well aware of Rutherford and his book. A Presbyterian minister, he was the only pastor to sign the Declaration of Independence.

Notes

1. Coffey, *Politics, Religion*, 159.
2. Taken from John Howie, "Scots Worthies," found at <http://www.puritansermons.com/ruth/howie1.htm> and, <http://www.constitution.org/sr/lexrex.htm>
3. Taken from Introduction to Coder and Smith, ed., *The Letters*, 19.
4. The Five Articles of Perth ordered the observance of traditional holy days, confirmation of the laity of bishops, private baptism, communion for the infirm, and kneeeling at communion. They were decidedly non-Presbyterian articles.
5. A body of Scottish church leaders closely tied to the Church of England.
6. Coffey, *Politics, Religion*, 37.
7. Loane, *Makers of Religious Freedom*, 61.
8. *Quaint Sermons*, 311.
9. Coffey, *Politics, Religion*, 48.
10. Coder and Smith, eds., *The Letters*, 19-20.
11. Letter to M. McKnaught, March 2, 1634. Coder and Smith, eds., *The Letters*, 85.
12. Loane, *Makers of Religious Freedom*, 69-70.
13. Ibid, 70.
14. Ibid.
15. Letter to Lady Culross, July 30, 1936. Coder and Smith, eds., *The Letters*, 116.
16. Coffey, *Politics, Religion*, 45.
17. Letter to Alexander Gordon, February 23, 1637. Coder and Smith, eds., *The Letters*, 173.
18. Coffey, *Politics, Religion*, 47.
19. Smith, ed., *The Letters*, 112.
20. Coffey, *Politics, Religion*, 208.
21. Tables were bodies of the supplicants, mainly noblemen, lairds, and ministers, who met to further elaborate their grievances against Charles I.
22. Fissel, *The Bishop's War*, 21-39.

23. Coffey, *Politics, Religion*, 162.

24. Schaeffer, *A Christian Manifesto*, 100.

25. Coffey, *Politics, Religion*, 53.

26. Ibid, 257.

27. Ibid, 61.

28. All quotes from Rutherford's deathbed taken from John Howie, "Scots Worthies," <http:\\\www.puritansermons.com/ruth/howie1.htm>, and Loane, *Makers of Religious Freedom*, 101-02.

29. Schaeffer, *A Christian Manifesto*, 32.

Chapter 12

THOMAS MACDONOUGH

"God Armeth Me"

On the night of February 3, 1804, as the moon slipped in and out behind the clouds, a small ship silently knifed its way across the rough waters of the Tripolian harbor.

"How much farther?"

Thomas Macdonough peered through the blackness of the dark night as he heard his friend and captain, Stephen Decatur, whisper through the hatch of the ship.

"Not much farther," was the hoarse reply from the Sicilian pilot, Salvadore Catalono.

In the faint light of the moon, Thomas could see Decatur nod and lean back in the darkness, resting his head against the solid oak planks of the ship's hull. The captain glanced over at Thomas, who sat with a naked cutlass across his knees. Both were young but hardened by the rigors of naval war. And now, both men were tensed, ready for action. The 58 other men who sat huddled below decks with them were quiet as well. All had volunteered for this mission. Most were from Decatur's ship, the *Enterprize*.

The *Enterprize* was far behind now, anchored with the rest of the American fleet as the 60 American sailors and their Sicilian pilot sailed into the Tripolian harbor.

The objective was the *Philadelphia*. Only months before, on October 22, 1803, the *Philadelphia*, under the command of William Bainbridge, was blockading the Barbary pirate ships anchored in the Tripolian harbor. But in the midst of chasing a smaller pirate ship, the *Philadelphia* ran aground. Within minutes, Tripolian gunships were racing toward the *Philadelphia*. Four hours later, unable to return fire and outnumbered, the *Philadelphia* struck its colors.[1]

The dilemma that faced Commodore Edward Preble, commander of the United States fleet, was evident. The Tripolians now possessed a ship far superior to any they could have ever built or purchased. As for political damage, the loss of the *Philadelphia* was a serious blow to American prestige on the international level. For months the Americans were powerless to rescue the men held captive by the Tripolians or to recapture or destroy the *Philadelphia*. The answer to Preble's problem came in the form of Lieutenant Stephen Decatur, who suggested that a select group of men enter the harbor at night and burn the *Philadelphia*.

Desperate for a solution, Preble agreed to the plan. Decatur would have the honor of leading the mission. On February 3, 1804, Decatur and his 59 men sailed into Tripolian harbor. For two-and-a-half hours their small ship struggled across the harbor before it reached the *Philadelphia*.

As it neared the ship a voice aboard the *Philadelphia* called out in Arabic, "What ship are you?"

"We are from Malta," Salvadore Catalono replied in perfect Arabic. "We have lost our anchor. Can we tie up alongside you until morning?"[2]

In reply to his request, a line was thrown over the side as the smaller ship jarred into the *Philadelphia*.

Instantly, Decatur, Macdonough, and the others scrambled up onto the deck of the *Intrepid* and then onto the deck of the *Philadelphia*. The Tripolian crew recoiled in surprise as the 60 American seamen armed with cutlasses swept over them. With ten men under his command, Macdonough raced to the berth deck and the storeroom of the *Philadelphia*. He knew the ship well. Only weeks before its capture, Macdonough had been transferred off it to the *Enterprize*.

Fighting their way into the storeroom, Macdonough and his men quickly set fire to it. As they raced back to the upper deck, flames began to burn the dry timbers of the *Philadelphia*. In a sharp struggle, the Americans overpowered the Tripolians, leaving 20 of them dead on the deck as the rest jumped overboard and swam for shore.

Within 25 minutes of boarding the Philadelphia, the frigate was engulfed in flames as Decatur, Macdonough, and the others retreated. Under heavy fire from the harbor guns as well as from Tripolian gunships, their small ship miraculously escaped with only one hole in its sail. By midnight they cleared the harbor. Gripping the rail of the ship, Macdonough watched the *Philadelphia* illuminate the night sky. The roar of her exploding powder magazine blended with the cheers of the American sailors.

The mission would go down in the annals of Navy history as one of the greatest feats of bravery and courage of the nineteenth century. Not only was American honor restored, but Decatur and his men established a reputation for the American Navy that was not lost upon the European powers. Admiral Nelson, the famous British admiral, wrote of Decatur's triumph, "[it is] the most bold and daring act of the age."[3] However, this bold and daring act would receive only one line in Thomas Macdonough's journal. "I...joined the *Enterprize*, Lieutenant Stephen Decatur, commander. Was with him when the frigate Philadelphia was burned in the harbor of Tripoli...."

Thomas Macdonough and the others involved in the mission to destroy the *Philadelphia* were honored as national heroes. Many of the officers were promoted. Macdonough himself went from midshipman to first lieutenant aboard the *Enterprize* and in the years that followed he served aboard the *Wasp*, the *John Adams*, and the *Essex*. It was written of Macdonough during this time that he was "a deeply religious man...he quoted scripture readily, believed God was on his side and enjoyed the genuine respect of his men and superiors."[4]

More than once he received letters from his crew, a rare occurrence in that day. In the letter from the crew of the *Essex*, the crew wrote, "We…learn with heartfelt sorrow your intention of leaving the ship. Permit us, Sir, before your departure to return our most sincere thanks and acknowledgements of your officer-like conduct and Philanthropy during the time we have had the happiness of being under your command as Second officer."[5]

After years of uneasy peace with the major European powers, war again loomed on the horizon for Macdonough and his young nation. By 1812 the United States was again headed for a major conflict with a foreign nation, this time with a familiar foe—Great Britain. Unlike the American War for Independence, a land-centered conflict, this war began on the sea, and many of the major conflicts were contested there.

For years, the British Navy, engaged in several major theaters of war, relied upon press gangs to force sailors of various nationalities to serve in the British Navy. Between 1794 and 1804, nearly 2,400 American sailors alone were impressed into the British Navy. It is believed that during the Napoleonic conflict, the number tripled. Records show that many of the sailors taken from American ships were British subjects or deserters, and as long as the practice of impressment was reserved to merchant vessels, the Americans endured the impressment. However, when the British Navy began taking American sailors off American warships, the mood changed dramatically. American naval officers and the American public would not stand for the ignominy of having a foreign power removing sailors off American ships. One of the American officers impressed was Thomas Macdonough.

On shore leave in Liverpool, England, in 1805, while first lieutenant, Macdonough was overpowered by a press gang. In spite of his loud declarations that he was an officer in the United States Navy, Macdonough was dragged away. Taken aboard a British ship, he was thrown into sleeping quarters with a British officer. Waiting for the man to fall asleep, Macdonough grabbed his clothes and ran for the deck. When the British officer pursued him, Thomas turned around and knocked him down, jumped aboard a rowboat, and rowed himself back to shore, swearing out loud to himself as he rowed that, "If I live, I will make England remember the day she impressed an American sailor."[6]

On June 1, 1812, tired of England's denials of the impressments, President James Madison sent a war message to Congress. The House quickly approved and close upon that vote came the Senate's approval. Having been in existence less than 40 years and only 31 years after Yorktown, the United States was again at war.[7]

Military strategists from both sides acknowledged that one of the keys to victory for either side were the Great Lakes. For the Americans, the Great Lakes were the passageway for an invasion of British-held Canada. In return, the Great Lakes were also the doorway for a British invasion from the North.

Stalemated on Lake Ontario by the effort of American commander Isaac Chauncey, the British turned to Lake Erie. There, Lieutenant Oliver Hazard Perry faced the British veteran of Trafalgar, Captain Robert Barclay. Outnumbered and badly provisioned, Barclay, forced to fight, sailed to meet Perry's fleet on September 9, 1813. In a furious battle that left two-thirds of the crew dead on Perry's flagship, the *Lawrence*, and all the British commanders and their second-in-commands either dead or wounded, Perry destroyed the British fleet. Shortly after his victory he penned to General William Henry Harrison the immortal words, "We have met the enemy and they are ours."[8]

Now British hopes for victory lay on Lake Champlain.

The necessity of holding Champlain had not been lost on the Americans and early in the war, on September 12, 1812, Lieutenant Thomas Macdonough was ordered to take command at Lake Champlain. In his orders, the new Secretary of the Navy, William Jones, gave Macdonough the "unlimited authority" needed to regain "the ascendancy which we have lost."[9]

At best, Macdonough's fleet, as it was generously called, was simply a collection of two leaky gunboats and six small sloops. Seemingly unperturbed, Macdonough gave the orders to begin transforming the sloops from troop transports to fighting ships and then left to attend to personal business. On December 12, 1812, Macdonough married Lucy Ann Shaler and promptly took a honeymoon while Lake Champlain was ice locked.

By spring of 1813, he and his motley collection of ships were ready for action. As soon as the ice broke on the lake, Macdonough took three sloops, the *Growler*, the *Eagle*, and the *President*, onto the lake. Until June of that year, the British were content to let Macdonough control the lake. By the first of June, however, the British came looking for a fight and sent a squadron of gunboats seeking Macdonough and his small fleet. Sending his senior lieutenant, Sidney Smith, to attack with the *Growler* and the *Eagle*, Macdonough watched and waited. Perhaps it was overconfidence in Smith, or perhaps it was Smith's overexuberance, but in a short span of time, the *Eagle* was resting on the bottom of Lake Champlain and the *Growler*, with Smith aboard, had surrendered. For all intents and purposes, the British now controlled the lake.

Withdrawing to his naval base at Burlington, Vermont, Macdonough was powerless as the British landed troops at Plattsburg, one of the American outposts. The American militia evaporated as the British troops destroyed the blockhouse, arsenal, barracks, and the public buildings before reboarding their ships and returning behind British lines. It appeared it was only a matter of time before the British would have the ability to funnel thousands of troops across Lake Champlain and into the northern states of America.

Thomas Macdonough had other plans. Conceding for a time that the British held superiority on the lake, he and his small fleet retreated to the small town of Vergennes, Vermont. There he began one of the most impressive feats of shipbuilding in American naval history. Under the guidance of the Brown brothers, Noah and Adam, Macdonough built a new fleet. Within 40 days of the first tree being felled, he built the *Saratoga*, a brig 143' long and armed with 26 cannons. Taking a large steamboat, he rigged her as a schooner and named her the *Ticonderoga*. In only 19 days, Adam Brown built and launched another new brig for Macdonough, christened the

Eagle for the ship lost only a short time before, while his brother supervised the building of nine gunboats, 75′ long ships with two small masts, 40 oars for rowing, and one large cannon.[10]

On the other side of the lake, the British were not idle. While Macdonough built his fleet, they built a large 36-gun ship and a 16-gun brig. In a race against time and each other, the two navies were heading toward another major conflict on the lake.

It came on September 11, 1814, a Sunday morning.

Word came from the American picket ship off Cumberland Head: Enemy in sight.

Macdonough was not surprised. Though outgunned and outmanned, his ships were positioned in Plattsburg Bay, open to the south, closed to the north. With the prevailing winds from the north, the situation made it difficult for enemy ships to approach. Taking advantage of the nearby shoals, Macdonough left the British fleet two options—sail within range of his heavy carronades or run aground on the shoals.

A student of naval history, Macdonough took a page from the history books. Emulating the tactics of British naval hero Horatio Nelson at the Nile, Macdonough placed anchors at the sterns and bows of each of his larger ships along with two kedge anchors. Thus, by using "spring lines," Macdonough's men could manually rotate the ships by hauling the cables, effectively spinning the ships in place so that both the port and starboard batteries could be used in firing on the British ships.

From the fighting tops of his larger ships, Macdonough could hear the voices of his sailors calling out the position of the British ships as their masts cleared the trees that lined the shore of Lake Champlain.

Summoning his officers to the quarterdeck, Macdonough removed his cap. As his grandson would write in later years, "There was now a hushed expectant moment like the stillness which precedes the storm. Macdonough, whose manly courage was supported by a childlike faith, knelt on the deck of the flagship with his officers around him."[11]

As he and his officers knelt on the deck of the *Saratoga*, Macdonough prayed. "Stir up Thy Strength, O Lord, and come and help us, for Thou givest not always the battle to the strong, but canst save by many or by few—hear us, Thy poor servants; imploring Thy help that Thou wouldst be a defence [sic] unto us against the face of the enemy. Make it clear that Thou art our Saviour and Mighty Deliverer, through Jesus Christ our Lord."[12]

When he finished, Macdonough rose and placed his hat on once more.

The situation facing him that morning was clear. Defeat the British here, and there would be no northern invasion of the United States. If he failed, the northern states would be overrun by the British. And though he did not know it, only two weeks before the British had succeeded in their thrust into the middle of the United States. On August 19, the British swept away the defenses of the Americans around Washington and had burned the American Capitol to the ground. A victory on Lake Champlain was critical for the young nation's survival.

"Beat to quarters," he cried, and the battle was quickly joined. As the British ship, the *Linnet*, passed the *Saratoga*, she fired at the American ship, but her shots fell well short, save one cannonball that struck a hen coop aboard the *Saratoga*. The gamecock inside flew out and landed on the *Saratoga's* deck, crowing lustily. The Americans, taking it as a good omen, cheered, and Macdonough, manning one of the cannons himself, fired the first answering shot at the British fleet.[13]

The English commander, Downie, came up the port side of the bay. As Downie's flagship, the *Confiance*, came abreast of Macdonough's flagship, she opened fire. With 27 long, 24-pound cannons to Macdonough's 8, the initial blast from the double-shotted British cannons was devastating. Of the 240 men aboard the *Saratoga*, 40 were struck down by the first British broadside. Macdonough himself was knocked down by the blast of cannonballs hitting his ship, remaining senseless for a few minutes. Yet, when he regained consciousness, he struggled to his feet and again began directing his gun crews. Moments later, another cannonball took off the head of the man next to Macdonough and drove it into Macdonough's face with such force that he was knocked out again. He struggled to his feet once more and continued directing his men.

Twice the *Saratoga* was hit by hot shot, heated cannonballs, that set her on fire. Yet, in spite of the fires and of having 55 round shot in her hull from enemy cannons, the *Saratoga* and her crew gave as good as they got.

Like thunder, volley after volley of cannon fire echoed across the stillness of Lake Champlain and through the surrounding forests. Julius Hubbell, a young lawyer from a nearby town, wrote, "The firing was terrific, fairly shaking the ground, and so rapid that it seemed to be one continuous roar, intermingled with the spiteful flashing from the mouths of the guns, and dense clouds of smoke soon hung over the two fleets."[14]

Among the first casualties aboard the British flagship was Downie himself as one of his own guns, struck by an American shell, recoiled on him and crushed him. With the death of their commander, things went badly for the British fleet. Two of their midsized ships, the sloops *Chub* and *Finch*, met unglamorous fates. The *Chub* simply drifted into the middle of the American fleet and quickly hauled down its colors. The *Finch's* part in the battle ended almost as quickly as it ran aground on the shoals and was effectively removed from the battle.

Though there were numerous gunboats and galleys in the fight, the battle quickly evolved to a struggle between the four largest ships.

After two-and-half hours of battle, the *Eagle* cut her cables and swung her portside battery, thus far unengaged, into battle. Following suit, the *Saratoga* did the same and soon the two British ships were being mauled by volley after volley from the American ships. Its captain dead and itself badly damaged, the *Confiance*, the British flagship, was the first to haul down its colors. The *Linnet* quickly did the same, and soon the whole British fleet was in American hands.

On the Canadian shore of Lake Champlain, Sir George Prevost, the British governor of Canada and commander-in-chief of the British forces, watched in disbelief. At his back were ten thousand veterans from the Napoleonic Wars. They were men who, according to the victor of Waterloo, the Duke of Wellington, "could go anywhere and do anything." Now they were powerless to do anything. The expected victory and ensuing transport of them across Lake Champlain was not to be. With no other option left to him, Prevost and his men turned and marched back into Canada. Lieutenant Colonel John Murray, one of the commanding officers of the British forces under Prevost, was heard to say, "This is a proud day for America—the proudest day she ever saw."[15]

As for Macdonough, he wrote to Secretary of the Navy William Jones, "Sir: The Almighty has been pleased to grant us a signal victory on Lake Champlain, in the capture of one frigate, one brig, and two sloops of war of the enemy."[16]

Only four days after the Battle of Lake Champlain came the conflict at Fort McHenry, the guardian fortress of Baltimore. The British, fresh off their razing of Washington, hoped to repeat their success at Baltimore.

But, as Francis Scott Key wrote, after a night of heavy bombardment, the American flag of Fort McHenry still waved "by the dawn's early light." Unable to crack the American defenses, the British withdrew. These two victories at Lake Champlain and Fort McHenry, though minor by some standards, breathed life into a dying American cause.

Inspired by the feats of their fellow Americans, the defenders of New Orleans gave a spectacular defense as the British turned their efforts to the south. On January 8, 1815, the blow that broke the British military back in America came at the Battle of New Orleans. After a second major conflict with the British Empire, the Americans were again victorious.

Following Macdonough's victory at Lake Champlain, the United States Congress presented him with a gold medal honoring his victory. He was honored in every city he visited, and his name became a household word. In future years, Theodore Roosevelt wrote of Macdonough:

> In this battle [he] won a higher fame than any other commander in the war, British or American. He had a decidedly superior force to contend against…and it was solely owing to his foresight and resource that we won the victory…His skill, seamanship, quick eye, readiness of recourse, and indomitable pluck, are beyond all praise. A thoroughly religious man, he was as generous and humane as he was skillful and brave; one of the greatest of our sea captains, he has left a stainless name behind him.[17]

In time, Macdonough returned home where he and his wife raised five children. He was given command of the *Constitution* on May 31, 1824, and sailed to the Mediterranean. In October of the same year he took command of the American squadron in the Mediterranean. His command was short-lived. In October of 1825, Macdonough received news that his wife had died suddenly. Fighting tuberculosis and weighing only 60 pounds, Macdonough handed over command of the *Constitution* and sailed for home. Realizing his illness was terminal, and fighting despair over his wife's death, Macdonough's goal was only to reach American soil before he died. His final wish was denied him as he died at sea on November 10, 1825.

His friend, Doctor Turk, wrote Macdonough's mother-in-law. "I have never witnessed a death before so perfectly free from pain and distress. He fixed his eyes on me with fortitude and composure and appeared to have fallen gently to sleep."[18]

Thomas Macdonough was 41 years old. Mourning his death, the nation that he had saved years before on Lake Camplain gave him a hero's funeral.

His grandson wrote of Macdonough:

> The Commodore's religion was an essential part of his character. It was not a garment to be assumed or cast aside as taste or convenience dictated. It was unostentatious and unobtrusive...His faith was that of a little child, simple and trusting. His motto might have been that of the Scottish patriot—"God Armeth Me"—for his confidence in the Almighty Power to save in peace or war never wavered. The most beautiful act of his life, an act which showed him true to himself and true to his God, was that supreme moment when, on the deck of the Saratoga, he publicly proclaimed Christ before men and involved his aid in the upcoming battle.[19]

Notes

1. Fowler, *Jack Tars*, 94-95.
2. Fowler, *Jack Tars*, 100-01, and Macdonough, *The Life*, 68-70.
3. Macdonough, *The Life*, 70.
4. Macdonough, "People and Stories," <http://www.galafilm.com/1812/e/people/macdonough.html>, February 4, 2002.
5. Macdonough, *The Life*, 91-92.
6. "Thomas Macdonough," <http://unitedstates-on-line.com/delaware/mcdobio.htm>, February 5, 2002.
7. Fowler, *Jack Tars*, 160-61.
8. Ibid, 228.
9. "Thomas Macdonough," <http://unitedstates-on-line.com/delaware/mcdobio.htm>, February 5, 2002.
10. Bird, *Navies in the Mountains*, 289-92.
11. Macdonough, *The Life*, 177.
12. Fowler, *Jack Tars*, 239.
13. Macdonough, *The Life*, 178,
14. "Thomas Macdonough," <http://unitedstates-on-line.com/delaware/mcdobio.htm>, February 5, 2002.
15. "The Battle for Lake Champlain," <http://www.surfpac.navy.mil/shipsnav/LakeChamp/lkchis.htm>, February 4, 2002.
16. Macdonough, *The Life*, 185.
17. Roosevelt, *The Naval War*, 238.
18. Macdonough, *The Life*, 250-51.
19. Ibid, 261-62.

Chapter 13

JOHN HARPER

"Believe on the Lord Jesus Christ!"

★　★　★

"Believe on the Lord Jesus Christ, and thou shalt be saved!"

The words reverberated across the waters, intermingling with the cries of the drowning people. It was the early morning of April 15, 1912. The *Titanic*, the ship that "not even God Himself could sink," had struck an iceberg and was slipping below the waters of the North Atlantic.

★　★　★

First had come an almost imperceptible blow, so slight that the hundreds of pasengers sleeping were not awakened. But as the *Titanic* tried to slip by the iceberg, the submerged, "knife-like edge of the iceberg cut through the *Titanic* like a can opener."[1] Soon a torrent of water was raging through the tear in the ship's side, quickly filling the bulkheads of the ship. Then, as the ship came to a standstill in the quiet waters and the crew fired flares into the night, came the realization that the *Titanic* was sinking and that there were not enough lifeboats for all the passengers.

As panic began to spread, men and women began pressing toward the lifeboats. Bruce Ismay, part owner of the *Titanic* and the man responsible for the shortage of lifeboats on board, crawled into a lifeboat and left hundreds of women and children to drown. Other men tried to pass themselves off as women in an attempt to save themselves. In the end, when it was realized all was lost, the officers of the *Titanic* threatened men with their pistols to keep them away from the lifeboats.

Through the press of panicked people, the Reverend John Harper of Glasgow, Scotland, shouldered his way toward an upper deck captain, holding in his arms his only daughter, Nana, while his sister-in-law, Miss Jessie Leitch, clung to his coat. Instructing the officer to get his daughter and Miss Leitch into a lifeboat, Harper handed Nana to him. Before he let his daughter go, Harper hugged her one last time and kissed her good-bye. Her mother had died six years before, and now he was her only family. He could have easily slipped into a lifeboat, but instead, as Nana and her aunt were lowered into the dark waters aboard lifeboat number 11, Harper turned to face the teeming masses behind him.[2]

"Let the women, children, and unsaved into the lifeboats!" he cried out as he began helping women and children aboard the last boats. Like all the other passengers aboard the *Titanic*, Harper hadn't been expecting this. In fact, he wasn't even supposed to be on the *Titanic*. He had originally meant to sail on the *Lusitania*, but due to a change in schedules, had instead bought a second class ticket on board the *Titanic*.

At 2:20 a.m., as the water crept up to the ship's bridge, the ship heeled over to a 45-degree angle. Harper and hundreds of other passengers plunged into the icy waters. With a tremendous groan and scream of wrenching metal and machinery, the ship broke in half, and the bow of the boat began its plunge to the ocean floor. Moments later, as floor after floor of lights went out and the band members of the *Titanic* played the old Episcopal hymn "Autumn," the stern of the massive boat slid beneath the waves.[3]

Now, along with over 1,500 others for whom there had been no lifeboat, Harper was left to die in the cold waters. As the lifeboats pulled away from the passengers thrashing about in the water, a "long, continuous moan" of screams and cries for help began to fill the night air.[4] Beneath a clear night sky filled with stars, surrounded by the cries for help, Harper began swimming among the teeming mass of dying people. He had been en route to Chicago, where he was to preach an extended series of revival sermons at Moody Tabernacle. Now he would never give those revival sermons.

Concerned not for his life, but for the dying around him, Harper with his last breaths swam to the dying souls and cried out for them to be saved.

"Believe on the Lord Jesus Christ, and thou shalt be saved!"

As his strength began to ebb, Harper called out to a young man clinging to a piece of timber, "Man, are you saved?"

"No," the young man, a Scotsman by the name of Aguilla Webb, replied. "I am not."

Harper then took off his life jacket and gave it to Webb. "Here then. You need this more than me."

Webb protested, but Harper replied, "Don't worry about me. I'm not going down. I'm going up."

As they were pulled apart by the current, Harper called back to Webb, "Believe on the Lord Jesus Christ, and thou shalt be saved!"

A few moments later, Harper and Webb came into contact again. Weakened by hypothermia and struggling to keep his head above the water, Harper gasped, "Are you saved now?"

"No," Webb replied again. "I cannot say that I honestly am."

"Believe on the Lord Jesus Christ, and thou shalt be saved!" Harper cried out one last time, and with that, slipped beneath the waves for the last time.

Of the more than 1,500 people who went into the water that night, only six were rescued by the lifeboats. One of them was Aguilla Webb. Four years later, at a reunion of *Titanic* survivors in Hamilton, Canada, Webb testified that he had been saved twice that night: once by the lifeboats, and the other by

John Harper. Shortly after Harper sank beneath the waves, Webb recounted: "There, alone in the night, with two miles of water under me, I believed. I am John Harper's last convert."[5]

John Paton, a friend of Harper's, wrote upon hearing of his death:

> Some of us can well imagine him in those last awful minutes on board the doomed *Titanic*, standing amidst a group of stricken, repentant souls pointing them to the Savior he had loved and served so well, and helping them to seize the eleventh-hour opportunity. God has not many servants whom He could trust with such a service, and that to me at least is the explanation of our brother being on board the *Titanic* instead of on the *Lusitania* as he had at one time planned.[6]

In recorded testimonies of John Harper's life and ministry, those who knew him best echoed the same theme: John Harper was a man of prayer whose one goal in life was to point souls to Christ no matter what the time, the place, or the cost.

Harper's public ministry for Christ began one June day in 1890. Alone in his house, the 18-year-old Harper felt "as never before the purpose of God in the Cross of Christ. In Christ's love for men as seen on Calvary he beheld anew, in fuller form, a door of hope opened for a sinning world, and along with that fresh revelation he felt that God was beckoning to him, and committing to him a part in the ministry of reconciliation."[7]

The very next day, Harper stood on the corner of a street in his village and began preaching the gospel. He never looked back, and for the next 21 years he preached Christ, and it was said that every street corner was his pulpit. In 1897, he and 25 others formed the Paisley Road Baptist Church in Glasgow,

Scotland. For 13 years he preached there, and when Harper accepted a position at Walworth Road Church, London, the Paisley Church had grown to 500 members.

In the fall of 1911, Harper was invited to preach at the Moody Tabernacle in Chicago, and from November of 1911 until January of 1912, Harper preached a series of revival sermons. "His devotion to the Lord Jesus Christ, his unstinting sacrifice, his power in winning men to God endeared him to those who heard him." The time at Moody went so well that Harper was invited to return in April of 1912 to preach again.

Yet it seemed God had a greater plan for John Harper than to preach a series of revival sermons in Chicago. There was the need for a strong soul to lead others through the valley of the shadow of death. When the personal testimonies were written shortly after the last fateful hours on the *Titanic*, the manner of Harper's death was not known. Yet Pastor Hugh Gunn wrote:

> I am intensely curious as to know how he acted in the closing moments of his life. Would he not, as his wont, be drying the tear away, comforting, and helping till the last moment of his life? Would he not in the midst of that sweltering mass of drowning men, women, and children be pointing them to the Cross, and thus as he lived, die with the one name upon his lips: Jesus! Jesus!! Jesus!!!?[8]

The night before the *Titanic* sank, Miss Leitch recounted that John Harper was doing what he had done countless of other times: He was pleading with a young Englishman to accept Christ. Later that evening, as Harper, Nana, and Miss Leitch walked on the decks, Harper looked over to where the sun was setting in the west, and noting the red tinge, said, "It will be beautiful in the morning."[9] For John Harper, it was a beautiful morning. When the sun rose again, he was with Jesus.

Ninety years have passed since John Harper died that night, yet his life and dying words still echo down to us across the years and stand as a memorial and a challenge: "Believe on the Lord Jesus Christ, and thou shalt be saved!"

It has been recounted that when the World Trade Centers were struck on September 11, 2001, and thousands of people were fleeing down the stairwells, a man was standing near the bottom of one of the stairwells, calling out, his words echoing and reverberating. His words were almost exactly the same as those John Harper cried out the night the Titanic sank: "Believe on the name of Jesus, and you will be saved!"

Notes

1. Marshall, ed., *The Sinking*, 50.

2. *Encyclopedia Titanica: Second Class Passenger: John Harper*, <http://www.encyclopedia-titanica.org/bio/o/2nd/harper_j.shtml>, February 10, 2002.

3. Marshall, ed., *The Sinking*, 79, 89-90, 111, 213.

4. Ibid, 112.

5. Tan, *Encyclopedia*, 1, 320.

6. Adams, *Titanic's Last Hero*, 90.

7. Ibid, 31.

8. Ibid, 71.

9. *Encyclopedia Titanica: Second Class Passenger: John Harper*, <http://www.encyclopedia-titanica.org/bio/o/2nd/harper_j.shtml>, February 10, 2002.

Chapter 14

C.T. STUDD

"Hallelujah!"

In the flickering gaslight, the young man sat quietly next to the bed, watching as his brother tossed restlessly in a feverish sleep. It was feared his brother was dying, and night after night the young man kept vigil, watching, waiting, praying, thinking.

These brothers came from great wealth, their father having made several fortunes in the indigo business in India. Now that wealth seemed meaningless. As C.T. Studd leaned back in his chair, his eyes still fixed on his brother George's face, he was lost in thought. Their great wealth, his own athletic career—everything seemed meaningless at this moment.

He buried his head in his hands, lost in thought. Considered by many to be the greatest cricketer in England at the time, the *Cricketering Annual* wrote of him, "Mr. C.T. Studd must...be accorded the premier position as an all-around cricketer...." In a society that craved social position and athletic ability, he had little need of anything.

His eyes moved from George's sweaty face to the painting above the washstand. There, in the dim light, he studied the painting. It was of the empty cross of Christ, with three Eastern travelers curiously gazing at it. Atop the cross was still nailed Pilate's edict: "The King of the Jews."

Studd's mind drifted to the time several years before when he had made a commitment to Christ. He had been sincere at the time, but the headiness of success had taken his full attention in the intervening years. He looked back to George. *Now, what is all this popularity in the world worth to George? What is all the fame and flattery worth?* Studd thought. *What is it worth to possess all the riches in the world, when a man comes to face Eternity?*

He leaned forward and laid his hand on his brother's head. Then, in the back of his mind, flashed another thought. *Vanity of vanities; all is vanity. For what shall it profit a man to gain the world and lose his soul?*[1] In that brief moment, everything—his life, his purpose, his career—came into focus for Studd.

George had decided years ago that he cared about nothing save the Bible and the Lord Jesus Christ, and Studd wondered,

What if I was in George's place? What if I was the one dying?
What would all my wealth and fame be compared with eternity?

Thousands had gathered in Exeter Hall to hear these young men speak. People from all walks of life were in the crowd—men and women of wealth intermingled with working women and shopmen. Regardless of station in life, all had come tonight to hear the Cambridge Seven, the seven young men going to China as missionaries. It was one thing to hear that young, nondescript persons were going on the mission field. It was quite another to see the captain of the Cambridge University eight rowing team, the captain of the Cambridge cricket team, an officer of the Royal Artillery, and an officer of the Dragoon Guards laying down successful careers and going halfway around the world as missionaries. Their sacrifice captured the attention of all of England. The crowd grew silent as the seven young men strode across the stage and then, in turn, began addressing the crowd, sharing why they were going to China.

The last of the seven to speak that night was C.T. Studd. As he looked out at the faces of the men and women, he told them, "I want to recommend to you my Master. I have tried many ways of pleasure in my time; I have been running after the best master—and, thank God, I have found Him. The Lord has sought me and brought me back to Himself." In his conclusion, Studd asked the gathering, "Are you living for the day or are you living for life eternal? The opinion of men won't avail us much when we get before the judgement throne. But the opinion of God will. Had we not, then, better take His word and implicitly obey it?"[2]

The night vigil by George's bed several years before had changed Studd's life forever. As soon as George had recovered, Studd had gone to hear the American evangelist, D.L. Moody, who was in England conducting revival meetings. It was at one of these meetings that Studd rededicated his life to Christ, and it changed the course of his life forever.

He wrote to a friend, "Formerly I had as much love for cricket as any man could have, but when the Lord Jesus came into my heart, I found I had something infinitely better than cricket. My heart was no longer in the game; I wanted to win souls for the Lord."[3]

He began taking his friends from the national cricket team to hear Moody, and began praying as to what God wanted for his life. He recounted, "I thought, how could I spend the best years of my life in working for myself and the honours and pleasures of this world, while thousands and thousands of souls are perishing every day without having heard of Christ, going down to Christ-less and hopeless graves?"

It was at this time that Studd came across a tract written by an atheist, which read:

> Did I firmly believe, as millions say they do, that the knowledge and practice of religion in this life influences destiny in another, religion would mean to me every-thing. I would cast away earthly enjoyments as dross, earthly cares as follies, and earthly thoughts and feelings as vanity. Religion would be my first waking thought, and my last image before sleep sank me into uncon-sciousness. I should labour in its cause alone. I would

take thought for the morrow of Eternity alone. I would esteem one soul gained for heaven worth a life of suffering. Earthly consequences would never stay my hand, nor seal my lips. Earth, its joys and its griefs, would occupy no moment in my thoughts. I would strive to look upon Eternity alone, and on the Immortal Souls around me, soon to be everlastingly happy or everlastingly miserable. I would go forth to the world and preach to it in season and out of season, and my text would be, WHAT SHALL IT PROFIT A MAN IF HE GAIN THE WHOLE WORLD AND LOSE HIS OWN SOUL?[4]

It seemed to Studd that this atheist had summed up how a Christian ought to live. After several months of prayer and studying for the Bar, waiting "until the Lord Jesus should show me what my life's work was to be for Him," Studd felt led to go to China as a missionary. He was not alone in this desire. One of his friends from Cambridge, Stanley Smith, the stroke of the varsity eight rowing team, also felt led to follow that course.

But when Studd made mention of his plans to his family, he met resistance.

"Charlie, I think you are making a great mistake," his older brother, Kynaston, said when he heard of C.T.'s plans. "You are away every night at the meetings and you do not see your mother. I see her, and this is just breaking her heart. I think you are wrong to go to China."

"Let us ask God," Studd replied. "I don't want to be pigheaded and go out there of my own accord. I just want to do God's will."

"Think about the influence you could have with young men right here in England," Kynaston argued. "Why go halfway around the world to be an evangelist?"

That night, as he lay in bed, it seemed to Studd, "...as though I heard someone say these words over and over, 'Ask of Me and I will give thee the heathen for thine inheritance, and the uttermost parts of the earth for thy possession.' I knew it was God's voice speaking to me, and that I had received my marching orders to go to China."[5]

An interview with Hudson Taylor, the head of China Inland Mission, quickly followed, and C.T. Studd and Stanley Smith were accepted as associate members of the Mission.

Before leaving for China, Studd and Smith were asked to go to Edinburgh University to share their testimonies. The night of the meeting found young men jostling and pushing to get into the crowded hall to hear the two speak. One of the young men there that night, a medical student, wrote, "...Studd couldn't speak a bit...it was the fact of his devotion to Christ which told, and he, if anything, made the greatest impression."[6]

After speaking, Studd and Smith were surrounded by a crowd of young men, who all wanted to hear more about Christ. The success of the meeting led to others, and soon Studd and Smith were traveling all over England, sharing their testimonies. As the day neared for their departure to China, they were joined by five other young men who'd also decided to go to China. Dubbed the Cambridge Seven, the young men held three last meetings at Cambridge, Oxford, and London, each attended by large crowds, then sailed for China in February of 1885.

Upon arrival in China, all of them, as was the habit of the China Inland Mission, adopted the dress of the Chinese. Studd wrote to his mother, "I have been laughing all day at our grotesque appearance....we put our clothes on this morning, were duly shaved and pigtailed...Monty, Stanley [Smith] and I make huge Chinamen." The following months were spent learning Chinese, traveling by foot, mule, or houseboat into inland China, and sharing the gospel with whoever would listen.

Then, in 1886, Studd received news from home. He was to receive his inheritance, a sum exceeding 29,000 pounds. Some years before, Studd had shared with Hudson Taylor his desire to give away all his money to Christ's work. Studd related that shortly before he received news of his inheritance, "I was reading the harmony of the Gospels, I came to where Christ talked with the rich young ruler. Then God seemed to bring back to me all the vows I had made."

He was determined not to pass up on this golden opportunity to obey Christ's words to the rich young ruler. But, before he could begin to give the money away, he needed the signature of one of Her Majesty's officers to gain power of attorney. Since he was staying in Chungking with the British Consul at the time, the matter seemed easily solved. One morning Studd broached the subject to his host.

"I need your signature on these papers," Studd began.

"What for?" his host asked.

"For power of attorney. I need you to sign these papers so that I can start giving away my inheritance."

The man stared at Studd as though he were crazy. "Give it away?" he struggled even to get the words out.

"That's right."

"Won't do it."

"I need you to," Studd replied.

"I won't sign. Consider what you're doing. Come back in two weeks. If you're still intent on giving all that money away, I'll sign the papers then."

Two weeks later Studd brought the papers back, and the consul, true to his word, signed them. On January 13, 1887, Studd calmly sat down with his checkbook and began writing checks. He wrote four checks for 5,000 pounds each to D.L. Moody, George Mueller, George Holland, and the Salvation Army in India. Another 5,000 pounds was dispersed in 1,000-pound quantities to various charities in England. He kept back 3,400 pounds to give to his future wife, Priscilla Stewart, another missionary working in China. But, upon their wedding day, when she was given the money, Priscilla looked at Studd.

"Charlie, what did the Lord tell the rich young man to do?"

"Sell all," Studd replied.

"Well then, we will start clear with the Lord at our wedding." And so the last sum of Studd's inheritance was sent off to England to General Booth of the Salvation Army.

Ten years were spent ministering in China, but in the tenth year, Studd came down with typhoid. Though he survived the disease, it left him with severe asthma, which was to trouble him for the rest of his life. In poor health, he was ordered back to England. So with his wife and four young daughters in tow, Studd returned home. He was met at the London Docks by his brother, Kynaston. Sending his wife and daughters ahead, Studd clambered into the next cab with his brother. Perhaps a bit taken aback at the sight of his brother in poor health with a wife and four young children, aware that C.T. had given away his entire inheritance, Kynaston turned to his brother and asked, "Charlie, how are you off for money?"

Studd looked thoughtful for a moment, then patted his pockets, giving Kynaston a smile. "I think I have ten shillings in my pocket!"[7]

Studd had left England a rich man, a successful athlete, and had returned ten years later with hardly a pound to his name, in poor health, and with a family to care for. Still he was at peace, and for the next five years, ignoring his health problems, he toured Britain and America, preaching. His daughter, Edith, wrote that wherever he spoke, "...no hall or church was ever empty. He preached Christ as though he would never preach again, and as a 'dying man to dying men.' "[8]

In 1900, Studd felt called to south India and, along with his family, spent the next six years there. It had been his father's dying wish that the Studd family, who had earned their fortune in India, would someday return there to preach the gospel of Christ. Studd became pastor of the Union Church at Ootacamund, and it was said of his church, "That church is to be avoided unless a man means to get converted."

He was invited to come to Tirhoot, the very region where his father had owned his indigo plantations, and for the next six months he ministered both to the natives and to the planters. It was at this time that Studd joined a cricket tour in order to get opportunities to hold meetings with the British soldiers at night after playing the regimental teams. It quickly became evident that though he'd been away from the game for years, he could still play very well. In 1904 he made two double centuries, a feat that had been performed only once before in Indian cricket.

Two more years were spent in India, and then in 1906 Studd and his family returned once more to England. Again, not content to rest, Studd began traveling throughout England, speaking at YMCAs, Police Institutes, and Wesleyan Central Halls. Tens of thousands of men, many of whom had never stepped foot inside a church, came to hear Studd speak.

At a businessmen's luncheon, Studd stood up after the meal and addressed the gathering.

"Gentlemen, I'm not going to tickle you with pulpit or academic display of language," Studd began with a smile. "I shall speak in ordinary language, which we are all accustomed to when engaged in the real battles of life." He paused, looking at the men's faces. "I once had another religion, mincing, lisping, but no obedience, no sacrifice. Then came the change. The real thing came before me." He thumped the back of the chair behind which he was standing for emphasis. "The commands of Christ became not merely Sunday recitations, but battle calls to be obeyed—assent to creed was born again into decisive action of obedience." Studd's voice was earnest now. "Do you begin to see? If a man is willing to obey and sacrifice, he soon learns what is the blest reality of the fellowship of God's Son Jesus Christ. I dropped cant and ceremony and became a Christian."[9]

Studd's ministry was not just to wealthy businessmen. Once, when asked to speak in a small town, Studd spent the night with the local fishmonger. Underneath the bed he slept on was the day's catch of fish, and in the morning he and his host washed up in the kitchen sink using the same towel. Another time, a cabbie taking Studd to the railroad station recognized him as the great cricketer. So Studd climbed up and rode outside with the cabbie to the station, sharing the gospel with him the entire way.

In 1908, Studd was considering a return to India when he came across a notice posted outside an office door. It read: "Cannibals want missionaries." Finding the notice humorous and intriguing, Studd ducked inside the office and listened to a Dr. Karl Kumm share about his journies across Africa.

"There are numerous tribes who have never heard the story of Jesus Christ," Kumm said. "Big-game hunters, Arabs, traders, and scientists have gone, but no Christians."

Hearing those words, Studd thought, *The shame sinks deep into one's soul. Why have no Christians gone?*

At that moment, Studd felt God ask, *Why don't you go?*

The doctors won't permit it, Studd replied.

Am I not the Great Physician? Can I not take you through? Can I not keep you there?[10]

Sitting there, Studd realized he was out of excuses. He had to go to Africa.

Of course, he had no money, and when the doctors refused to give him a clean bill of health, due in great part to his asthma, a group of businessmen who had been willing to help Studd get to Africa dropped their support. Even his wife wasn't sure it was the right thing to do, but Studd felt that God was calling him to Africa. "If Jesus Christ be God and died for me, then no sacrifice can be too great for me to make for Him," became his response to the naysayers and doubters. When a friend placed ten pounds in Studd's hands, he immediately booked passage to Port Said in Africa, even though the money would not cover the cost of the trip there. But God provided the rest of the money needed, and in 1913, having reached Africa, Studd and his young companion, Alfred Buxton, headed for the Belgian Congo.

Their first night in the Congo, Studd wrote home, "I know I am God's. I know I only want His glory, and I know He knows it. I never was better or stronger for years, but best of all, I know God is with us. He talks to me and His blessed Word means more than ever before and makes me burn to dare and do for Him."[11]

Their goal was Niangara, the very heart of Africa. However, between them and Niangara lay the Ituri Forest and its inhabitants, the Balenda tribe. A short while before, a white man had been stripped, beaten, and sent back naked by Chief Julu of the Balendas. An English elephant hunter had been shot recently by one of the Balenda with a poisoned arrow, and he had died before any help could arrive.

"You'll never come through alive," a trader warned Studd and Buxton.

"They'll be too interested in our bicycles to do anything to us," Studd replied coolly.

"Bicycles?!" the trader managed to ask, choking on his words. "You are going to bicycle through the jungle?"

"Certainly," Studd replied. "We'll get to the other end more quickly. And when they can't carry us, we'll carry them."

Studd and Buxton set off, clad in knickers and riding their bikes down the rough paths, overshadowed by the tall trees of the forest. The inhabitants of the forest came out, and as Studd wrote, "...all carried bows and arrows, even the young children, but they were quite friendly with us." As Studd and Buxton rode along, the natives ran alongside them, laughing, yelling, and singing. Day after day the scene repeated itself as Studd and Buxton moved farther into the forest. The natives would carry their bikes for them through streams and rivers, across broken and dilapidated bridges. "They would lead us by the hand; men, women, and children ran along with us...so we marched along amid the singing, laughing crowd."[12]

When the paths permitted the bikes to be used again, Studd related that the natives continued to run alongside, laughing, chasing the missionaries as though they were the hounds and Studd and Buxton were the foxes. As they passed villages, the inhabitants would stream out to see the two white men cycling by, and Studd wrote, "It was the funniest thing in the world to see a woman catch the first sight of one riding along. Her face would express terror as though she had seen the devil; then all of the sudden it would be changed into a huge, broad smile; then she would drop her work, and run after us, joining in the fun as only an African woman can."[13]

After months of traveling, Studd and Buxton reached Niangara in October of 1913. A concession was granted to them by the Belgian government at Niangara and Nala, and within weeks they had built two mission houses. Studd and Buxton were now in the heart of Africa, immersed in thousands of miles of jungle and surrounded by cannibals. Ten years before, the first expedition of white men had come to the regions of Nala; 34 of the 35 men had been killed, cooked, and eaten. Studd calmly wrote a friend, "Today they [the natives] are quiet and friendly."

The ministry among the natives began well, and as Studd traveled back to England to muster more recruits for what was now being called the Heart of Africa Mission, Buxton began working among the cannibals. In June of 1915, while another missionary fired his revolver into the river to scare off the crocodiles, Buxton baptized 12 cannibals.[14]

Back in England, Studd spent nearly two years going up and down the country, recruiting more missionaries. Appealing to his fellow Christians to "fight and sacrifice for perishing souls," he wrote:

> ...Christ's call is to feed the hungry, not the full; to save the lost, not the stiff-necked....this can only be accomplished by a red-hot, unconventional, unfettered Holy Ghost religion...The fiery baptism of the Holy Spirit will change soft, sleek Christians into hot, lively heroes for Christ, who will advance and fight and die, but not mark time....Nail the colours to the mast!...."To die is gain." Some wish to live within the sound of Church or Chapel bell; I want to run a Rescue Shop within a yard of hell.[15]

With eight new recruits in tow, including his daughter, Edith, Studd set sail for Africa in 1916. He was never to return to England.

Studd launched into the mission work in Africa like a general plotting a campaign. He sent his small group of missionaries out to cover territory that was nearly half the size of England, then commissioned the earliest native converts to go out as well. The day he sent out the native missionaries, Studd gathered them under a mango tree.

"Here's my final advice to you," he started. "If you don't desire to meet the Devil during the day, meet Jesus before dawn. If you don't want the Devil to hit you, hit him first, and hit him with all your might, so that he may be too crippled to hit back."

"How long do we stay out?" one of the natives asked.

"If you are tired, return at the end of the month," Studd replied. "If not, return at the end of two; if you can stick three months, very good!"

"Oh no!" cried another native. "You will not see me for a year." And with that, he and the other native missionaries slipped into the jungle, singing, "I love Jesus/ Jesus loves me/ And nothing else in the world matters/So abounding joy possesses me."[16]

Natives began traveling to Nala, some coming 20 days to hear Studd, because "All the world knows there is much knowledge of God at Nala." By 1923, native churches of up to 1,500 were in existence. Studd wrote home, "The work is reaching a sure foundation at last, and now we will go bounding forward. Oh, it is good to be in a stiff fight for Jesus."

By the late 1920s, Studd was suffering from very poor health, enduring heart attacks, asthma, and pain from gallstones. But, he refused to let his health stop his work. He translated the New Testament into the native language, often spending 18 hours a day on the work, so that visiting natives could return to their villages with a Bible in hand. He saw his wife only once in the last 15 years of his life. While he labored in Africa, she traveled the world raising support for the Mission. Yet, Studd counted everything as loss for the glory of God. In early 1931, he wrote:

> As I believe I am now nearing my departure from this world, I have but a few things to rejoice in; they are these: 1. That God called me to China and I went in spite of utmost opposition from all my loved ones. 2. That I joyfully acted as Christ told that rich young man to act. 3. That I deliberately at the call of God, when alone on the Bibby liner, gave up my life for this work, which was henceforth not for the Sudan only, but for the whole un-evangelized World. My only joys therefore are that when God has given me a work to do, I have not refused it.[17]

The end came quickly for Studd. On Sunday the twelfth of July, 1931, he spoke for five hours at a meeting at the mission station, but by Tuesday, he had developed a severe pain in his stomach. He realized he was suffering from severe gallstones, but nothing could be done for him. He grew weaker, and by Thursday he was asked how he felt.

"Heart bad," he whispered.

"Are you going to be leaving us this time?" he was asked.

"I don't know. It is very likely," he replied.

As he lay there, his breathing labored, surrounded by worried faces, thousands of miles away from England, Studd smiled. He hadn't been a fool to give every earthly thing away to gain eternal glory. "Hallelujah," he whispered. "Hallelujah."

With each successive breath, he whispered, "Hallelujah." When he lapsed into unconsciousness, a smile on his face, his last word was "Hallelujah." Later that evening, he breathed his last.

It was a stormy day when Studd was laid to rest. Thousands of natives and some of the most powerful chiefs in the region came, and as his native friends and missionaries carried Studd to his final resting place, the rain poured down on the silent brown and white faces. It was said that "even the great forest trees bowed their heads and dripped," great teardrops of water rolling off their leaves to fall on those below. But, it was not all sadness that day. A great man was laid to rest, and those attending knew it. Alfred Buxton, Studd's first companion to Africa, wrote of him shortly after his funeral:

> C.T.'s life stands as some rugged Gibraltar a sign to all succeeding generations that it is worth while to lose all this world can offer and stake everything on the world to come. His life will be an eternal rebuke to easy-going Christianity. He has demonstrated what it means to follow Christ without counting the cost and without looking back.[18]

Today, the Heart of Africa Mission is known as the World-wide Evangelism Crusade. The Crusade has missionaries across the world, from Africa to South America; from India to the United States and Canada.

Notes

1. Buxton, *Reluctant Missionary*, 28.
2. Pollock, *The Cambridge Seven*, 115-16.
3. Grubb, *C.T. Studd*, 34.
4. Ibid, 36.
5. Buxton, *Reluctant Missionary*, 30.
6. Pollock, *The Cambridge Seven*, 96.
7. Buxton, *Reluctant Missionary*, 14.
8. Ibid, 31.
9. Grubb, *C.T. Studd*, 123-24.
10. Ibid, 126
11. Buxton, *Reluctant Missionary*, 68-69.
12. Grubb, C.T. Studd, 156.
13. Ibid, 157.
14. Grubb, *Alfred Buxton*, 45.
15. Grubb, *C.T. Studd*, 163-66.
16. Ibid, 173-74.
17. Ibid, 239.
18. Buxton, *Reluctant Missionary*, 163.

BIBLIOGRAPHY

INTRODUCTION

Kennedy, John F. *Profiles in Courage.* New York: Harper and Row, 1964.

Marshall, Logan, ed. T*he Sinking of the Titanic and Great Sea Disasters.* Oakland, CA: Regent Press, 1912.

JOSEPH WARREN

Bancroft, George. *History of the American Revolution*. Boston: Little, Brown and Co., 1852–1874, Vol. 7, ch. 16.

"The Battle of Bunker Hill (Breed's Hill)." An article taken from William Farrand Livingston. *Israel Putnam, Pioneer, Ranger, and Major-General*. (The Knickerbocker Press, 1901). February 2002 <http://www.putnamelms.org/breeds.htm>.

Bowen, Catherine D. *John Adams and the American Revolution*. Boston: Little, Brown and Co., 1950.

Buckley, Gail. *American Patriots*. New York: Random House, 2001.

Cummings, Scott. "The Battle of Bunker Hill." (Copyright 2001-2002). February 2002 <http://www.patriotresource.com/battles/bunker.html#>.

Falkner, Leonard. *Forge of Liberty*. New York: Dutton and Co., Inc., 1959.

Frothingham, Richard. *The Battle of Bunker Hill (With a Relation of the Action by William Prescott)*. Boston: Massachusetts Historical Society, 1876.

Frothingham, Richard. *The Life and Times of Joseph Warren*. Boston: Little, Brown and Co., 1865.

Ketchum, Richard. *Decisive Day: The Battle for Bunker Hill*. New York: Doubleday and Company, Inc., 1974.

Lewis, Paul. *The Grand Incendiary: A Biography of Samuel Adams*. New York: The Dial Press, 1973.

Loring, James S. *The Hundred Boston Orators*. Boston: J.P. Jewett and Company, 1853.

Morrissey, Addie. "General Jospeh Warren." January 2002 <http://geocities.com/Heartland/Meadows/3361/GJWarren.html>

Novak, Michael. *On Two Wings: Humble Faith and Common Sense of the American Founding*. San Francisco: Encounter Books, 2002.

Ramsey, David. *The History of the American Revolution, Volumes I and II*. Philadelphia: 1789. Reprinted by Russell and Russell, New York, 1968.

Sparks, Jared. *The Library of American Biography. Vol. 10*. Boston: Hillard, Gray and Company, 1838.

Stories about General Warren, by a Lady of Boston. Boston: James Loring Publisher, 1835.

Thomas, Peter. *Tea Party to Independence: The Third Phase of the American Revolution*. Oxford: Clarendon Press, 1991.

Warren, Dr. Joseph. *An oration delivered March 5th, 1772*. Boston: Edes and Gill, 1772.

_____ . *An oration delivered March 6th, 1775*. Boston: Edes and Gill, 1775.

Williams, Robert W. III. "Joseph Warren: Martyr of Bunker Hill." January 2002 <http://www.warrentavern.com/tav_warr.htm>.

WILLIAM WILBERFORCE

Allen, William. *Life of William Allen*. London: Charles Gilpin, 1846.

Belmonte, Kevin. *Hero for Humanity: A Biograpohy of William Wilberforce*. Colorado Springs, CO: NavPress, 2002.

Everett, Betty Steele. *Freedom Fighter: The Story of William Wilberforce*. Fort Washington, PA: Christian Literature Crusade, 1994.

Harford, James. *Recollections of William Wilberforce*. London: Longman, Green, Longman, Roberts and Green, 1864.

Lean, Garth. *Brave Men Choose*. London: Blandford Press, 1961.

Lean, Garth. *God's Politician: William Wilberforce's Struggle to Abolish the Slave Trade and Reform the Morals of a Nation*. Colorado Springs, CO: Helmers & Howard, 1987.

Pollock, John. "The Little Abolitionist, William Wilberforce." *Christianity Today*. April 21, 1978: 23.

Pollock, John. *Wilberforce*. New York: St. Martin's Press, 1978.

The Parliamentary History of England from the Earliest Period to the Year 1803. Vol. XXIX [the period from 22 March 1971 to 13 December 1792]. London, 1817.

Romilly, Sir Samuel. *Sir Samuel Romilly: The Friend of the Oppressed*. C.G. Oakes, ed., London: George Allen and Unwin Ltd., 1935.

Wilberforce, A.M. *Private Papers of William Wilberforce*. New York: Burt Franklin, 1968.

Wilberforce, Robert and Samuel. *The Life of William Wilberforce*. Freeport, NY: Books for Library Press, 1972.

Wilberforce, William. *A Practical View of Christianity*. Kevin C. Belmonte, ed., Peabody, MA, 1996.

Wilberforce, William. *The Speech of William Wilberforce, Esq., Representative for the County of York, On the Question of the Abolition of the Slave Trade.* London: The Logographic Press, 1789. This edition of Wilberforce's speech was edited by Kevin Belmonte, Director of The Wilberforce Project, Gordon College.

CHRISTOPHER GREENE

Adams, Gretchen. "Deeds of Desperate Valor" (a paper handed in at the University of New Hampshire. <http://revolution.h-net.msu.cdu/essays/adams2.hml>.

Bray, Robert and Paul Bushnell, ed. *Diary of a Common Soldier in the American Revolution: An annotated edition of the military journal of Jeremiah Greenman*. DeKalb, IL. Northern Illinois University Press, 1978.

Buckley, Gail. *American Patriots*. New York: Random House, 2001.

Falkner, Leonard. "Captor of the Barefoot General." *American Heritage*. August 1960: 29-31, 98-100.

George Washington Papers at the Library of Congress, 1741–1799. January 2002. <http://memory.loc.gov/ammem/gwhtml/gwhome.html.

Green, Lorenzo. "Some Observations of the Black Regiment of Rhode Island in the American Revolution." *The Journal of Negro History*. April 1952: 142-72.

Kaplan, Sidney. *The Black Presence in the Era of the American Revolution*. New York: New York Graphic Society in conjunction with the Smithsonian Institution Press, 1973.

Lippitt, Charles Warren. "The Battle of Rhode Island." Newport Historical Society. Number 18. (October 1915).

Lossing, Benson J. *Pictorial Field Book of the Revolution, Volume II*, 1850. <http://freepages.history.rootsweb.com/~wcarrl/Lossing1/Chap35.html>.

Nell, William C. *The Colored Patriots of the American Revolution*. Philadelphia, 1855. Reprint 1968.

Puckrein, Gary. *The Black Regiment in the American Revolution*. Providence, RI: Rhode Island Black Heritage Society, 1978.

Raymond, Marcius. "Colonel Christopher Green." *The Magazine of History* XXIII Number 1 (July 1916).

Rider, Sidney S. "The Black Regiment of the Revolution." Rhode Island Historical Tracts, Number 10, Providence, 1880.

Showman, Richard, ed. *The Papers of General Nathanael Green*, Volumes I–III. Chapel Hill, NC: University of North Carolina Press, 1976.

Voelz, Peter. *Slave and Soldier*. New York: Garland Publishing, Inc., 1993.

Walker, Anthony. *So Few the Brave*. Newport, RI: Seafield Press, 1981.

Wallcut, R.F. *The Negro Soldier*. Boston, 1861. New York: Negro Universities Press, 1970.

RICHARD ALLEN

"The American Colonization Society." 2002. <http://webby.cc.denison.edu/~waitc/libcria/history/acs.htm>.

Allen, Richard. *The Life Experience and Gospel Labors of the Rt. Rev. Richard Allen*. Nashville, TN: Abingdon Press, 1960.

Cannon, N.C.W. *A History of the African Methodist Episcopal Church, the Only One in the United States of America, Styled Bethel Church (Gen. xxviii. 19). To Be Held Forth in Remembrance of the Right Reverend Richard Allen, First Bishop of the Connection*. Rochester, NY: Strong & Dawson, Printers, 1842.

George, Carol V.R. *Segregated Sabbaths: Richard Allen and the Emergence of Independent Black Churches 1760–1840*. New York: Oxford University Press, 1975.

Matthews, Marcia M. *Richard Allen*. Baltimore, MD: Helicon, 1963.

ADONIRAM JUDSON

Anderson, Courtney. *To the Golden Shore: The Life of Adoniram Judson*. Valley Forge, PA: Judson Press, 1987.

Judson, Edward. *The Life of Adoniram Judson*. New York: Anson D.F. Randolph and Company, 1883.

McElrath, William N. *To Be the First: Adventures of Adoniram Judson, America's First Foreign Missionary*. Nashville, TN: Broadman Press, 1976.

Warburton, Stacy R. *Eastward! The Story of Adoniram Judson*. New York: Round Table Press, 1937.

Wayland, Francis. *A Memoir of the Life and Labors of the Rev. Adoniram Judson, D.D*. Boston: Phillips, Sampson and Company, 1853.

ELIJAH LOVEJOY

Alton Observer, November 7, 1837. <http://www.altonweb.com/history/lovejoy/aol.html>.

Beecher, Edward, *Narrative of the Riots at Alton: In Connection with the Death of Rev. Elijah P. Lovejoy*. New York: Haskell House Publishers, 1970.

Dillon, Merton. *Elijah P. Lovejoy, Abolitionist Editor*. Urbana, IL: University of Illinois Press, 1961.

Ford, Thomas. *History of Illinois*. Chicago: S.C. Griggs, 1854.

Lincoln, William S. *Alton Trials of Winthrop Gilman*. New York: John F. Trow, 1838.

Lovejoy, Joseph and Owen. *Memoir of the Rev. Elijah Lovejoy*. Freeport, NY: Book for Library Press, 1970.

Simon, Paul. *Freedom's Champion*. Carbondale, IL: Southern Illinois University Press, 1994.

Tanner, Henry. *The Martyrdom of Lovejoy: an account of the life, trials, and perils of Rev. Elijah P. Lovejoy, who was killed by a proslavery mob at Alton, Illinois, the night of November 7, 1837. By an eye-witness*. New York: A.M. Kelley, 1971.

ANGELINA GRIMKÉ

Barnes, Gilbert H. and Dwight L. Dumond. *Letters of Theodore Dwight Weld, Angelina Grimké Weld and Sarah Grimké, 1882–1844*. New York: D. Appleton-Century Company, Inc., 1934.

Birney, Catharine. *The Grimké sisters: Sarah and Angelina Grimké, the first American women advocates of abolition and woman's rights*. Westport, CN: Greenwood Press, 1969.

_____. *The Sisters Grimké*. New York: Haskell House Publishers, 1970.

Grinké, Angelina. *Appeal to the Christian Women of the South*. New York: Arno Press and The New York Times, 1969.

Lerner, Gerda. *The Grimké Sisters from South Carolina: Rebels Against Slavery*. Boston: Houghton Mifflin Company, 1967.

Thomas, Benjamin P. *Theodore Weld: Crusader for Freedom*. New York: Octagon Books, 1973.

FATHER DAMIEN
DE VEUSTER

Beevers, John. *A Man for Now*. New York: Doubleday, 1973.

Bunson, Margaret R. *Father Damien*. Huntingdon, IN: Our Sunday Visitor Publishing, 1997.

Crouch, Howard E. *Damien and Dutton: Two Josephs on Molokai*. New York: The Damien-Dutton Society for Leprosy, 1998.

Daws, Gavan. *Holy Man*. New York: Harper and Row, 1973.

DeBroey, Stephen. *Father Damien: The Priest of the Lepers*. Dublin: Clonmore and Reyonds LTD, 1966.

Quinlan, May. *Damien of Molokai*. London: MacDonald and Evans, 1909.

Stoddard, Charles Warren. *Diary of a visit to Molokai in 1884*. The Book Club of California, San Francisco, 1933.

PETER MUHLENBERG

Barton, David. "The Myth of Separation." <http://www.truthinhistory.org/NoKing.htm>.

Hocker, Edward. *The Fighting Parson of the American Revolution.* Philadelphia: published by author, 1936.

Muhlenberg, Henry A. *The Life of Major General Peter Muhlenberg of the Revolutionary Army.* Philadelphia: Carey and Hart, 1849.

Tappert, Theodore and John Doberstein, trans. *The Journals of Henry Melchior Muhlenberg.* 3 volumes. Philadelphia: The Muhlenberg Press, 1982.

Wallace, Paul A. *The Muhlenbergs of Pennsylvania.* Philadelphia: University of Pennsylvania Press, 1950.

Wright, General Marcus. "A Sketch of the Life of General John Peter Gabriel Muhlenberg." Southern History Association. Volume V, Number 3, May 1901.

EDITH CAVELL

Clarke-Kennedy, A.E. *Edith Cavell: Pioneer and Patriot*. London: Faber and Faber, 1965.

Got, Ambroise, ed. *The Case of Miss Cavell: Unpublished Documents of the Trial*. London: Hodder and Stoughton, 1916.

Gray, Elizabeth. *Friend Within the Gates*. Boston: Houghton Mifflin Co., 1961.

Hoehling, A.A. *A Whisper of Eternity: The Mystery of Edith Cavell*. New York: Thomas Yoseloff, Inc., 1957.

Judson, Helen. *Edith Cavell*. New York: The MacMillan Company, 1941.

Protheroe, Ernest. *A Noble Woman: The Life Story of Edith Cavell*. London: Charles H. Kelley, 1916.

Ryder, Rowland. *Edith Cavell*. New York: Stein and Day, 1975.

van Til, Jacqueline. *With Edith Cavell in Belgium*. New York: H.W. Bridges, 1922.

SAMUEL RUTHERFORD

Coder, S. Maxwell and Wilbur Smith, ed. *The Letters of Samuel Rutherford*. Chicago: Moody Press, 1951.

Coffey, John. *Politics, Religion and the British Revolutions: The Mind of Samuel Rutherford*. Cambridge: Cambridge University Press, 1997.

Fissel, Mark. *The Bishop's War*. Cambridge: Cambridge University Press, 1994.

Horne, A. Sinclair. *Torchbearers of the Truth: Sketches of the Scottish Covenanters*. Edinburgh: The Scottish Reformation Society, 1968.

Loane, Marcus L. *Makers of Religious Freedom in the 17th Century*. Grand Rapids, MI: William B. Eerdmans Publishing Co., 1961.

Quaint Sermons of Samuel Rutherford. London: Hodder and Stoughton, 1885.

Schaeffer, Francis. *A Christian Manifesto*. Wheaton, IL: Crossway Books, 1981.

Stevenson, David, ed. *Government under the Covenanters* (1637–1651). Edinburgh: Clark Constable LTD., 1982.

THOMAS MACDONOUGH

Bird, Harrison. *Navies in the Mountains: The Battles of Lake Champlain and Lake George*. New York: Oxford University Press, 1962.

Buckley, Gail. *American Patriots*. New York: Random House, 2001.

Burdick, Virginia. *Captain Thomas Macdonough: Delaware Born Hero of the Battle of Lake Champlain*. Wilmington, DE: Delaware Hertiage Press, 1991.

Fowler, William M. *Jack Tars and Commodores: The American Navy, 1783–1815*. Boston: Houghton Mifflin, Co., 1984.

Macdonough, Rodney. *The Life of Thomas Macdonough, U.S. Navy*. Boston: The Fort Hill Press, 1909.

Muller, Charles G. *Hero of Champlain*. New York: The John Day Company, 1961.

_____. *The Proudest Day*. New York: The John Day Company, 1960.

Papers of Thomas Macdonough, 1815–1825. microfilm MMC-0996, Library of Congress.

Roosevelt, Theodore. *The Naval War of 1812*. New York: G.P. Putnam's Sons, and Lond, 1882.

JOHN HARPER

Adams, Moody. *The Titanic's Last Hero*. Columbia, SC: The Olive Press, 1997.

Encyclopedia Titanica: Second Class Passenger: John Harper. February 10, 2002. <http://www.encyclopedia-titanica.org/bio/o/2nd/harper_j.shtml>.

Encyclopedia Titanica: Articles. February 10, 2002. <www.encyclopedia-titanicca.org/documents/harper_j_prog.shtml>.

Marshall, Logan, ed. *The Sinking of the Titanic and Great Sea Disasters*. Oakland, CA: Regent Press, 1912.

Tan, Paul Lee. *Encyclopedia of 7,700 Illustrations*. Rockville, MD: Assurance Publishers, 1982.

C.T. STUDD

Buxton, Edith. *Reluctant Missionary*. London: Lutterworth Press, 1968.

Grubb, Norman. *C.T. Studd: Cricketer and Pioneer.* London: Lutterworth Press, 1970.

_____ . *Alfred Buxton of Abyssinia and Congo*. London: Lutterworth Press, 1942.

Pollock, John. *The Cambridge Seven*. Hants, England: Marshalls Paperbacks, 1985.

Additional copies of this book and other
book titles from DESTINY IMAGE are
available at your local bookstore.

For a complete list of our titles,
visit us at www.destinyimage.com
Send a request for a catalog to:

Destiny Image® Publishers, Inc.
P.O. Box 310
Shippensburg, PA 17257-0310

*"Speaking to the Purposes of God for This
Generation and for the Generations to Come"*